Ban The Bomb

BAN THE BOMB

A History of SANE, the Committee for a Sane Nuclear Policy, 1957–1985

MILTON S. KATZ

CONTRIBUTIONS IN POLITICAL SCIENCE, NUMBER 147

GREENWOOD PRESS
New York • Westport, Connecticut • London

Library of Congress Cataloging-in-Publication Data

Katz, Milton S., 1945–
    Ban the bomb.

    (Contributions in political science, ISSN 0147–1066 ;
no. 147)
    Bibliography: p.
    Includes index.
    1. SANE, Inc.—History.   2. Nuclear disarmament—
United States—History.   I. Title.   II. Series.
JX1974.7.K274   1986   327.1'74'06   85–24824
ISBN 0–313–24167–8 (lib. bdg. : alk. paper)

Library of Congress Catalog Card Number: 85–24824
ISBN: 0–313–24167–8
ISSN: 0147–1066

First published in 1986

Greenwood Press, Inc.
88 Post Road West
Westport, Connecticut 06881

Printed in the United States of America

The paper used in this book complies with the
Permanent Paper Standard issued by the National
Information Standards Organization (Z39.48–1984).

10 9 8 7 6 5 4 3 2 1

Copyright Acknowledgments

The author and publisher are grateful to the following for granting the use of:

"Safe" is reprinted from LATEST WILL: New and Selected Poems of Lenore Marshall,
by permission of W. W. Norton & Company Inc. Copyright © 1969 by Lenore Marshall.

Reproductions of advertisements and posters courtesy of SANE, Committee for a Sane
Nuclear Policy, Washington, D.C., and the Swarthmore College Peace Collection,
Swarthmore, Pennsylvania.

The chapter "Vietnam and the Politics of 'Responsible' Protest" appeared in slightly
different form in *Peace and Change* 9 (Summer 1983).

For my mother and father
who made peaceful concerns and scholarship
important parts of my life

Contents

Illustrations

Preface

> The people in the long run are going to do more to promote
> peace than our government. Indeed, I think that people want
> peace so much that one of these days government better get
> out of the way and let them have it.
> —Dwight David Eisenhower, 1959[1]

On June 12, 1982, the largest political demonstration in U.S. history
took place in New York City where estimated crowds from 700,000 to
perhaps a million people jammed the streets of Manhattan and the Great
Lawn in Central Park to protest the nuclear arms race. Although *Newsweek* felt it important to comment that this "gigantic turnout was a
remarkable reminder of the extraordinary speed with which anti-nuclear
sentiment has swept the world," there is a small group of American
citizens who have actively participated against nuclear weapons for over
a quarter of a century. Exactly twenty-five years before, in June 1957,
twenty-seven prominent citizens met at the Overseas Press Club in New
York City and formed the "Provisional Committee to Stop Nuclear
Tests." In the fall, the group adopted the name the National Committee
for a Sane Nuclear Policy, commonly known as SANE, placed a full-
page advertisement in the *New York Times* which read "We Are Facing
A Danger Unlike Any Danger That Has Ever Existed," and quickly
became the largest and most influential nuclear disarmament organization in the United States.[2]

This book is the twenty-eight-year history of this little known yet significant organization and the men and women like Norman Cousins, Clarence Pickett, Lenore Marshall, Norman Thomas, Steve Allen, Dr. Benjamin Spock, H. Stuart Hughes, Sanford Gottlieb, Seymour Melman, and David Cortright, who published full-page advertisements, wrote letters, signed petitions, staged impressive rallies, and took to the streets to pressure U.S. leaders to lessen the risk of nuclear war. From the first large American anti-bomb rallies of the late 1950s and early 1960s, through the organizing of the then largest anti-Vietnam War demonstration in November 1965, to helping bring about the June 1982 disarmament march and rally, SANE has been at the forefront of the liberal nuclear disarmament movement in the United States. This case study is not only designed to assess the historical and philosophical roots of SANE and its role in American society, but also to provide a window on the post–1945 American peace movement. In the same way, SANE will be examined as an important reflection of Cold War American liberalism.

SANE was founded on the basic liberal premise that mistaken U.S. policies can be remedied and set right; and that in order to do so, the imperatives are effective communication, dialogue, public education, and direct political action. Given certain facts on an issue, SANE liberals believed the government had the intelligence, courage, and willingness to change. Thus, the organization limited its direct action methods to persuasion and protest; it made no attempts to use noncooperation or civil disobedience. SANE's leaders chose specific goals, at least partially, because as executive director Donald Keys once stated, they were "moral, realistic, politically possible and pragmatically feasible next steps."[3]

This strategy balanced between advocacy and acceptability accounts for both the organization's strengths and weaknesses. The nuclear pacifists gathered around SANE legitimized the protest, gave it political scope and meaning, and thereby enlarged the area of accepted political action. Within American politics, SANE offered a retreat bunker for liberals who couldn't find a place to take a stand in the structure of political parties. Within the peace movement, it filled the gap that had opened among nuclear pacifists following the decline of the world government cause in the early 1950s and the shift among internationalists to the support of America's interventionist policies. And it should be given considerable credit for bringing a coalition together out of the

McCarthy days to work for such achievements as the establishment of the Arms Control and Disarmament Agency in 1961 and the 1963 partial Nuclear Test Ban Treaty. In 1965, SANE helped lead the opposition to President Lyndon Johnson's escalation of military involvement in Vietnam. Less than two years later, it helped form the "Dump Johnson" coalition and spearheaded the Eugene McCarthy presidential campaign in 1968.

That same liberal strategy, however, limited SANE's vision and methods and curtailed its impact both within the peace movement and within American politics. A product of Cold War liberalism, the organization spent too much time and energy grappling with the issue of working with Communists and more radical peace activists and protecting the process of consensus-formation as the way to influence American foreign policy. Dodging right-wing attacks from the beginning, SANE's dominant liberal leadership aimed to assemble a progressive movement that would, according to Norman Cousins, "strengthen America's relationship with other peoples through the creation of a nuclear policy that can serve as a basis for world leadership." Historian Charles DeBenedetti has written, "Members of SANE wanted the nuclear-pacifist movement to become a respectable endeavor, and they felt that it could best become respectable—and effective—as it first met American security concerns through the international control of nuclear weaponry."[4]

In the 1970s, SANE fought the proposed Anti-Ballistic Missile (ABM) system, played a key role in the passage of the Strategic Arms Limitation (SALT) Agreement of 1972, helped bring down the costly B–1 bomber in 1977, and, most recently, led the fight against the MX missile, and has assumed a leadership position in the nuclear freeze campaign. At the same time, these nuclear disarmament activists developed and refined a long-range strategy to scale down the power and wealth of the military and its governmental and industrial allies and drew up plans to channel resources into life-serving pursuits. In 1982, the organization created a Political Action Committee to translate the vast swell of public opposition, which has surfaced in recent years into concrete political activity, to halt the nuclear arms race.

Surviving the apparent lack of concern about nuclear warfare that culminated in the mid–1970s, SANE has experienced a dramatic growth, increasing its membership to over 120,000 people and making it once again the largest and one of the most respected and effective peace organizations in the country. And yet, as Charles DeBenedetti has pointed out, "Organized peace seeking has never succeeded as a movement in penetrating the dense layers of American society." Although having only moderate success in influencing government policy, peace liberals in SANE and like-minded groups had and continue to have importance in that they articulate foreign policy alternatives and help to establish the climate of opinion of which governmental decisions are made. With public concern and opposition to nuclear war reaching an all-time high, SANE is convinced the time has come to undertake a drive for nuclear sanity that is unprecedented in its scope and scale and is more committed than ever in turning the tide in the arms race and fulfilling its original mission of leading humanity "away from nuclear war and toward peace with justice."[5] It is my hope that this history will provide insight into and appreciation for the many citizen peace activists that have worked over the years in this committee and thus, in some modest way, to help make their vision of a peaceful and just world a step closer to reality.

In the course of the research and writing of this book, I benefited from the help and cooperation of many individuals. The idea for the manuscript was inspired by my association with various scholars in the Conference for Peace Research in History (CPRH), among them Charles Chatfield, Lawrence Wittner, and Solomon Wank. More immediately, three friends and colleagues provided provocative ideas and invaluable criticisms. Former president of CPRH Charles DeBenedetti, Robert Schulzinger, and Ralph Levering read the manuscript in its entirety, and their critical advice improved the study in many important ways.

I acknowledge my debt to the many people I interviewed during the course of my research, especially Norman Cousins, Benjamin Spock, and Sanford Gottlieb who all read at least parts of the manuscript and were more than generous with their time and dedication to this project. Gracious assistance was afforded me at all the various libraries and manuscript collections I visited, especially by executive director David Cortright and Charlie Kraybill of the SANE staff at the national office in Washington, D.C., and Jean Soderlund, curator of the Swarthmore College Peace Collection in Pennsylvania. I am grateful to Mimi Pettegrew, Linda Whiteside, Carol McLaughlin, and Faye Intrater, all of whom typed large parts of this manuscript, and to Production Editor Michelle Scott of Greenwood Press for her skilled guidance in the preparation of the final version. The National Endowment for the Humanities, the Union of Independent Colleges of Art, and the Kansas

City Art Institute provided me opportunities for travel and research, including a summer study fellowship.

Finally, I thank my twin brother, Neil, for introducing me to the wonderful resources at the Swarthmore College Peace Collection, thereby implanting the idea of peace research in my heart and head, and my daughters, Stephanie and Tamara, for their tolerance and understanding and most importantly their joy of life that makes working for peace and everything else worthwhile. Most of all, I thank my wife, Sharon, who edited the entire manuscript and gave me the criticism, love, and encouragement I needed to complete it.

Ban The Bomb

1

Nuclear Pacifism in Cold War America, 1945–1957

The madmen are planning the end of the world. What they call continued progress in atomic warfare means universal extermination, and what they call national security is organized suicide. There is only one duty for the moment: every other task is a dream or a mockery. Stop the atomic bomb. Stop making the bomb. Abandon the bomb completely. Dismantle every existing bomb. Cancel every plan for the bomb's use.... Either dethrone the madmen immediately or raise such a shout of protest as will shock them into sanity.

—Lewis Mumford, 1946[1]

On the night after the atomic destruction of Hiroshima, the young editor of the *Saturday Review*, Norman Cousins, sat down to compose one of the most famous editorials in American history, "Modern Man is Obsolete." "On August 6, 1945, a new age is born," he declared; the dropping of the bomb "marked the violent death of one stage in man's history and the beginning of another." The "new age" created a "blanket of obsolescence not only over the methods and products of man but over man himself." Cousins contended that Americans had to be made aware of the changes that had taken place on that day. For this purpose a movement that came to be known as "nuclear pacifism" was created. The nuclear-pacifist movement in the United States emerged from the traditional liberal internationalist groups composed of writers, intellectuals, university faculty, scientists, and other professionals who had supported World War II but had come to believe, along with Cousins, that "man's survival on earth is now absolutely dependent on his ability to avoid a new war."[2]

Liberal nuclear pacifists, who twelve years later organized the National Committee for a Sane Nuclear Policy, consisted initially of two sometimes overlapping groups: advocates of world government and atomic scientists. Out of these two groups emerged the United World Federalists and the Federation of Atomic Scientists, both of which in the relatively friendly postwar atmosphere became influential in American life. Along with traditional pacifists from the American Friends Service Committee and other organizations and radical pacifists like A.J. Muste who were committed to Gandhian nonviolent resistance, nuclear pacifists emerged after World War II to spearhead the movement against nuclear war in the United States.

The idea of world government had existed for a long time, but Hiroshima gave new impetus to the movement. As one world government advocate recalled, the atomic bomb "forced us to look at which we had all been trying not to see: namely that no agreements between sovereign nations to do something, or not to do something, are likely ever to amount to much." "Of this sad fact we have been amply warned," he added, "and yet—even yet, until Hiroshima—we continued to hope. Since Hiroshima, we have begun to see the fallacy of hoping, and have at least begun to demand something more." Cousins, who was one of the leading advocates of the world government movement and one of the founders of SANE, observed: "The need for world government was clear long before August 6, 1945, but Hiroshima and Nagasaki raised that need to such dimensions that it can no longer be ignored." National sovereignty was "preposterous now."[3]

In October 1945, Cousins joined with fifty influential persons, including prominent New York lawyer Grenville Clark and former U.S. Supreme Court Justice Owen J. Roberts, who shared his conviction in the necessity for the extension of peace and order through federal world structure. Meeting in Dublin, New Hampshire, the conferees acknowledged the value of the new United Nations but insisted that it did not go far enough in reordering world politics. They called instead for "a world federal government with limited but definite and adequate powers to prevent war'' and prepared to galvanize a popular movement in its behalf.[4]

World federalism indeed was seen by many at this time to be a viable and workable notion. Federalists believed that world peace required a clearcut authoritative definition, both of the limits of national power and of the area of effective jurisdiction of the world body. The nations should retain the right to maintain their own cultures and political institutions, wrote Cousins, but the UN should have authority in matters related to world security and world development. Recognizing that restructuring the UN, taking into account all the ideological, historical, political, and cultural differences within it, ''may be the most difficult problem yet to be undertaken by the human mind,'' Cousins and other federalists followed the lead of Grenville Clark and explored in depth specific problems relating to the full development of the UN into a genuine world security authority.[5]

The world government movement's political power rose accordingly with the increasing numbers of people sympathetic with the idea. Even more important, however, was the number of influential supporters. As historian Dexter Perkins correctly observed, although world government proponents were ''not very powerful numerically,'' they were ''a part of the elite opinion . . . which deserves to be regarded as of more importance than mere numbers suggest.'' Influential people they were, for by mid–1946, of a total of ninety-six U.S. senators, seven openly advocated world government, while a dozen others admitted privately that they supported it. Between 50 and 100 of the 435 members of the House of Representatives favored some form of world government, as did Minnesota's Governor Harold Stassen, considered a leading contender for the Republican nomination for president in 1948. A Greenville, North Carolina, attorney, Robert Lee Humber, persuaded fourteen state legislatures to adopt a resolution urging Congress to establish a world government. By 1946 nineteen others were considering it or had already passed the resolution in one house. And in his annual message to Congress in 1946, President Harry Truman declared:

The United Nations Organization now being established represents a minimal essential beginning. It must be developed rapidly and steadily. . . . Our ultimate security requires more than a process of consultation and compromise. It requires that we begin now to develop the United Nations organization as the representative of the world as one society.[6]

Although public opinion data must be used cautiously, a Gallup poll taken in 1946 suggested that the general public was not far behind its leaders. In stark contrast to the isolationist mood that followed World War I, 52 percent of the American public expressed support of U.S. participation in the liquidation of national armed forces, with an international police force to be given the responsibility of keeping the peace. Only 24 percent were opposed to this idea, and 22 percent still remained undecided.[7]

Encouraged by this at least potentially strong public support, five of the groups dedicated to world government convened in February 1947 in Asheville, North Carolina, and combined to form the United World Federalists for World Government With Limited Powers Adequate To Prevent War (UWF). Further identifying their mutual aim as "the mobilization of public opinion and action toward world government so that the local and national representatives of the people will be impelled to world federation by an irresistible political force," they announced the following credo:

We believe that peace is not merely the absence of war but the presence of justice, of law, of order—in short, of government; that world peace can be created and maintained only under world law, universal and strong enough to prevent armed conflict between nations.[8]

UWF officers included some of the most respected and influential men in America. Cord Meyer, Jr., a young war hero who had served as Harold Stassen's aide at the founding of the United Nations and wrote the bestselling *Peace or Anarchy*, was elected president of the organization. Grenville Clark; Norman Cousins; Thomas K. Finletter, a New York attorney and future secretary of the Air Force; W.T. Holliday, president of Standard Oil; Robert Lee Humber; liberal news commentator Raymond Gram Swing; and historian Carl Van Doren all served as vice presidents of the new organization.

The UWF was successful in attracting members. By the end of 1948, membership rose to 40,000 people organized in 659 chapters, and Cord Meyer, Jr., announced the expenditure of $550,000 in an expansion program toward the goal of one chapter in every community. Earlier that year, Meyer jubilantly cited a new poll conducted by the Roper organization that showed an increase in public support to 63 percent for a UWF proposal that the United States initiate action to change the United Nations into a strong federation of nations.[9]

In June 1949, 8,000 people came to Madison Square Garden for a UWF rally in support of a congressional resolution introduced by Democratic Senator Glen Taylor of Idaho, which advocated the official announcement by the State Department that the goal of American foreign policy involved the development of the United Nations into a world federation. The chief speaker of the evening, Supreme Court Justice William O. Douglas, was followed by Cord Meyer, Jr., and Senator Charles W. Tobey of New Hampshire, the man who joined with twenty-one others to sponsor the resolution in the Senate and who was supported by more than 100 sponsors in the House of Representatives.[10]

Although the growth of the world federalist idea was important, none of the groups spurred to action by the atomic crisis seemed as profoundly converted as the atomic scientists. Their concern began with their role in the creation of the bomb during the war and carried over into postwar organization. The Federation of Atomic Scientists, which played a leading role in the anti-nuclear movement, was formed in Chicago on November 16 and 17, 1945 when thirteen local groups came together "to promote the use of scientific discoveries in the interest of world peace and the general welfare of mankind." The main local group organizing the federation was the Atomic Scientists of Chicago which claimed the support of "over 90 percent" of the scientists from the atomic bomb project. As of mid–1946, the Federation of American Scientists, which earlier absorbed the Federation of Atomic Scientists, had 2,000 members. The *Bulletin of the Atomic Scientists*, originally the journal of the Chicago group, became the official organ of the new federation. The *Bulletin* first appeared, observed its editor, "to make fellow scientists aware of the new relationships between their own world of science and the world of national and international politics," as well as "to help the public understand what nuclear energy and its application to war meant for mankind."[11]

Albert Einstein, a longtime pacifist himself, would set the tone of the organization when, on December 10, 1945, he told a Nobel anniversary dinner crowd in New York:

Physicists find themselves in a position not unlike that of Alfred Nobel. Alfred Nobel invented an explosive more powerful than any then known—an exceedingly effective means of destruction. To atone for this "accomplishment" and to relieve his conscience he instituted his award for the promotion of peace. Today, the physicists who participated in producing the most formidable weapon of all time are harassed by a similar feeling of responsibility, not to say guilt. As scientists, we must never cease to warn against the danger created by these weapons.[12]

Some scientists naively believed that atomic bombs made war obsolete; but others saw that only the establishment of a peaceful world would keep men from destroying themselves, and they threw themselves into the struggle against war. Many also became involved in the campaign for world government. It was "necessary that the individual state be prevented from making war by a supranational organization," Einstein maintained. In light of the "political mentality prevailing at present," he conceded, this might "seem illusory, even 'fantastic,' " nevertheless, it was the "only . . . way out." Many scientists began to see that peace was an absolute necessity. As one physicist told a scientific gathering: "The atomic bomb is the final and conclusive proof of the fact that there must be no more wars." It seemed that pacifist Roy Finch was right when he stated that "science is intrinsically more revolutionary than any ideology or political or social movement . . . ;" and "nowhere is the revolutionary character of science more evident than with regard to war."[13]

In the years immediately following Hiroshima, American nuclear pacifists were critical of the foreign policies of both the United States and the Soviet Union. The United World Federalists considered these nations the main obstacles to the coming of federal world government. Yet, according to historian Lawrence Wittner, despite the criticism world government proponents directed at American foreign policy, most followed other American liberals in accepting Washington's developing commitment to the containment of Soviet power.[14]

This was strikingly demonstrated in a Town Meeting debate of December 30, 1947. The assistant editor of the *New York Herald Tribune* opened with the statement: "Let's have peace based on international respect for the power of America. Let's have the most powerful Army, Navy and Air Force in the world. . . . Civilization preserved through force." Cord Meyer labeled this program "peace by intimidation" and said that such a policy "may work for a time, but it will end inevitably in the collective suicide of a Third War." But paradoxically, after an eloquent plea for world federation, Meyer concluded: "Until this world federation is established and the nations agree to disarm under its protection, I would agree with Mr. Forrest [of the *Herald Tribune*] that we must maintain our defensive military strength." Later in the program he further justified the current U. S. position: "I think we have to follow a policy of military preparedness now, given the fact that other nations are arming."[15] As critics have pointed out, here lay the core contradiction of the world federalist position: simultaneous support for the arms race and world government.

There seemed to be a similar inconsistency with the atomic scientists' position, although at first their position seemed crystal clear. "The founding of the *Bulletin of Atomic Scientists* in 1945," said its editor Eugene Rabinowitch, "was a part of the conspiracy to preserve our civilization by scaring men into rationality." The basis of their program was simple; "The arms race must be stopped." The most militant scientific organization was the Emergency Committee of Atomic Scientists consisting of Einstein, Harold Urey, Hans Bethe, Selig Hecht, Thorfin Hogness, Phillip Morse, Linus Pauling, Leo Szilard, and Victor Weisskopf. As chairman of the committee, Einstein spoke for the members in 1946 when he declared "a world authority and an eventual world state was not just 'desirable' in the name of brotherhood, they are 'necessary' for survival."[16]

Addressing a rally of student federalists that same year, Einstein charged that the United States had not made "a really serious effort" toward an understanding with the Soviet Union. "It seems to me that America has done just the opposite.... There was no need to keep on producing more and more atomic bombs." Instead, he argued:

Enduring peace will come about, not by countries continuing to threaten one another, but only through an honest effort to create mutual trust. One should assume that the desire to bring about decent conditions for mankind on this planet as well as the fear of unspeakable annihilation would render those in positions of responsibility wiser and more dispassionate.[17]

As the Cold War heightened in 1947–1948, the Emergency Committee again prophesized disaster if the trend toward military power was not reversed and reiterated that there was but one hope for mankind—"world government." In spite of tensions between the two power blocs, Einstein felt strongly that the Soviet Union should be included in the world federation from the very outset. Einstein told a reporter from the *New York Post* in 1948: "Should this be impossible, efforts should nonetheless be made to organize other nations into world federation, provided that it be done in such a way that Russia were free to join at any time, with all the privileges and duties of other nations."[18]

Like the world federalists, however, there was a similar flaw in the scientist's position. In a public reply to an "Emergency Appeal" by Einstein in 1946, A.J. Muste issued an incisive critique contending that if Einstein and the rest of the Federation of American Scientists refused to make atomic weapons, "the American people would at last realize that you were deadly serious about the bomb. . . . What is infinitely more important," wrote the pacifist leader, "they would be shaken out of moral lethargy and despair and would become capable of inspired action to abolish war and build a democratic society, because they would behold the spectacle of men who do not try to shift the responsibility for their actions onto the military or the state, who refuse to make conscience subservient to them." There is "a deep cleavage in our souls and our society because our moral and social development has not kept pace with technological advance," Muste stated. "That cleavage must be healed first and basically within the morally responsible human being. It will be healed in the scientist who becomes a prophet, a man whose words and actions are in true accord." Mankind's destiny, concluded Muste,

is being decided by the scientists who take, or fail to take, upon themselves the awful responsibility of being prophets, conscientious objectors, persons, whole human beings, and not technicians or slaves of a war-making state, albeit heavy-hearted and unenthusiastic ones.[19]

Einstein replied that Muste's criticism was largely justified and later asserted: "Non-cooperation in military matters should be an essential moral principal for all true scientists." Others, like Leo Szilard, who agreed with Muste "on the moral issue involved," noted that "considerations of expediency" on the part of "the majority of scientists" would doom Muste's proposal to failure. Although Szilard was right, Muste's challenge to the scientists persuaded many, as individuals, to begin to withdraw their support from the arms race. Their organization and most of its members, however, believed a scientific walkout would somehow be undemocratic and illegal and would weaken the United

States, accepting thereby the paradoxical position of other world government advocates.[20]

With the Bikini Island bomb tests in the summer of 1946, public opinion began to desert the scientists and their position began to lose strength. Many Americans, upon learning about these tests, found the atomic bomb less destructive than expected. After watching the first explosion of the test series, a reporter remarked to Cousins: "The next war's not going to be so bad after all." Also, the scientists' movement was undercut by two other developments. Americans became fascinated with the "peaceful uses" of atomic power, and many responded to the fear of nuclear destruction by a belief in nuclear deterrence. Norman Thomas ironically put it: "Nobody can escape the logical conclusion that if our best hope is fear of retaliation, then our best defense is not disarmament, but scientific armament." The scientists knew their early reliance on fear might present a problem, especially when the fears created by the Cold War heightened, but they had no answers for this dilemma. As Eugene Rabinowitch remarked in *The Bulletin* in late 1951, "While trying to frighten men into rationality, scientists have frightened many into abject fear or blind hatred."[21]

Sensing their decline in public support, American scientists united behind the more conservative Acheson-Lilienthal proposals for the international control of atomic energy, subsequently presented to the United Nations by Bernard Baruch. The Russians united behind Andrei Gromyko's proposals, but neither led to serious discussion. Nuclear pacifists generally found the Gromyko proposals "inadequate," while a number of world federalists had reservations about the Baruch plan. As Cousins and Thomas Finletter observed in the *Bulletin of Atomic Scientists*, "While all the nations in the world would be asked to surrender their sovereignty in the mining, processing, and manufacture of fissionable materials," the United States "would still be permitted to stockpile its own atomic bombs." Muste, who often criticized the superpowers' piecemeal gestures, remarked about one element of accord in both the American and Soviet proposals: "Both say to the other 'I don't trust you and will not take any chances, but I ask you to trust me and take the chances which that involves.' "[22]

The scientists' movement lost even more strength during 1947–1948 as the Cold War intensified and as President Truman prepared to contain the Soviet Union militarily and domestic dissidents politically. As early as 1946, Harold Urey wrote that the scientists were "in danger of being internationally minded and not loyal'' and were ''afraid of being accused of being communists, or something of that sort.'' After President Truman initiated the Loyalty Order of March 21, 1947, the tension heightened. Confronted with such threats, the scientist movement dissipated; although a small minority, led by Philip Morrison, Linus Pauling, and Harlow Shapley continued to call for the international control of atomic energy. A larger and more influential group, however, began to argue that with the intensification of the Cold War, military containment of the Soviet bloc took precedence over any plans for international control.[23]

After winning the 1948 election, Truman moved from the advocacy of a mixed economic-military response to the Soviet challenge to support of one based primarily upon military power; and in 1949, with the Soviet atomic explosion and the Communist victory in China's Civil War, his administration proposed to develop the hydrogen bomb. This action brought about the final revolt of many remaining scientists against military policies. One of them, Hans Bethe, expressed the view of many of his colleagues: ''I believe the most important question is a moral one. Can we, who have always insisted on morality and human decency, introduce this weapon of total annihilation into the world?'' But another sector of the atomic scientists took quite a different position. Edward Teller, the driving force behind the H-bomb, argued: ''It is not the scientist's job to determine whether the hydrogen bomb should be constructed, whether it should be used or how it should be used. This responsibility rests with the people and with their representatives.'' Backed by the administration, this group soon prevailed.[24]

From then on it was a downhill fight, and an atmosphere of despair settled over the once-spirited scientists' movement. With the outbreak of the Korean War in 1950, the atomic scientist movement virtually collapsed. The Emergency Committee of Atomic Scientists, inactive since January 1, 1949, ceased functioning entirely by the end of 1950. Einstein sadly remarked: ''How can we presume to reassure the American people from their uncertainties if we cannot agree among ourselves?'' Einstein and Leo Szilard wanted to give the balance of the committee's funds to the American Friends Service Committee rather than to the *Bulletin of Atomic Scientists*, which Einstein considered to have degenerated into ''no more than a publication of neutral information,'' but the money eventually went to the *Bulletin*. Eugene Rabinowitch, editor of the *Bulletin*, wrote sadly in January 1951: ''The break between the two camps appears all but complete. . . . Scientists—

whose profession requires a recognition of facts, however unpleasant—cannot but admit their campaign has failed.''[25]

Much the same thing occurred in the movement for world government. During 1948 and 1949, the United World Federalists continued to grow larger, although correspondingly more conservative, until its membership stood at 50,000. But by early 1950 the world government movement had begun to crumble. In explaining the collapse, one proponent of world government stated: ''A climax was reached June 25, 1950, when the North Koreans crossed the 38th Parallel.'' World government organizations almost universally accepted the American role in the Korean War, believing the United States was participating in an ''international police action,'' and fighting under the United Nations flag. UWF chapters in about thiry cities and towns across the country ran an advertisement proclaiming: ''United World Federalists are wholeheartedly behind our nation in this and every fight that may darken the nation's future.'' Federalist sentiment gave way to nationalist fervor. ''The world government movement will disintegrate as the world war movement accelerates,'' Milton Mayer predicted in May 1950. ''The end is in sight. . . . War will come faster than world government.''[26] Personifying the way the UWF had begun to support rather than castigate American nationalism, honorary president Cord Meyer, Jr., left the UWF in 1951 to become a ranking official in the Central Intelligence Agency. His duties there included covertly channeling funds to the National Student Association and other liberal left organizations.[27]

Yet, in spite of their clear nationalistic enthusiasm, nuclear-pacifists, like other American liberals, failed to find the American political climate hospitable to their cause. On the contrary, a right-wing political resurgence—known generically as McCarthyism—pushed them so forcefully to the defensive that they nearly went out of business. Public fears of atomic spies and espionage made the atomic scientists a focal point of public concern. The scientists were subjected to constant political pressures in a long-running struggle over questions of loyalty and national security that came to a head in 1954 in the Oppenheimer hearings. This investigation labeled the prominent physicist a ''security risk'' and denied him reinstatement to his post in the Atomic Energy Commission. The proceedings of this case enraged the scientific community, and some fled from government service rather than commit themselves to the new security regulations. In late 1954, Einstein showed his utter despair with the times by remarking:

If I would be a young man again and I had to decide how to make my living, I would not try to become a scientist or scholar or teacher. I would choose rather to be a plumber or a peddler in the hope to find that modest degree of independence still available under present circumstances.[28]

Individuals prominently identified with the cause of world government, whom Senator Joseph McCarthy often sneered at as "one worlders," did not fare much better than the atomic scientists. In 1950, the Senate Foreign Relations Committee heard testimony from such witnesses as the Women's Patriotic Council on National Defense, National Society of New England Women, National Society of Women Descendants of the Ancient and Honorable Artillery Company, Dames of the Loyal Legion of the United States of America, and the Veterans of Foreign Wars, branding the United World Federalists as subversive. The following year the Senate Appropriations Committee, under the leadership of Pat McCarran, approved a bill banning funds from any organization which "directly or indirectly promoted one world government or world citizenship." In February 1953, *Newsweek* reported that "loyalty investigators are now asking would-be government employees if they ever were members of the United World Federalists." The question was plainly designed "to satisfy congressional suspicions of any group's plugging projects in which Communist nations participate."[29]

Liberal peace activists who championed the cause of world government found it a definite liability. In March 1958, at the performance of a play in Hagerstown, Maryland, sponsored by a local chapter of UWF, four American Legion posts picketed and distributed mimeographed statements of the alleged "facts" about Norman Cousins, Rex Stout, and Oscar Hammerstein II, as gathered from the files of the House Committee on Un-American Activities. At the end of the play the American Legion adjutant for the state of Maryland climbed on to the stage and charged that Cousins had been cited by the House Committee on Un-American Activities for speaking at the Scientific and Cultural Conference for World Peace, a Communist-front meeting, in New York in 1949. Cousins later explained that he had indeed been "cited" in the House Committee on Un-American Activities report, but for speaking at the conference at the request of the State Department in order to present the United States' anti-Communist views, and that he had been roundly booed and hissed and needed a police escort to leave the hall.[30]

World Federalists generally became more and more feeble and defensive in countering these attacks and thus indirectly aided in their own demise. Cousins, who became president of the UWF in 1952, tried to encourage world government advocates to retake the political offensive. He refused to confront every charge that federalists were pro-Communist and insisted instead on carrying the fight to the public. Rather than avowing our anti-Communism, Cousins wrote in 1952, ''let us say instead that we are moving heaven and earth to create a human community on this planet, that world citizenship is the ultimate goal and no one need apologize for it.''[31]

In editorials and speeches Cousins denounced the extreme Right ''a menace to the United States'' for creating a climate of ''uneasiness and insecurity.'' He held that ''there could be no more ghastly irony than is presented today by those who in the name of Americanism are actually helping to prepare the country for the eventual triumph of Communism,'' by their assault on constitutional government through attacks on people's reputations, purges, and the assigning of guilt by association. He wanted to fight Communism, but by means of liberal humanitarianism. ''Instead of fighting Communism by strengthening and enlarging humanitarian objectives,'' he editorialized, ''we turned on humanitarism itself.''[32]

Cousins and other world federalist leaders won some token victories of public apologies or retractions in their counterattacks; but the anti-Communist hysteria decimated the rank and file of the already declining movement. In 1951, the UWF had an income of more than $180,000 obtained from about 40,000 members. Within five years these figures had shrunk to about $65,000 and 17,000 respectively. ''Seven years ago, when world law was mentioned, people said it was too soon,'' complained Cousins in late 1952. ''Now, when it is mentioned, they say it is too late.''[33]

Nuclear pacifists were rendered almost impotent mainly because of their belief that international liberal values were best served through unconditional commitment to one side in a polarized world. Like their liberal counterparts in the American labor movement, the newly formed Americans for Democratic Action, and the intellectuals who wrote for the *Partisan Review*, *Commentary*, *New Republic*, and the *Reporter*, most nuclear pacifists embraced America's anti-Communist world mission and ironically helped to forge the post-World War II Cold War consensus. Veteran peace activist and socialist Norman Thomas, in replying to a plea from A.J. Muste for America to take a ''unilateral initiative'' in disarmament, was symptomatic of the liberal pacifists' position when he succumbed to some extent to Cold War views by replying, ''Repeatedly men have been forced to use clumsy and self-defeating tools in their struggles for a larger freedom and justice. I desperately want to avoid war,'' he added, ''but for America to avoid war simply by surrender to communism would in no way avoid the ultimate violence'' of ''Stalin's imperialist communism.''[34]

Hope within the nuclear-pacifist camp nonetheless persisted through the dolorous 1950s. Some federalists and atomic scientists, as individuals, began to withdraw their support from the arms race and, like Albert Einstein and Norman Cousins, maintained an emphatic opposition to any and all plans for atomic war. While convinced of a very real Soviet threat, these confirmed nuclear pacifists nurtured the post-Hiroshima spirit of species ''survivalism,'' but they lacked an issue that would renew liberal interest in confronting the nuclear menace. Quite unexpectedly, a galvanizing issue presented itself in March 1954, when a U.S. H-bomb test explosion accidentally scattered radioactive dust on twenty-three Japanese fishermen and shocked the world into fear over the generalized health hazards attendant upon atomospheric testing. ''If there is still a peace movement left in America,'' journalist I.F. Stone pleaded a few months later, ''this must be its platform. As a first step away from mutual destruction, no more tests.''[35]

The conflict between the claimed U.S. security need for atmospheric testing and the demonstrable immediate and long-term health dangers gripped anti-nuclear activists and policy makers in an angry dispute for the next nine years. In the November 1954 issue of the *Bulletin of Atomic Scientists*, physicist Ralph Lapp gave the American people the first detailed description of fallout and its perils. He explained that, unlike atomic bomb tests which only produced local fallout, hydrogen bomb tests produced forms of radiation that circled the globe and returned to the ground thousands of miles from the point of the explosion. An Atomic Energy Commission report finally released to the public in February 1955 confirmed Lapp's analysis of the dangers of fallout, admitting that ''the most frightening and insidious characteristic of radioactivity was its invisible nature.'' Warning that ''no one yet knows just how much radiation a human being can take without jeopardizing his offspring,'' *Newsweek* declared that the issue of '' 'how dangerous is fallout' is potentially the most dangerous gap in modern man's scientific knowledge.''[36]

Disturbed by these reports of fallout danger, the British philospher Bertrand Russell joined Einstein and nine other renowned international scientists in July 1955 in issuing an appeal for governments to acknowledge the suicidal nature of modern nuclear war and to seek peaceful means of settling their disputes. Signers of this statement included Percy W. Bridgman, Herman J. Muller, Linus Pauling, and Einstein of the United States; Cecil F. Powell, Joseph Rotblat, and Russell of England; Frederick Joliot-Curie of France; Leopold Infeld of Poland; Hideki Yukawa of Japan; and Max Born of Germany. The text, drawn up by Einstein and Russell, began: "We are speaking on this occasion, not as members of this or that nation, continent or creed, but as human beings, members of the species man, whose continued existence is in doubt." We have taken steps, the authors contended, "to prevent a military contest of which the issue must be disastrous to all parties." "Shall we . . . choose death because we cannot forget our quarrels," the statement concluded. "We appeal, as human beings to human beings: Remember your humanity and forget the rest."[37]

About the same time, the leaders of the newly emerging nations in Asia and Africa, meeting in Bandung in Indonesia, expressed concern over the exposure of their peoples to nuclear radiation. At the opening of the conference, both India's Prime Minister Jawaharlal Nehru and Indonesia's President Sukarno called on the nuclear powers to end their tests. Pending the negotiations of such a ban, the Bandung delegates appealed to the United States and Russia "to suspend experiments for such weapons." At the Vatican, Pope Pius XII called for an international agreement to achieve an end to nuclear explosions, the renunciation of atomic weapons, and effective air and ground observation to insure arms control appliance.[38]

In the United States, Democratic presidential candidate Adlai Stevenson, prompted by Cousins and other of his foreign policy advisors, introduced the test ban controversy into the 1956 election campaign. On April 21, speaking to the American Society of Newspaper Editors, Stevenson suggested halting nuclear weapons tests as "a step which would reflect our determination never to plunge the world into nuclear holocaust, a step which would affirm our purpose to act with humility and a decent concern for public opinion." Ignoring those who accused him of exploiting public fears to win votes, Stevenson felt a strong moral commitment to speak out on an issue which he believed went to the very heart of the Cold War, and he proceeded to make the test ban a central theme of his campaign. Although Stevenson found this a poor political issue in a nation committed to the maintenance of military strength at all costs, he, with Cousins's encouragement, brought the test ban issue out of obscurity and into the forefront of public discussion.[39]

Cousins's own concern with the issue intensified sharply in August 1956, when a small group of professors at Washington University in St. Louis, including the biologist Barry Commoner, showed him scientific analyses of the human costs of radioactive fallout. One of the research studies, undertaken under the auspices of the U.S. Atomic Energy Commission, demonstrated that radioactive fallout was causing increased contamination of milk supplies with the element Strontium–90, a known carcinogen that particularly threatened children whose bodies mistook radioactive strontium for calcium in the building process. Cousins emerged from this meeting with a determination to help bring nuclear testing under control. Testing was no mere abstract issue. It powered the arms race, abetted the spread of nuclear weapons, and presented immediate harm to children and the unborn.[40]

Shortly thereafter, Cousins visited Dr. Albert Schweitzer at his hospital in Lambaréné, French Equatorial Africa, to ask him to speak out against nuclear tests. A world famous musician, philosopher, theologian, physician, and Nobel Peace Prize recipient, Schweitzer had gone to Africa in order to tend the health needs of the people. By the 1950s, he had earned virtually cultic status within the United States as a saintly grandfather whose very name was a synonym for humanitarianism. Cousins believed that "there was no one in the world whose voice would have greater carrying power than his own." Although Schweitzer had been concerned with the nuclear danger since Hiroshima, he hesitated first upon hearing Cousins's request that he issue a public appeal against continued testing. After several days' reflection, however, he told Cousins that he would speak out in an attempt to stimulate public opinion.[41]

On April 24, 1957, under the auspices of the Nobel Prize Committee in Oslo, Norway, Schweitzer issued his famous "Declaration of Conscience." Entitling his remarks "Peace or Atomic War," Schweitzer focused his attention on the danger that nuclear fallout posed for human life and concluded that "the end of further experiments with atom bombs would be like the early sun rays of hope which suffering humanity is longing for." His statement produced a powerful response throughout the world. But the governments of the United States, the Soviet Union, and the People's Republic of China declined to broadcast the full text of the message, and the American press generally ignored Schweitzer's appeal. The *New York Times* printed a front-page story, and Cousins's *Saturday Review* published the full text. But opinion-shaping elites in the United States chose to downplay the strongest appeal issued by a man regularly identified by ordinary Americans as one of the most admired men in the world.[42]

Indeed, as historian Robert Divine pointed out, Schweitzer's statement might have gone virtually unnoticed in the United States had not tomic Energy Commissioner, Willard Libby, decided to give an official reply. His rebuttal took the form of an eight-page public letter which, while voicing great respect for Schweitzer, contended that his appeal was not based "on the latest scientific information on radioactive fallout." Libby maintained that AEC records showed that human exposures "are very much smaller than those which would be required to produce observable effects in the population" and, therefore, that the risk was slight. He concluded that "it would be far more dangerous to run the terrible risk of abandoning the defense effort which is so essential under present conditions to the survival of the free world. . . . "[43]

Libby's defense of the justification of the harmfulness of fallout in light of national security needs precipitated a lively debate in the United States. Both *Time* magazine and the *New York Times* found his words persuasive and agreed that there was no real cause for alarm as Schweitzer believed. But Rabinowich's editorial in the *Bulletin of Atomic Scientists*, although agreeing that Schweitzer's data was unverified and exaggerated, stated that his words expressed a moral truth that transcended scientific evidence. People responded to Schweitzer's appeal, Rabinowitch explained, because it was based "on a sound and highly rational desire of mankind to reverse the trend which brings it closer every day to a suicidal situation."[44]

One person who was deeply affected by the Schweitzer appeal was the Nobel Prize winning scientist Dr. Linus Pauling. In the test ban movement, he discovered a cause to which he could devote his great energy and intelligence and wholeheartedly enlisted in the crusade which would ultimately bring him the Nobel Peace Prize. On May 15, 1957, Pauling spoke to an honors day assembly at Washington University in St. Louis. Citing Schweitzer's appeal, he dealt at length with the test ban issue, describing his own position as stemming from "humanitarian" rather than scientific concerns. He declared:

I believe that no human being should be sacrificed to a project, and in particular I believe that no human being should be sacrificed to the project of perfecting nuclear weapons that could kill hundreds of millions of human beings, and could devastate this beautiful world in which we live.[45]

Pauling's reception was so favorable that he decided to go ahead in framing a petition by American scientists, appealing for an international agreement to halt all nuclear tests. Two Washington University professors, Barry Commmoner and physicist Edward Condon, helped him draft the petition and circulate it among faculty members across the nation. Nearly 2,000 scientists signed Pauling's petition by June 1, and two days later he released it to the press and sent a copy to the White House. The petition called for an international agreement to halt nuclear testing as soon as possible. An end to testing, the scientists claimed, would help break the disarmament stalemate and prevent the spread of nuclear weapons to other nations. For all these reasons, the appeal concluded, "We deem it imperative that immediate action be taken to effect an international agreement to stop the testing of all nuclear weapons."[46]

On May 27, a Subcommittee on Radiation of the Joint Committee on Atomic Energy, under the chairmanship of a liberal Democratic congressman from California, Chet Holifield, began to hold hearings on the fallout question. For the next several days more than forty witnesses appeared; many were AEC employees, but several academic scientists known to be critical of the government's nuclear policies were also included. Holifield's goal was to preside over a scientific seminar which would present the American public all the known facts on fallout. The hearings ended on June 7 without arriving at any consensus on the fallout danger. In the absence of firm data on the effects of low-level radiation, the experts could not agree whether there was a threshold below which fallout did not injure human health. But the hearings did serve, however, to shake confidence in the AEC's assertion that fallout posed no problem for the American people. As Robert Divine pointed out, "Nuclear tests could no longer be taken for granted; the AEC would have to prove they were a necessary evil."[47]

Schweitzer's appeal had stirred the imagination of millions; Pauling's petition revealed a growing revolt among scientists; and the Holifield subcommittee hearings put the burden of proof on the government to show how the potentially serious hazards from fallout could be justified in the name of national security. A Gallup poll in May 1957 showed that 63 percent of Americans agreed that the United States should stop such tests. Only six months earlier, 56 percent of those Gallup had asked opposed a test ban. The percentage who knew what fallout was had risen to 28 percent compared to 17 percent in 1955. More than half of this knowledgeable group believed that there was "real danger" from test fallout, and 69 percent favored a multilateral agreement to halt nuclear testing. Commented *Newsweek*:

Not since Hiroshima had such a bitter and fateful debate raged over the building, testing, and ultimate use of the A-bomb—and its vastly more destructive offspring, the H-bomb. Governments, scientists, military men, just plain citizens—all were caught up in the controversy."[48]

The issue, as seen by the liberal nuclear pacifists, spoke to matters of right morality and working democracy. Atomic tests were by nature murderously indiscriminate. Shifting winds bore radioactive debris throughout the Northern Hemisphere and across much of the world. In this way, atomic testing was not only harmful in its own terms; it also symbolized perfectly the utter vulnerability of the world's peoples to the ongoing nuclear menace and the government's failure to bring it under control. If the United States or the Soviet Union took the position that other peoples should be expected to sustain the radioactive hazard because it contributed to security, the other nations, according to Cousins, could not be blamed if they asked that they not be taken for granted. And, regardless of health dangers, continued nuclear testing severely reduced the chances for bringing the nuclear arms race under control. It indeed sped the race forward.[49]

Convinced that "world public opinion will compel all other nations to do likewise," Cousins urged the United States to undertake a unilateral suspension of tests. The Dwight Eisenhower Administration, however, insisted that the development of bigger and better bombs, capable of intimidating the Russians and thus enhancing U.S. national security, outweighed the possible damage to human life caused by the tests; and on January 24, 1957, the AEC announced a new series of atomic tests scheduled for the Nevada proving grounds in late spring and early summer. Former President Harry Truman agreed. In a newspaper article in May, Truman called the fallout "a small sacrifice" compared to "the infinitely greater evil of the use of nuclear bombs in war.'' He asked the American people "not to be panicked by the Soviet campaign of fear" which was "intended primarily to cripple the defense of the West."[50]

Moreover, it was not surprising that both the administration and its supporters suggested that the test ban proponents were following the Communist party line and implied that they were subversive of the national security. President Eisenhower opened up this line of attack at a press conference on June 5 when he commented that the call for test cessation "looks like almost an organized affair." The *U.S. News* had no doubt about what organization the president had in mind, calling the anti-testing movement "Communist-inspired." In Congress, Representative Francis Walter of Pennsylvania pointed to Pauling's long association with Communist-front groups to accuse him of spreading Soviet propaganda, and Representative Lawrence H. Smith of Wisconsin identified Cousins as a Communist dupe for enlisting Schweitzer in the test ban cause. Claiming that Communists and their apologists were "stirring up a national hysteria," Smith appealed to the American people not to "let the superficial, disputed fear of radioactivity blind us to the greatest threat of all—atheistic Communism."[51]

This time, however, not even "red baiting" could still the debate. Nuclear pacifists understood that radiation was one topic that touched a sensitive nerve and that the fear of fallout was alone capable of arousing the American people to press for a nuclear test ban treaty. By 1957 liberal organizations such as the Federation of American Scientists, the American Friends Service Committee, the Women's International League For Peace and Freedom, United World Federalists, Americans For Democratic Action, and the World Council of Churches were all speaking out and asking the three nuclear powers to reach agreement to suspend their nuclear tests. "It may or may not be too late," Cousins editorialized in the *Saturday Review*, "but at least we owe it to sanity to make the effort."[52] All that was needed was a central organization to coordinate the campaign. Thus the controversy over the atmospheric testing of nuclear weapons became the central issue of nuclear-pacifist concern and the one out of which the National Committee for a Sane Nuclear Policy would soon develop.

2

Bringing the Voice of Sanity to the People, 1957–1959

Within, at the most, ten years, some of these bombs are going off. I am saying this as responsibly as I can. That is the certainty. On the one side, therefore, we have a finite risk (negotiated nuclear test ban agreements). On the other side we have a certainty of disaster. Between a risk and a certainty a sane man does not hesitate.

—Sir Charles (C.P.) Snow, 1960[1]

The spring of 1957 was felt to be what Norman Cousins referred to at that time as "a magic moment," when the popular outcry over radiation led to reconsideration of American policy regarding nuclear testing. With this in mind, a temporary committee to stop H-bomb tests was formed when Lawrence Scott, the American Friends Service Committee peace education director in Chicago, "came east obsessed with nuclear testing and began agitating constantly for an end to this." Scott went to New York and gained the support of leading pacifists such as Muste, civil rights and peace activist Bayard Rustin, and Robert Gilmore, the New York executive secretary of the American Friends Service Committee. Using their names to attract other leading pacifists from the established peace organizations and church peace groups, Scott called all of them together for a meeting in Philadelphia on April 22. These pacifists talked about forming a "Proposed Committee to Stop H-Bomb

Tests'' and decided that the committee would "be broadly based with both pacifists and non-pacifists included.''[2]

Two very important questions were discussed at that April meeting: how to deal with the differences between the radical pacifists and the liberal nuclear-pacifists and whether to work for disarmament or to only focus on the nuclear testing issue. The first question was settled when they decided to form two groups—one for radical pacifists who would engage in Gandhian nonviolent resistance as their major tactic and the other for liberal nuclear-pacifists which would be "more educational and conventional orientated.'' The second question was easily answered when Henry Hitt Crane, a Methodist pastor from Detroit, jumped excitedly from his seat and proposed that both groups should focus on the "nuclear testing issue as the first step towards disarmament.'' Finally, it was decided to operate through a threefold organization: (1) an ad-hoc liberal nuclear-pacifist organization that would later be known as SANE, (2) an ad hoc radical pacifist, direct action oriented organization that would become the Committee for Non-Violent Action, and (3) the older peace organizations such as American Friends Service Committee and the Women's International League For Peace and Freedom, which would increasingly focus on the nuclear-testing issue, thus giving support and encouragement to the two ad hoc organizations.[3]

Scott made it clear that although there would be two separate ad hoc committees, he wanted a close working relationship between them. "While the two aspects are not organizationally tied together,'' he said, "I hope there will be some organic and spiritual relationship between the two aspects within a larger movement of Creative Truth.'' Scott was himself a radical pacifist and thus had more sympathy with that wing, so while he and Muste were forming the Committee for Non-Violent Action, he asked Robert Gilmore, who worked well with both types of pacifists, to organize the liberal organization. Initially, the two groups got along very well—some people, like Gilmore and Homer Jack, a Chicago Unitarian minister, were active in both—even though in later years they drew increasingly apart.[4]

During May an initiating committee formed and decided that Scott would contact Norman Cousins and Clarence Pickett, the secretary emeritus of the American Friends Service Committee, to see if they would join in calling leading liberals and churchmen to a meeting in New York to consider what citizens might do to end all nuclear weapons tests. Cousins agreed, as did Pickett, but he also expressed two concerns:

that the issue of nuclear tests should be taken out of the context of political polarization as had occurred in the presidential campaign the previous year and that it must be pointed up as a moral issue in which the clergy and other acknowledged leaders of moral thought and action would take the lead. Cousins strongly believed that the scientific facts and the important moral question at issue in the tests needed to be driven into the consciousness of all Americans and people of other lands. Thus on May 29, Pickett, Scott, Cousins, and Jack met in Cousins' New York office and decided to call together people of national stature who were concerned with the issue of cessation of bomb tests. The meeting was called at the Overseas Press Club in New York on June 21 by both Cousins, who contacted the leading nonpacifists concerned with peace work, and Pickett, who contacted the leading pacifists.[5]

Present at this formative meeting on the first day of summer 1957 were twenty-seven national leaders including churchmen, scientists, businessmen, labor representatives, authors, editors, and public figures. Pickett, a gentle, gray-haired man whose experience in such problems spanned half a century or more, opened the five-hour meeting by stating that Cousins and he "felt that something ought to be done to bring out the latent sensitivity of the American people to the poisoning effect of nuclear bombs on international relations and on humanity." The tone of the meeting was one of caution, of searching for clarity in approach, because everyone realized that the group and each of its members would be subject to attack from the advocates of increased armament.[6]

Cousins indicated that the day's meeting had no agenda but that at some point the United States must come to grips with the problem of nuclear testing. "We cannot sit back and wait for radioactive burden to settle over us," he stated. "The cessation of tests will not in itself make peace, but it will stop something dangerous in itself and gain firmer ground to stop future problems." Towards the end of five hours, Henry Hitt Crane tried to summarize the meeting in three points: the delegates should be encouraged by the London (Disarmament) Conference then going on; they should keep the United States from backing down; and they ought to recognize the immorality of poisoning the air of others by our continued nuclear tests. The conferees also decided to form a small steering committee, led by Pickett and Cousins, to name Homer Jack as secretary and coordinator of the group, and to issue a weekly newsletter to prospective members. Finally, they agreed to make a complete prospectus for the operation of an ad hoc committee of which

Norman Thomas was put in charge. The group temporarily named itself the Provisional Committee to Stop Nuclear Tests and decided to meet again in September.[7]

As Robert Divine has pointed out, the organizers of SANE faced a series of difficult problems, of which one was money. The Friends Committee on National Legislation supplied small sums for the newsletter, while Norman Cousins borrowed against the stock of the *Saturday Review* and spent several thousand dollars of his own money. Lenore Marshall, a wealthy New York writer and peace activist, soon became the group's sustaining patron.[8]

A name became a second consideration. The famed psychoanalyst and author, Erich Fromm, a refugee from Nazi Germany who had already in his lifetime watched mass madness overcome one great power, insisted that American public life first recognize the revalidation of simply saving sanity. According to Fromm, "The normal drive for survival" had been overwhelmed by the Cold War, and the role of informed citizens was to "try to bring the voice of sanity to the people." Admitting that it was "pathological" for people to be afraid when there was nothing to fear, he told Pickett that the lack of fear over the current arms race was even worse, "a symptom of a kind of schizophrenic indifference . . . which is so characteristic of our age." Heeding his suggestion that they advocate a return to sanity, the organizers finally settled on the name: the National Committee for a Sane Nuclear Policy.[9]

The final issue was how SANE could best influence national policy. Some members wanted a broad attack on the whole problem of disarmament; others preferred a quiet approach to policy makers, following the model of the Council of Foreign Relations. Catherine Cory, a West Coast organizer for the Friends Committee on National Legislation, struck the note that prevailed. "Ending bomb tests is the issue," she wrote to Cousins and Pickett. "The man on the street becomes paralyzed at the complexities of 'general disarmament.' " But in calling for an end to bomb tests, she continued, "at last we have an issue that the average Joe understands. Let's start with him and move on from there."[10]

SANE started out as an informal national committee for the purpose of putting important information before the American people and stimulating a great debate on the nuclear testing issue. It soon became apparent, however, that there was a larger need for a national organization with finances and personnel available. "The people are ready for leadership," wrote Catherine Cory to Cousins and Pickett, "and we are ready for that change in the level of our operations which your group can provide." The majority of SANE activists accepted this analysis. Thus, at the first organizing meeting in October, Homer Jack volunteered to serve as executive secretary on a part-time basis; and Cousins and Pickett, as co-chairmen. An organizing committee of five to six people, including Cousins, Pickett, Jack, Thomas and Gilmore, were chosen to draft a statement of purpose, hire a full-time executive secretary, and choose a larger committee of fifteen to twenty persons.[11]

Erich Fromm liked the idea of a national committee, "distinguished by one quality: sanity, realism, and concern," and though not overly optimistic, felt it was "worth trying everything to avoid a catastrophe." In a letter to Cousins, he expressed the sentiment of many nuclear pacifists when he pleaded: "We cannot sit and wait until a happy chance straightens out world history for us. Time is after us, with the speed of a sputnick." He added, "If we want to save ourselves from the inventions of our intelligence, then we must begin to exercise self-control and to turn this world into a place where one can live."[12]

Later that month, Trevor Thomas, who secured a leave of absence from the Friends Committee on National Legislation of Northern California, was hired to be the temporary executive secretary. Although the American Friends Service Committee became the organizational base for the new organization, an executive committee was formed which, besides for Cousins, Pickett, Jack, Thomas, Gilmore, and Lenore Marshall, included a wide diversity of peace activists and prominent public figures. Representing the established world peace organizations were Orlie Pell, president of the U.S. Section of the Women's International League for Peace and Freedom; Josephine Pomerance of the Committee for World Development and World Disarmament; and Clark Eichelberger, director of the American Association for the United Nations. Businessman Eugene Exman, vice president of Harper Brothers; Lawrence Mayers, Jr., president of L.C. Mayers Co.; Alan Wilson, vice president of the Advertising Council; and Clarence Low, a retired businessman, added their names and efforts to this distinguished list. Edward Sparling, president of Roosevelt University in Chicago, and Rev. Donald Harrington, minister of Community Church in New York, joined the executive committee. Professors Charles Price, director of the Department of Chemistry of the University of Pennsylvania, and

Hugh Wolfe, chairman of the Department of Physics at Cooper Union, added scientific prestige to the SANE cause and enlisted other scientists in the organizations' behalf.[13]

The organizing committee met in October and drafted a statement of its goals and purposes which included "developing public support for a boldly conceived and executed policy which would lead mankind away from nuclear war and toward world peace with justice." To this end they proposed the immediate cessation of all nuclear weapons tests by all countries enforced through a United Nations monitored agreement, the international control of missiles and outerspace satellites through a United Nations agency, and the support and reinforcement of all agencies concerned with upholding and strengthening the United Nations as an instrument of effective world law. The functions of the organization were also established: the committee would be a rallying point and a clearing house; it would prepare and reprint materials, distribute films, encourage the formation of local committees, issue public statements, sponsor visits to the major policy-making leaders, call conferences, and stimulate national organizations to take a stand on disarmament. Beyond these precise policy objectives, SANE leaders established their operation upon "a strong moral premise." In this way, SANE intended to speak intelligently about complex political and military considerations without floundering in endless technicalities. In this way, too, SANE activists planned to realize their main ambition of galvanizing "an aroused, articulate humanity that said to governments everywhere that a halt now [to nuclear testing] is not only possible, but imperative to survival."[14]

SANE's most successful effort toward rallying public support took place on November 15 when it ran a full-page newspaper advertisement in the *New York Times* beneath the banner "We Are Facing A Danger Unlike Any Danger That Has Ever Existed." Largely written by Cousins, the statement stressed going beyond the "national interest" to "the sovereignty of the human community" where "man has natural rights . . . to live and grow, to breathe unpoisoned air, to work on uncontaminated soil." It called on Americans to press their government for an immediate suspension of nuclear testing and proceed toward the development of "a higher loyalty—loyalty by man to the human community."[15]

As Robert Divine has pointed out, the sponsors signing this call to arms leaned heavily toward the liberal side of the political spectrum.

"We Are Facing A Danger Unlike Any Danger That Has Ever Existed..."

First of a Series of Statements For Americans in A Nuclear Age

A deep uneasiness exists inside Americans as we look out on the world.

It is not that we have suddenly become unsure of ourselves in a world in which the Soviet Union has dramatically laid claim to scientific supremacy.

Nor that the same propulsion device that can send a man-made satellite into outer space can send a missile carrying a hydrogen bomb across the ocean in eighteen minutes.

Nor is the uneasiness only the result of headlines that tell of trouble between Turkey and Syria and a war that could not be limited to the Middle East.

The uneasiness that exists inside Americans has to do with the fact that we are not living up to our moral capacity in the world.

We have been living half a life. We have been developing our appetites, but we have been starving our purposes. We have been concerned with bigger incomes, bigger television screens, and bigger cars — but not with the big ideas on which our lives and freedoms depend.

We are facing a danger unlike any danger that has ever existed. In our possession and in the possession of the Russians are more than enough nuclear explosives to put an end to the life of man on earth.

Our uneasiness is the result of the fact that our approach to the danger is unequal to the danger. Our response to the challenge of today's world seems out of joint. The slogans and arguments that belong to the world of competitive national sovereignties — a world of plot and counter-plot — no longer fit the world of today or tomorrow.

Just in front of us opens a grand human adventure into outer space. But within us and all around us is the need to make this world whole before we set out for other ones. We can earn the right to explore other planets only as we make this one safe and fit for human habitation.

The sovereignty of the human community comes before all others — before the sovereignty of groups, tribes, or nations. In that community, man has natural rights. He has the right to live and to grow, to breathe unpoisoned air, to work on uncontaminated soil. He has the right to his sacred nature.

If what nations are doing has the effect of destroying these natural rights, whether by upsetting the delicate balances on which life depends, or fouling the air, or devitalizing the land, or tampering with the genetic integrity of man himself; then it becomes necessary for people to restrain and tame the nations.

Indeed, the test of a nation's right to survive today is measured not by the size of its bombs or the range of

What You Can Do

1. What you say and what you do make public opinion. Let the people who serve you in public office know of your apprehensions and your hopes. Above all, make your ideas known to the President of the United States.

2. You can join the signers of this statement.

3. You can help make it possible for this statement and other statements like it to appear in newspapers throughout the country and the world.

4. You can talk to your friends and neighbors about the points in this message. You can discuss these matters in your church or synagogue, your club, your school, your union.

5. You can fill out the two coupons below: Send one to the President and the other to the National Committee For a Sane Nuclear Policy.

its missiles, but by the size and range of its concern for the human community as a whole.

There can be no true security for America unless we can exert leadership in these times, unless we become advocates of a grand design that is directed to the large cause of human destiny.

There can be no true security for America unless we can establish and keep vital connections with the world's people, unless there is some moral grandeur to our purposes, unless what we do is directed to the cause of human life and the free man.

There is much that America has said to the world. But the world is still waiting for us to say and do the things that will in deed and in truth represent our greatest strength.

What are these things?

FIRST, AS IT CONCERNS THE PEACE, AMERICA CAN SAY:

That we pledge ourselves to the cause of peace with justice on earth, and that there is no sacrifice that we are not prepared to make, nothing we will not do to create such a just peace for all peoples;

That we are prepared to support the concept of a United Nations with adequate authority under law to prevent aggression, adequate authority to compel and enforce disarmament, adequate authority to settle disputes among nations according to principles of justice.

NEXT, AS IT CONCERNS NUCLEAR WEAPONS, AMERICA CAN SAY:

That the earth is too small for intercontinental ballistic missiles and nuclear bombs, and that the first order of business for the world is to bring both under control,

That the development of satellites or rocket stations and the exploration of outer space must be carried on in the interests of the entire human community through a pooling of world science.

AS IT CONCERNS NUCLEAR TESTING, AMERICA CAN SAY:

That because of the grave unanswered questions with respect to nuclear test explosions — especially as it concerns the contamination of air and water and food, and the injury to man himself — we are calling upon all nations to suspend such explosions at once;

That while the abolition of testing will not by itself solve the problem of peace or the problem of armaments, it enables the world to eliminate immediately at least one real and specific danger. Also, that the abolition of testing gives us a place to begin on the larger question of armaments control, for the problems in monitoring such tests are relatively uncomplicated.

AS IT CONCERNS OUR CONNECTIONS TO THE REST OF MANKIND, AMERICA CAN SAY:

That none of the differences separating the governments of the world are as important as the membership of all peoples in the human family;

That the big challenge of the age is to develop the concept of a higher loyalty — loyalty by man to the human community,

That the greatest era of human history on earth is within reach of all mankind, that there is no area that cannot be made fertile or habitable, no disease that cannot be fought, no scarcity that cannot be conquered;

That all that is required for this is to re-direct our energies, re-discover our moral strength, re-define our purposes.

SIGNED

CLIP AND MAIL TO:

PRESIDENT DWIGHT D EISENHOWER
THE WHITE HOUSE, WASHINGTON 25, D. C.

Dear Mr. President:

I respectfully urge you to go before the United Nations and propose:

That nuclear test explosions, missiles and outer-space satellites be considered apart from other disarmament problems;

That, as there is now agreement in principle on the need for supervision and inspection necessary to verify a cessation of tests, all nuclear test explosions by all countries be stopped immediately and that the U N then proceed with the mechanics necessary for monitoring this cessation;

That missiles and outer-space satellites be brought under United Nations-monitored control, and that there be a pooling of world science for space exploration under the United Nations.

Now, more than ever before, mankind waits for some sign that it can be released from the terror of sudden attack and the grip of armaments. We look to you for guidance and direction in that aspiration.

Sincerely,

Name _____

Address _____

CLIP AND MAIL TO:

NATIONAL COMMITTEE
FOR A SANE NUCLEAR POLICY
P. O. BOX 1750
NEW YORK 17, N. Y.

Note: Make contributions to
"Sane Nuclear Policy".

☐ I am enclosing $_____ as my contribution toward advancing the work of the Committee and in helping to place this message in other towns and cities throughout the United States and the world. (This statement is available for reprint in your local paper.)

☐ I wish to know if a group to forward these ideas exists in my community.

☐ Send me further information about the Committee and its program.

Name _____

Address _____

City _____
(please print)

They included clergymen Henry Emerson Fosdick and Paul Tillich, scholars Lewis Mumford, James Shotwell, and Pitirim A. Sorokin, novelists James Jones and John Hersey, and such diverse public figures as Eleanor Roosevelt, Norman Thomas, and Cleveland Amory. Neither the former AEC commissioner Gordon Dean nor General Electric board chairman Charles Wilson, both of whom had attended the June 21 meeting, appeared on the list; and one businessman who did, General Mills board chairman Harry H. Bullis, insisted that his name be removed. Other nonsigners included Hermann J. Muller, Chester Bowles, Bentley Glass, Graham DuShane, Hans Bethe, and Max Ascoli. Their reasons for refusing varied, but Eugene Rabinowitch summed up the attitudes of many when he objected to such emotional phrases as "poisoned air" and "uncontaminated soil." While such qualitative language was "colorful," he felt that most scientists believed their task was to "help replace qualitative attitudes by quantitative judgments."[16]

The advertisement also drew mixed reactions from the public. Critics complained that the ad was too one-sided. Some of the respondents wondered whether the appeal would not aid Soviet policies and Communist propaganda. Others did not just wonder. There was an organization in Colorado Springs, Colorado, under the leadership of Robert and Virginia Heinlein, who published an advertisement in the local papers that read: "Who Are The Heirs of Patrick Henry? Stand Up and Be Counted." After quoting Patrick Henry's famous speech of "give me liberty, or give me death," it said that even if the people in the national committee were not all Communists, their manifesto was "the rankest sort of Communist propaganda." The New York Daily News adopted a milder approach toward SANE's efforts. "Far be it from us," their editorial declared, to charge SANE's leaders "with consciously trying to do a job for the Kremlin. We merely think that as regards nuclear weapons tests they are as nutty as so many fruitcakes."[17]

On the positive side, however, the response seemed to the committee to be overwhelming. People throughout the country shared their deep concern with the signers whose appeal expressed the fears, the desires, the hopes of many. Typical of most reactions were ones from two religious leaders. One said, "Some powerful national movement, with the intentions expressed in your advertisement, is desperately needed. I hope that you will grow to be the voice of countless citizens allied for the constructive use of atomic power." The other one read: "At a time when we seem frantic with hysterical fears it is good to have a voice calling for sanity and a new direction to our efforts on behalf of the human community."[18]

One Denver resident sent in a check for $2 with the words, "This is THE idea I have been waiting for." And the *Denver Post* reproduced a condensed version of the November 15 statement on its editorial page accompanied by a lead editorial which concluded:

Almost casually begun, as this National Committee for a Sane Nuclear Policy may have been, it looks like the spark that could call forth the expression of one great amen of the apprehensions common to men everywhere over whether or not they will be able to survive the awesome power their species has acquired with technical knowledge.

And the *Des Moines Tribune* in another lead editorial concluded:

There may be an element of naivete in the specific proposals advanced (by the National Committee), but the urgency is real, the dangers are real, the ultimate goal is hard to quarrel with. We are facing a danger unlike any danger that has ever existed.[19]

An ad hoc venture intended by its founders to serve a temporary educational purpose, SANE was not designed to become a permanent membership organization, but this one advertisement, as an organizational report later acknowledged, "started a movement." Within six weeks of its appearance approximately 2,500 letters, the vast majority of them enthusiastic, poured into the understaffed SANE office in New York. The $4,700 cost of the ad was recovered in the first few days after its publication. People in all parts of the country voluntarily placed reprints of this original advertisement in thirty-two different newspapers by January and donated an additional $12,000 to the new organization. There were requests for 25,000 reprints of the statement, and thousands of people wrote in to ask how they could help or join the committee. Grass-roots response was so electrifying that SANE leaders, who were originally ambivalent toward the idea of a mass membership organization, decided to redefine the SANE operation along these lines. By the summer of 1958 SANE had about 130 chapters representing approximately 25,000 Americans. Powerfully SANE swept into a vacuum in the American peace movement, energizing people to politically relevant action on specific issues of the arms race. "SANE gave anxious citizens from varied background," one of its leaders recalled later, "a single meaningful issue on which to act—the cessation of nuclear weapons testing."[20]

Yet this view seems only partially correct. SANE did attract many young people and liberals who were sympathetic to the nuclear-pacifist movement; however, it also drew upon the peace movement's more traditional sources of strength. As sociologist Nathan Glazer had observed, SANE "was actually based on a coalition of two major groupings, both of which had their origins in older issues: the proponents of world government on the one hand and the pacifists on the other."[21] For example, prominent SANE spokesmen like Norman Cousins, Oscar Hammerstein, and Walter Reuther had all been officers in the United World Federalists. In addition, Donald Keys, SANE's first full-time executive director, had been on the UWF staff. Because of the latter's desire to avoid "eyebrow-raising" activities, SANE received little cooperation from the world government organization. Although a considerable number of SANE leaders were moderate and traditional pacifists, including Clarence Pickett, Robert Gilmore, and Norman Thomas, SANE itself was "pragmatic, not absolutist." Radical pacifists like A.J. Muste gave SANE strong support in the beginning, but most became involved in the more direct-action groups such as the Committee For Non-Violent Action.

An early profile of SANE membership also indicated a considerable unevenness in SANE's appeal as evidenced by the fact that almost 80 percent of the responses and contributions came from New York, New Jersey, Connecticut, California, Illinois, and Pennsylvania; while no responses were received from eleven states and only a few from twenty-two others. New York and San Francisco responded well to the advertisement; Manhattan alone contributed almost one quarter of the total funds raised. On the other hand, a full-page advertisement in the *Wichita* (Kansas) *Beacon* (circulation 100,000) elicited total contributions of $8; and Buffalo, Indianapolis, Minneapolis, New Orleans, Dallas, and San Antonio did not respond at all.[22]

Despite the fear created by the Soviet launching of the Sputnik satellite that orbited the earth in a stunning display of Russian technological advancement and missile capability, the public campaign against nuclear weapons tests continued to grow in the early months of 1958; and SANE played an important role in giving the movement an organizational focus. Feeling that the Eisenhower Administration needed to be goaded into pursuing a nuclear test ban treaty, SANE approached Democratic Senator Hubert Humphrey of Minnesota with a draft resolution calling for a moratorium on testing under international supervision and asked if he would introduce the resolution in Congress. Although Humphrey had emerged as the leading congressional advocate of a test ban, he declined to sponsor the SANE resolution. He did promise, however, that, as chairman of the Senate Subcommittee on Disarmament, he would hold a new round of hearings on the test ban issue and would give a major speech on disarmament in the Senate on February 4. Praising Humphrey's speech urging a test ban with an adequate system of inspection and detection, SANE's executive director Trevor Thomas sent telegrams to fifty-five local chapters asking them to solicit at least twenty-five individual letters to Congress endorsing the senator's remarks. In a letter to the *New York Times*, New York City SANE members, including Erich Fromm, Norman Thomas, and Robert Gilmore, called attention to the Senate address and urged Humphrey to put his proposal in the form of a resolution and prompt action to implement it. A test ban, they wrote, would be "the one most obvious step toward halting a world competition in destructiveness which can have only one end."[23]

With President Eisenhower still doubting the wisdom of the test ban proposal, SANE decided to capitalize on the fallout scare that gripped the American people. The committee's second advertisement appeared in the *New York Herald Tribune* on March 24, 1958. Entitled "No Contamination without Representation," the text, taken from an editorial by Norman Cousins in the *Saturday Review* and published earlier, charged that the American tests were poisoning the atmosphere of the entire world. "We do not have the right—nor does any nation—to take risks, large or small, for other peoples without their consent," SANE declared. Some critics felt the ad was too emotional, appealing to people's fears and anxieties; but others like Bill Attwood, the editor of *Look*, favored a frontal assault that would shock the American people into action. "The appeal has to be made to the emotions first," he wrote. "The intellectual arguments come later." Civil rights leader and pacifist Martin Luther King, Jr., liked the advertisement and signed it enthusiastically, but others wanted SANE to deal less with education and more with action. Lewis Mumford signed the ad reluctantly but wrote to Trevor Thomas that he thought this ad "underestimates the amount of knowledge the people have already acquired about radioactivity. . . . What they need more information about is what they shall do to bring our leaders to their senses," he stated. "and this problem occupies the smallest part of the whole appeal."[24]

After Soviet Foreign Minister Andrei Gromyko informed the world on March 31 that the USSR was unilaterally halting all further tests of nuclear weapons, SANE directed its efforts toward similar action by the United States. For the first time the committee took to the streets in direct action protest by staging a nineteen-day rally in New York City, held public meetings, and picketed at the United Nations. On April 11 the leaders of SANE placed another full-page ad in the *New York Times* frankly designed to frighten the American people. Half the page was taken up by a mushroom cloud with the caption, "Nuclear Tests Are Endangering Our Health Right Now." After calling for an immediate cessation in American testing, the ad closed with the injunction, "We must stop the contamination of the air, the milk children drink, the food we eat. While there is still time, let us come to life on this issue and take the moral initiative."[25]

Several signers of the two earlier SANE ads disagreed with what one called "the frenzied tone" of this statement, but Norman Cousins, who again wrote the copy for SANE, went even further in his *Saturday Review* editorials. In the April 12 issue he called the Soviet suspension "a moral disaster for the United States." A week later he wrote an editorial reprinted in an advertisement in the *New York Times* stating that the people of the world were "worried about the obscene competition in creating weapons that can incinerate millions at a time" and stressed his belief that there was "a real threat of contamination to air and food and human tissue." The only solution was for the United States to stop all tests immediately. "No nation has the right to contaminate or jeopardize the air or water or food that belongs to other people," he declared. "If we are to hold our own in the world and move towards a meaningful peace, then we must come up with a daring program of our own. This is where sanity begins. . . ."[26]

Advocates of testing again charged that those who called for suspension were helping the Communist cause. *Time* did a feature in mid-April in which the editors pointed out that Pauling and several others who signed the SANE ads had been active in Communist-front groups. Under pictures of the signers, *Time* ran the caption, "Defenders of the unborn . . . or dupes of the enemies of liberty?" And to a surprising degree the American people agreed with the opponents of the test ban.

NUCLEAR BOMBS CAN DESTROY ALL LIFE IN WAR

NUCLEAR TESTS ARE ENDANGERING OUR HEALTH RIGHT NOW

WE MUST POSTPONE OUR COMING TESTS

1. The Soviet Union states it is calling off further nuclear tests. The easiest way for us to convert this announcement into a moral disaster for the United States is to stand pat on this issue. The least we can do today—if we hope to restore America's moral standing in the world—is to postpone our tests while we negotiate a satisfactory agreement. President Eisenhower's April 1 letter to Khrushchev regains some of the ground lost by our first response to the Soviet announcement. The President's recommendation for technical studies preliminary to a broad disarmament agreement deserves the widest possible support. But much more has to be done!

2. It is true that the Soviet Union waited until it completed its Spring tests which sharply increased poisonous radioactive strontium in the atmosphere. But it makes no sense for the United States to complain about radioactivity from the Russian tests and then plan to add to it with our own tests. Estimated nuclear box score to date: United States—100-odd tests; Soviet Union—50-odd tests.

3. The U. S. Atomic Energy Commission now admits that radioactive fallout is a matter for genuine concern and that the United States is the hottest radioactive place in the world. Scientists warn that thousands of babies will be born malformed because of tests to date. Many thousands more people will prematurely die of diseases of blood and bone.

WE MUST CALL FOR A UNITED NATIONS INSPECTED BAN ON TESTS

1. We must challenge Moscow's bid by proposing a permanent end to tests under effective inspection. Khrushchev said on April 4: "Russia is willing to accept supervision." Let's call his hand.

Dr. Libby of the Atomic Energy Commission concedes that detection of nuclear explosions is feasible, contrary to the much publicized doubts of Dr. Edward Teller. The AEC has said that last year's underground test in Nevada was detected only 250 miles away. Now it is revealed that the test was detected in Alaska, 2300 miles away. A hydrogen bomb is many thousands of times more powerful than the "tiny" bomb used in the underground test.

Tests deemed necessary for peaceful purposes can be conducted by an international agency. Nuclear weapons tests must be stopped.

WE MUST NOT SUPPLY BOMB MATERIALS TO OTHER COUNTRIES

Bills now before Congress would authorize transfer of bomb materials, parts and weapons design blueprints to other countries.

This would mean more nuclear powers and so extend the "suicide club." Korea is pressing for nuclear arms. NATO powers are seeking them. Turkey will certainly want them. Then Pakistan. Moscow will make Communist China a nuclear power. Fuses could be set all over the world.

We would increase the chance of accidental war, launched by some minor military commander. Witness the anonymous French colonel who ordered the attack on a Tunisian village, using American-made planes.

AMERICAN SECURITY AND WORLD SECURITY ARE NOW ONE

America must give leadership for world disarmament and conditions that make for a just and workable peace. We must stop the contamination of the air, the milk children drink, the food we eat.

While there is yet time, let us come to life on this issue and take the moral initiative.

ACT NOW—FOR MAN'S SAKE

Write President Eisenhower, The White House, Washington, D. C., and Vice-President Nixon, The Capitol, Washington, D. C.

Write your U. S. Senator and Representative in Washington opposing the bills to transfer bomb materials to other countries and favoring an end to nuclear tests as a first step toward a broader disarmament. Send a copy to Senator John O. Pastore of the Joint Committee on Atomic Energy.

Write your newspaper editor, or news commentator.

Organize a group, or work with existing ones in your community.

Write the National Committee for permission to reprint this advertisement in your home paper. We'll tell you how to do it.

Send a contribution to this Committee to keep it going and expand its influence. Your moral support is heartening. YOUR FINANCIAL SUPPORT IS *IMPERATIVE*. Use the coupon below.

NATIONAL COMMITTEE FOR A SANE NUCLEAR POLICY, 202 East 44th Street, New York 17, N. Y. OXFORD 7-2295

Chairmen: Norman Cousins, Clarence Pickett. Treasurer: Clarence H. Low. Comptroller: Lawrence S. Mayers, Jr. Staff: Trevor Thomas, Alfred Williams

---

CLIP AND MAIL TO:

In a Gallup poll in mid-April, by a two-to-one margin the American people rejected a unilateral halt to nuclear testing. The same poll revealed, however, that 46 percent believed that continued testing might harm future generations. Apparently, as Robert Divine has pointed out, many still felt that national security required that this risk be taken.[27]

Not easily disheartened, however, nuclear pacifists were already going beyond the testing issue to an emphasis upon the dangers of nuclear weapons themselves. This step was predictable, for the weapons always represented the greatest concern of SANE disarmament advocates. In June 1958, pondering what would happen if the United States did ban nuclear weapons tests, Norman Cousins maintained that such an action would "not represent the be-all and end-all of world peace and nuclear sanity. A truly sane nuclear policy will not be achieved," he stated, "until nuclear weapons are brought completely under control." Two months later, Cousins's thoughts gathered greater salience when the United States followed the lead of the Soviet Union and voluntarily suspended nuclear weapons tests, and both nations agreed to meet in Geneva to begin negotiations for a test ban treaty. SANE co-chairmen Cousins and Pickett sent a telegram to the president on August 22 praising him for his "wise and courageous action" and stating their hope that the stage was now set "for an early agreement signed by all nations for the permanent cessation of weapons tests followed by a dramatic series of moves looking towards the world control and reduction of nuclear stockpiles." With the testing issue thus in negotiation, SANE turned its attention to intercontinental ballistic missiles and to the threat of nuclear annihilation. At a fall 1958 national conference, the organization resolved to broaden its goal from a nuclear test ban to general disarmament.[28]

As historian Lawrence Wittner has noted, this growth of nuclear pacifism beyond the fallout issue indicated "that while some Americans may have concerned themselves solely with the problem of avoiding a dosage of radiation, many others were reexamining the nature of war in light of the development of thermonuclear weapons." Nuclear pacifists believed that the development of nuclear weapons and their sophisticated delivery systems had made the use of war as an instrument of national policy totally self-defeating, impractical, and immoral. The best hope for a world without self-destroying war, SANE agreed, was in the achievement of universal, total disarmament with adequate inspection and control, down to levels required for maintenance of internal order.[29]

Nuclear pacifists considered various crucial steps towards disarmament to include the conclusion of an international agreement for the cessation of all nuclear weapons testing under adequate inspection, an international security system that required a strengthened United Nations to settle disputes and to carry out inspection and control, a World Court whose jurisdiction was accepted without reservation by all nations, and some form of international peace force or police. The early stages of a phased-in disarmament should, they felt, be accompanied by political settlements and the mutual withdrawal of armed forces and nuclear weapons from danger areas. Thus both disarmament and disengagement under proper inspection would reduce international tensions.[30]

With the committee's policy branching out into general disarmament, it seemed to many that SANE was becoming the American equivalent of Britain's Campaign for Nuclear Disarmament (CND), even though contact between SANE and CND seems to have been limited. Homer Jack of SANE had gone to London to help start the Campaign for Nuclear Disarmament in January 1958 in protest against Britain's explosion of its first H-bomb test the preceding November, and a year later the group that founded CND wished to model the organization after SANE in mapping a strategy that was directed solely toward influential established figures. Like SANE, the early CND executive committee possessed the qualities of rather mild radicalism combined with the social prestige necessary to make the success of such a campaign plausible.[31]

As Americans became more conscious of the potential for nuclear disaster, SANE grew rapidly in size and influence. On June 4, 1958, Senator Humphrey on the floor of the Senate praised the national committee and stated that it had "done much to encourage a constructive and thoughtful discussion of the problems inherent with development of nuclear weapons and the proposals to ban nuclear weapons testing by international agreements providing for an effective system of inspection and detection." During the 1958–1959 Geneva talks on disarmament, the committee gathered thousands of signatures on petitions urging a test ban, culminating when Donald Keys and Robert Gilmore flew off to the Geneva Conference and left them with the bewildered delegates. SANE also arranged for nineteen world leaders, including Albert Schweitzer, Gunnar Myrdal of Sweden, Dimitri Shostakovich of the Soviet Union, Bertrand Russell, Eleanor Roosevelt, and Martin Luther King to address an appeal "To The Men at Geneva." Published as a full-page ad in the *New York Times* on October 31, 1958, the day the one-year halt in U.S. nuclear testing went into effect and the nuclear powers commenced their meeting in Geneva, the petition stressed both the fallout danger and the problem of nuclear proliferation and concluded with the statement: "Today is a day that could make an historic beginning in controlling the new power and in safeguarding those fragile conditions on this earth that would make human life possible." Mr. T.G. Narayanan, personal representative of the secretary general of the United Nations, indicated that this appeal was the most helpful effort that had been made in support of the Conference on Discontinuance of Nuclear Weapons Tests in Geneva.[32]

Believing that a moratorium had been secured, SANE did not foresee the long struggle to achieve even a partial test ban treaty. As the talks dragged on, the members realized that they had to face the difficult task of supporting the marathon Geneva negotiations despite diminishing interest by the public and concerted attacks by the Atomic Energy Commission and the Department of Defense. John McCone, head of the AEC, declared that his agency was ready to resume testing at a moment's notice. He openly regretted the moratorium and stated the AEC's belief that additional tests were needed to perfect new weapons, especially the desired "clean" bomb which the Eisenhower Administration had talked about a year earlier. At the end of 1958 with the Geneva discussions well under way, Eisenhower received an AEC report on Operation Hardtack which cast doubt on the ability of the Geneva network to detect all underground tests. This information, Eisenhower later wrote, "threw a pall on the conference at Geneva." Not wanting to break off the talks completely, Eisenhower still refused to give up the quest for a test ban.[33]

To give the president support in this endeavor, SANE published another advertisement in February 1959, titled "Mr. Eisenhower, Mr. Khrushchev, Mr. Macmillan, The Time is Now!" "The answer to the present deadlock," the statement declared, "is an inspection system divorced from political considerations, and staffed by an international team of scientists." The Atomic Energy Commission came in for sharp attack, as SANE called attention to the misleading way the AEC used "new evidence on underground tests" to exaggerate the difficulties of establishing a workable inspection system. The statement challenged the Atomic Energy Commission's record on "the clean bomb," the hazard of the fallout and the use of tactical nuclear weapons, and declared that "the political judgments of the Atomic Energy Commission and the Defense Department provide dangerous counsel for Americans and the World.'' SANE appealed to the Geneva representatives for substantial progress, warning that ''the price of failure may very well be the price of human life itself.'' Fifty-eight eminent Americans signed this statement including Gordon W. Allport, psychologist; Stuart Chase, author; Rev. Harry Emerson Fosdick of Riverside Church in New York; Nobel Prize winning scientists H.J. Muller, Linus Pauling, and Harold C. Urey; playwright Clifford Odets; and cartoonist Walt Kelly, creator of ''Pogo.''[34]

The appearance of the advertisement signaled the beginning of a month-long campaign during March by local SANE committees throughout the country in an effort to make the Eisenhower Administration as well as the British and Soviet governments aware of the deep desire of Americans for the success of the Geneva Conference. The campaign was focused around what was called ''Acts For Sanity,'' to protest the insanity of continued nuclear testing and the nuclear arms race and to appeal for reasonable solutions to international conflict. ''We must see to it that nothing is left undone by ourselves and our country that might contribute to agreement and settlement,'' National SANE declared in a letter to every local group in the country focusing attention on ''Acts For Sanity'' and initiated a major effort in its behalf.[35]

As part of this spring campaign SANE inaugurated peace demonstrations patterned after Britain's ''Ban the Bomb'' Aldermaston march and worked in support of a Senate resolution endorsing efforts to secure a test ban treaty, giving special praise to Senator Humphrey for his efforts in this endeavor. The New York Easter demonstration, one of several in American cities, was sponsored by SANE and the American Friends Service Committee, with Robert Gilmore, a director in both organizations, as chairman. The *New York Times* estimated that 600 people, mostly high school and college students, attended the rally in 32° weather where they heard a series of speakers, headed by Norman Thomas and A.J. Muste, call for a halt to nuclear bomb testing and for agreement of atomic disarmament. These Easter-time Aldermaston marches, as they were called, became annual events in Britain and marked the end of apathy in that country on the peace question. When SANE inaugurated these marches in 1959, the same held true in the United States but to a much lesser degree.[36]

At the same time, the American people found themselves in the grip of a full-scale fallout scare. ''The fallout issue has become our hottest,'' commented SANE's Washington lobbyist Sanford Gottlieb that spring, "and we have a real chance to make a significant breakthrough which will affect our drive against testing." In New York City, SANE responded by setting up a storefront information center for two weeks in Times Square. A vivid window display held a geiger counter, marked magazine articles explaining the effect on Strontium–90 in the milk we drink, statements by Albert Schweitzer and Linus Pauling on the dangers of nuclear fallout, a long photograph showing the flattened landscape of Hiroshima after the A-bomb, and a flashboard hooked to an "Electronic Brain" device that challenged all comers to a game of Tic-Tac-Toe. A loudspeaker told the passing stream "Strontium 90 falls to the earth like rain. It can cause leukemia, cancer, and bone disease. . . . " Inside, there were displays of books and pamphlets, including Nevil Shute's *On the Beach*, a widely read novel published in 1957 on how fallout from a nuclear war fought in 1961 gradually wiped out the entire population of the globe. And each day speakers including Dr. Algernon Black of the Ethical Culture Society, Stanley Issacs of the City Council, the Reverend Donald Harrington of the Community Church, and Dr. Hugh C. Wolfe, head of the Physics Department at Cooper Union, addressed the crowds that gathered at lunch time.

The exhibit was part of the committee's "Acts for Peace." Though planned for only two weeks, public response and donations were such that it held out for four. An estimated 40,000 people visited the display taking away some 80,000 pieces of literature, which included more than 1,000 reprints of a *Consumer's Reports*' article on Strontium–90 in milk. Nearly 6,000 people signed the "Time is Now" petition, over 200 letters and 800 postcards were written at the center, and visitors contributed $2,200. For all its efforts, SANE received at least some of the publicity it was seeking. The *New York Post* carried four feature stories on the center; the *Nation* ran a special feature article called "Beachhead on 42nd Street;" and the committee gained national television exposure on Dave Garroway's "Today" show.[37]

The protests mounted in intensity as the spring went on. Linus Pauling, addressing a SANE rally in Brooklyn, warned that the increased level of Strontium 90 would lead to 100,000 deaths in the next generation. "The only safe amount of Strontium 90 in the bones of our children," he declared, "is zero." Norman Cousins was equally indignant. "There is no known way of washing the sky," he wrote, "no way to keep the strontium and cesium from falling like rain; no way to keep it from getting into food and milk and thence into the bones of children. . . . '' The argument that only a tiny fraction of the world's population would be affected did not impress Cousins. ''The heart of the matter is that we have not asked—nor have the Russians nor the English—the permission of other peoples to foul up their air, dust their lands with radioactive poisons, and jeopardize the lives of children in particular.''[38]

On May 5 the special Congressional Committee on Radiation headed by Representative Holifield began a four-day series of hearings on the hazards of fallout and concluded that future testing in the atmosphere would soon lead to dangerous burdens of Strontium–90 in the bodies of everyone on earth. But when Holifield released the report to the AEC's General Advisory Committee, the scientists on the panel concluded that the hazard from Strontium–90 was slight, amounting to less than 5 percent of the radiation exposure the average American received from natural background sources and medical and dental x-rays. This small risk was well worth running, the panel concluded, pointing out that ''weapons tests have been an essential part of our effort to prevent the occurrence of nuclear war.''[39]

SANE took the hearings to task and demanded that they be reopened to allow critics of testing to present their case to the American people. In another full-page ad in the *New York Times*, SANE claimed that the hearings had ignored the high level of radiation in the American food supply. Calling for a new Congressional inquiry, the Committee stated its belief that ''Humanity Has A Common Will And Right To Survive.'' Stressing the dangers of psychological fallout, the statement declared, ''More dangerous than nuclear fallout or nuclear war is the psychological fallout that blinds men to the peril and drives nations to seek solutions to world problems in ways that threaten world disaster.'' Among the sixty-nine signers were actors Steve Allen and Robert Ryan; Dr. William Davidon, chairman, Atomic Scientists of Chicago; Dr. David Inglis, senior physicist, Argonne, National Laboratory; and such well-known public figures as academics C. Wright Mills and David Riesman, Mrs. Eleanor Roosevelt, and author Tennessee Williams. The ad pointed out that only a direct appeal to President Eisenhower would be effective in thwarting the distribution of nuclear weapons to other countries and asked the president to announce a continuation of the moratorium to support the continuing test ban talks in Geneva.[40]

The following September, interpreting the exchange of visits between

HUMANITY HAS A COMMON WILL AND RIGHT TO SURVIVE!

These are the shocking facts 3 Congressional Committee Hearings disclosed, and failed to disclose, about Nuclear Testing and Nuclear Warfare

THE HEARINGS ON FALLOUT

These Facts Were Revealed:

- A "very serious hazard" would result from continued unrestricted testing of nuclear weapons.
- In a few years, the average concentration of Strontium-90 in American children will likely reach 10 "Sunshine (strontium) units," and in some, 30 s. u., even if no more tests are held.
- The AEC now admits that the total numbers injured throughout the world will be very large.

These Key Issues Were Not Even Discussed:

- A new international recommendation shows a growing danger. The International Commission on Radiological Protection says that the radioactivity which populations can safely absorb is only one-third (33) strontium units of that currently considered "safe" by the AEC (100 s.u.).
- Fallout conditions in several United States locations including areas of North Dakota, Utah, and Minnesota are well beyond the new "permissible" level. In a few years radioactivity in many areas will reach or pass this danger level.
- There is practically no information available on the levels of radioactivity in everyday foodstuffs throughout the U.S., despite the millions spent by the AEC.
- There is no advice available to consumers on how to reduce dietary levels of radioactivity.
- There is no biologist member on the AEC, and no one in actual charge of the program on fallout.

THE HEARINGS ON NUCLEAR WAR

These Facts Were Revealed:

- That a relatively small nuclear raid on the United States involving 263 hydrogen bombs would kill and injure 68,000,000 Americans.
- ...raise from 23,000,000 to 800,000,000 new mutations over 30 generations, which would result in increased malformations and stillbirths.
- ...render comfortable half of all the dwellings in the U. S. for an extended period.
- ...raise the average level of Strontium-90 in human bones to 300 strontium units, more times the now recommended "maximum" level.
- ...leave the survivors to "eke out an existence on land contaminated by radioactivity, swept by forest fires, and ending into new dark lands."
- He says, the U. S. has answered its ability to cure to viable every Russian city of consequence in the first few minutes of such a war.

Again Many Key Issues Were Not Even Discussed:

- Nor is it clear why the size of weapons in the hypothetical attack was held to 10 megaton raw without tons of TNT equivalent, when both Russia and the United States have exploded much larger weapons.
- The study showed that civil defense efforts in the immediate area of the attack will be useless.
- The "immediately" area — or "hopelessly congested" area, to one or ten or more active area — "The ignition hazard from the thermal radiation of a 10 MT surface burst will extend over a circle of about 25 miles in radius ... everyone and everything within this tremendous area (1,200 square miles) would probably be consumed or killed."
  — Testimony of William F. Hines.
- A civil defense program of "do-it-yourself" fallout shelters is an admission that target-area populations will be written off. Such shelters will only save the lives of those far outside the attack periphery.
- No estimate was given of the problems of communication, food supplies, economic recovery, or human behavior under the conditions stated.
- No realistic appraisal was given of the pulse at which type and order break down, or when a radium cannot be a nation.
- No reference was made to the use of other new weapons of mass destruction—"Biologicals" and gas are now being brought forward as "main humane" weapons. We are being told that our adversaries will use biological, and that, consequently, we must be fully prepared, both materially and psychologically, to do the same.

THE HEARINGS ON DISPERSAL OF NUCLEAR WEAPONS PARTS

These Facts Were Revealed:

- Nuclear weapons delivery systems will be installed in Germany and in other NATO countries.
- The warheads themselves will be stockpiled in these countries and will remain, at least initially, under American control.
- Several of the agreements, including the one with West Germany, can only be terminated at the will of both parties.

The Key Issues Received No Floor Debate In The Senate And Little In The House:

- The agreements will give Germany a veto over any efforts for nuclear arms control in Europe.
- They will prejudice the negotiations on the reunification of Germany.
- They will contribute to the creation of additional nuclear powers.

(These agreements now go into force automatically unless the President himself delays their implementation.)

But more dangerous than nuclear fallout or nuclear war is the psychological fallout that blinds men to the peril and drives nations to seek solutions to world problems in ways that threaten world disaster. It is psychological fallout that encourages belief that security can be based on the threat of annihilation or war "limited" by a new set of rules. It is psychological fallout which prompts well-meaning persons to insist that continued nuclear testing is "moral" and desirable, and this is what leads to apathy and to a denial of the problems. THE PLAIN FACT IS THAT THE SYSTEM FOR SETTLING DIFFERENCES BY WAR HAS BROKEN DOWN. It has broken down under the impact of man's inventiveness and cannot be restored. THE PLAIN FACT IS THAT THE RULE OF FORCE CAN NO LONGER REGULATE THE RELATIONS BETWEEN NATIONS, and that nations can no longer provide "security" for themselves. They can only find world security in an effective and strengthened United Nations. THE PLAIN FACT IS THAT HUMANITY HAS A COMMON RIGHT AND A COMMON WILL TO SURVIVE. Because of this, Russians and Americans have a common goal in negotiated settlements and in those arrangements which will lift off the world the burden of the multi-billion dollar nuclear arms race, which is a tragic betrayal of human need, and can only lead to disaster.

NATIONAL COMMITTEE FOR A SANE NUCLEAR POLICY, INC.
202 EAST 44th STREET · NEW YORK 17, N. Y.

WHAT CAN YOU DO FOR A SANE NUCLEAR POLICY?

- Wire the President at once, urging no distribution of nuclear weapons systems to other countries.
- Urge that the U. S. announce a policy of no nuclear tests to support the treaty talks in Geneva.
- Urge your friends and business associates, members of your church or temple, your club or organization, to take a stand and send wires to the President on this issue.
- Work with your local SANE committee, and send your dollars to help bolster the efforts for a sane nuclear policy.

National Committee for a Sane Nuclear Policy, Inc.
Clarence H. Low, Treasurer
Box 1705, New York 17, N. Y.

☐ Enclosed is my contribution for a Sane Nuclear Policy
☐ $1,000 ☐ $500 ☐ $100 ☐ $25 ☐ $____
☐ I have wired the President opposing the nuclear giveaway program.
☐ Send me more information about your committee.

Name _____

Address _____

City _____ Zone ____ State ____

Premier Nikita Khrushchev and President Eisenhower as an opportunity to indicate the overwhelming public support for a permanent end to nuclear testing, SANE launched a nationwide appeal campaign in the form of an open letter to the premier and the president. Welcoming the exchange, and stating the committee hope that this direct approach would make a durable peace more possible, the statement declared:

There is one tangible act you can perform that will be a clear unmistakable sign to all humanity that your meetings have been fruitful. You can remove the few remaining obstacles to a permanent end to nuclear weapons tests under inspection and control. . . . Your historic meeting can be the turning point that will guarantee human survival. . . . "[41]

In conjunction with its second annual meeting in October, SANE held a rally in New York's Carnegie Hall, where almost 3,000 people crowded in to hear Linus Pauling denounce the menace of nuclear weapons and call for complete disarmament. Pauling declared that probably not more than one million Americans could survive a nuclear attack of the size that could then be expected, and he urged the United States to press for success in the current Geneva talks. The American people evidently agreed. A Gallup poll taken in mid-November showed that an overwhelming 77 percent of those asked wanted to see "the agreement to stop testing H-bombs extended for another year." While SANE published another full-page ad in the *New York Times* with the caption "Three Out of Four Americans Favor a Ban on Atomic Testing," the editors of the *Bulletin of Atomic Scientists* rejoiced that the "good old days when the AEC felt free to test as it pleased" are over. "The general agreement that the air we breathe is the common property of mankind and not to be polluted at the will of sovereign nations," the *Bulletin* concluded, "is a step forward in the education of the human race."[42]

In this period, SANE grew rapidly with 150 local committees organized in many communities, including chapters in Canada and Puerto Rico, and prominent personalities volunteering to become sponsors. The international lists were compromised largely of those who had signed the earlier statement "To the Men at Geneva:" Albert Schweitzer; Max Born of Germany; Lord Bertrand Russell, Canon L. John Collins, and Lord Boyd-Orr of Great Britain; Gunnar Myrdal of Sweden; Francois Mauriac of France; D. Rajagopalachari from India; Pablo Casals from Puerto Rico; and Brock Chisolm from Canada. A wide diversity of notable national sponsors were also enlisted which ranged from Pauling and King to singer Harry Belafonte, cartoonist Jules Feiffer, architect Walter Gropius, and conductor Bruno Walter.[43]

SANE activists were equally proud of their other accomplishments during the previous year. The committee was more financially stable than it had ever been. Emerging from a period where the national organization was literally struggling on a week-to-week basis to meet a reduced payroll and keep the telephones operating, it was now able to have paid off most of its debt and had raised and spent $50,000 in behalf of its program. During 1959 SANE had prepared and distributed 202,000 pieces of literature and had published three full-page ads in the *New York Times* which resulted in 11,708 mail responses and direct contributions of $9,393. National SANE issued twenty-five Action Memos during the year dealing with the ads, the petitions, the Geneva talks, and related subjects—an average of about one every two weeks—and placed representatives of the committee on more than fifty television and radio programs.[44]

SANE was becoming so popular that it spread to Hollywood, where actor Steve Allen was host to the first meeting of the Hollywood chapter of SANE at the Beverly Hills Hotel. At a subsequent meeting at the home of Robert Ryan, more than 150 actors, writers, directors, and producers gathered to hear Cousins speak on the dangers of nuclear testing and a nuclear-based foreign policy. According to Allen, "In SANE the nation at long last had a magnet that would attract people from all walks of life." Hollywood, which had been for so many years politically inactive, "sparked to this organization as if by magic." Allen and Ryan became co-chairmen of the committee; Max Youngstein, vice president of United Artists, treasurer; Maxine Gomberg, secretary; and Marianna Newton became executive director. A statement of purpose from the newly formed committee declared:

We wish to lend the resources of Hollywood to the work already being done in alerting the American public to the catastrophic danger facing us all today. . . . Now that the survival of mankind is at stake, we are calling upon ourselves, our time, our talents, and dedication to help acquaint the public with the facts.

Within a few days they added to the letterhead of Hollywood for SANE the names of more than fifty of some of the most influential and prominent people in the entertainment industry, including Marlon Brando,

Kirk Douglas, Gregory Peck, Milton Berle, and Henry Fonda, and raised $5,000 for National SANE.[45]

As more and more Americans became involved in the nuclear testing debate, college students also for the first time since the 1930s began agitating for peace. The National Student Council for a Sane Nuclear Policy, which came to be commonly known as Student SANE, was organized by a group of seven students in the summer of 1958. Timothy Shopen of Swarthmore College drafted their first policy statement, and at their first National Conference in September Michael Arons of Cooper Union was elected chairman. By March 1959, the students had participating committees on more than twenty-five college campuses and individual supporters in over fifty colleges. Student SANE collected over 10,000 signatures directed to the Geneva Conference and started a campaign of individual letters calling attention to the specific concerns of youth. "Never before has youth been faced with the possibility of being robbed of its future; the mistakes of today will be irredeemable tomorrow," one of the letters said in part; and copies were also sent to Washington officials.[46]

The nuclear-pacifists gathered around SANE spoke out as no group had done since the Cold War had begun over a decade before. To many Americans who had witnessed the McCarthy days, it seemed almost unbelievable. H. Stuart Hughes, a noted historian who was later to become co-chairman of SANE, observed that he was surprised that a respectable organization like SANE even existed, much less that it was speaking out the way it was. "I've often talked in retrospect that the founding of SANE was the sign that the McCarthy pall was really lifting," he declared. Peace was no longer regarded as a suspect word in the United States. I.F. Stone wrote on October 5, 1959, in an article in his *Weekly* on the exchange of visits between Premier Khrushchev and President Eisenhower, that "quite suddenly peace has become respectable."[47]

Diverse public figures as Senator Humphrey, Edward Teller, and a representative of the U.N. secretariat all credited SANE with discouraging nuclear tests and maintaining the conditions for the continuation of the dialogue. And although President Eisenhower realized that the American people were more concerned about national security than fallout, an aroused public opinion was, according to many observers, the clinching factor for the moratorium on nuclear testing. Nuclear pacifists in SANE and other organizations played a prominent role in this endeavor, and as the new decade approached they felt confident in their power and in the future. Cousins echoed this sentiment when he stated at the second annual Conference of the Committee that although the movement had been in existence only two years he believed "victory was within the means of this organization. The President of the United States or the head of any other country cannot do the job," he concluded, "but this organization can. . . . " Nuclear pacifism with SANE leading the way seemed to be flourishing, but its intellectual rigor and vitality would be severely tested in the years to come.[48]

3

Communist Infiltration in the Nuclear Test Ban Movement, 1960

If decent organizations like the Committee for a Sane Nuclear Policy wish to protect themselves against the danger of Communist infiltration, I cannot emphasize too strongly the need for an organizational climate that is openly inhospitable to Communists. This is a situation where a tepid declaration simply will not suffice while a neutral silence is an open invitation to disaster.

—Senator Thomas J. Dodd, 1960[1]

In May 1960, at the height of its influence and prestige, SANE held a major rally in New York City's Madison Square Garden to coincide with the planned summit conference between President Eisenhower and Premier Khrushchev. The rally was successful despite the fact that, because of the U–2 incident, the summit was cancelled. Twenty thousand persons heard a roster of distinguished citizens, including Norman Cousins, Mrs. Eleanor Roosevelt, former Republican presidential nominee Alfred M. Landon, Governor G. Mennon Williams of Michigan, Norman Thomas, civil rights leader A. Philip Randolph, and Walter Reuther of the United Auto Workers, speak about the human right to live without the fear and danger of fallout and nuclear disaster. Harry Belafonte headed the entertainment and was joined by Elaine May, Tom Posten, and Orson Bean. Telegrams were read from Senators Hubert

Humphrey and Jacob Javits and from Adlai Stevenson, praising the efforts of these nuclear pacifists. Following the rally, Reuther, Thomas, and Belafonte led a march of 5,000 persons to the UN for midnight prayer. On the West Coast, the Hollywood for SANE Committee presented "An Evening with Harry Belafonte" attended by 6,500 persons at the Shrine Auditorium, with the rush for tickets being so great that all were sold two weeks in advance. "For a moment," one critic observed, "it looked as though SANE might grow into a really powerful force in American politics." But this prediction never came true. The reasons for this failure tell us a great deal about the difficulties that faced SANE and the nuclear-pacifist movement in the United States.[2]

SANE's troubles began on the eve of the rally, when Senator Thomas J. Dodd (D-CT.), temporary chairman of the Senate Internal Security Subcommittee in place of James Eastland of Mississippi and the most conspicuous congressional opponent of the nuclear test ban policies of the Eisenhower Administration, demanded that SANE "purge their ranks ruthlessly" of Communists. He charged that "the unpublished chief organizer of the rally was a veteran member of the Communist Party" and that "the Communists were responsible for a very substantial percentage of the overflow turnout." While admitting that SANE was "headed by a group of nationally prominent citizens about whose integrity and good faith there is no question," Dodd contended that "evidence" existed "of serious Communist infiltration at chapter level."[3]

The threat of being identified with the Communist issue had long concerned SANE's leadership. Larry Scott expressed his concern in a memo dated April 30, 1957, when the committee was in its planning stages. While writing to the Proposed Committee to Stop H-Bomb Tests, he stated, "An ad-hoc committee such as we propose on this of all subjects will be vulnerable to both villification of Communist front on one hand and vulnerable to infiltration by Communists on the other hand." He urged the proposed committee to follow a middle ground and stated, "We will be neither naive concerning this problem nor hysterically expend our energy refuting false charges." Scott added that although "this is a problem that most peace organizations have had," he believed "a morally sound program is impervious to either villification or infiltration."[4]

After the organization formed and Trevor Thomas became the first executive secretary, Cousins cautioned him about the issue of Communist infiltration in a letter stating: "We must develop a razor-sharp vigilance against the danger of Communist infiltration or control as the issue of nuclear testing, perhaps more than any other issue in recent years, provides an attractive sphere of action for Communists.'' Cousins wanted SANE to remain ''completely free of Communist infiltration or taint.'' Although he sensed the situation in the local chapters in New York, Oregon, and Missouri ''could be potentially harmful,'' he had been assured, he wrote Thomas, ''they are under control.'' Cousins did realize, however, that this situation ''serves as a stern warning that we must have both the policy and the means to deal effectively with the problem when it arises.''[5]

Thomas noted the importance of Cousins's concern but pointed out that SANE had resisted the organization necessary for chartering local groups; and therefore, it ''must rely on the integrity and good sense of most people, recognizing that the batting average will be less than 100 percent.'' ''Unless the Committee faces up to the fact that it has no 'policy' or means to deal effectively with the problem when it arises,'' he warned Cousins, ''then you will have to rely on my successor to 'run' the local committees out of hand.''[6]

By the summer of 1958, Cousins had become so concerned about this issue that he approached the Federal Bureau of Investigation (FBI) asking for the bureau's help in furnishing SANE with the names of any subversives who might be attempting to infiltrate any of the local committees in New York or other cities. According to an FBI office memorandum, Cousins indicated that he ''recognized the committee was a 'natural' for attempts at infiltration by subversive individuals or organizations'' and that he felt so strongly about the aims of the committee that he ''did not wish to see it hampered by being used by an individual who did not have the best interests of the United States at heart.'' The FBI wrote back that it ''could not legally give him any assistance,'' and SANE continued without the policy and the means to deal with what it considered to be a pressing problem.[7]

By 1960, the situation in the local committees had deteriorated. Norman Thomas, who had faced this situation before with other organizations and wanted to be able to speak from what was clearly a non-Communist position, warned the executive committee in early 1960

that unless it faced up to the Communist issue, this organization placed itself in dual jeopardy: on the one hand, there was the danger that increasing Communist activity on the local level would compromise or undermine the organization; on the other hand, there was the danger that our inability or unwillingness to recognize the problem would increase the likelihood of official attack, with our defense crippled in advance.

At the January 1960 national board meeting, Thomas continued warning the committee about "the whole system of ruthless manipulation and deception practiced by these types (fellow travelers) and the destructive effects this brings to an organization." He therefore pleaded to the committee to take steps to avoid this danger.[8]

Agreeing with Thomas's position, Cousins tried to put the problem into perspective, noting that "any directives on this matter may seem distasteful" and that "in a few instances there may be strenuous protests and charges that we are reverting to the kind of action that disfigured so much of American life a few years ago." Yet he thought SANE could be firm without being irresponsible, because firmness was necessary in order "to build an effective peace movement in the United States."[9] Although Cousins, Thomas, and the rest of the board recognized the importance of this issue and the inherent problems involved, no action was taken; and the Dodd crusade precipitated a major crisis within SANE.

Senator Dodd's first step was to subpoena Henry Abrams on May 13, 1960. A former leader of the American Labor Party and the 1948 Henry Wallace campaign, Abrams was then co-chairman of the West Side New York Committee for a Sane Nuclear Policy. More importantly, he had played a leading role in planning and promoting the Madison Square Garden Rally scheduled for the following week. Abrams was a well-known political figure in New York, and some people thought that at one time he might have been a Communist party member; but, according to A.J. Muste, he had "recently engaged in some political activity which the Communist Party opposed." Before the Dodd Senate Subcommittee, Abrams took the Fifth Amendment and charged that the sole purpose of the closed hearing was to "interfere with public discussion of the most important single issue facing the American people, preventing the nuclear arms race, and proceeding beyond this to total disarmament."[10]

Cousins, who was understandably upset when he heard of Dodd's actions and plans, immediately called Abrams into his office and "begged him" to be frank with SANE's board members so that they would be able to defend him against the inquisition of the Dodd committee. He asked Abrams to tell him man to man that he was not a Communist. Abrams answered him by saying: "You have the right to ask me two questions: Have I always followed the policy set down by the national board?, and Have I done a good job? I think the answer to both is in the affirmative." Although Abrams went on to assure Cousins and the other board members present that, according to Cousins, "he was not under the orders or instruction of any outside agent or organization, and that his sole concern was to make SANE a success," that assurance was not enough in Cousins's opinion, and he asked Abrams to resign. Abrams was incredulous, particularly since he had talked to Robert Gilmore, chairman of New York SANE, before agreeing to head up the Madison Square Garden Committee to make sure there would be no opposition to him from SANE's leaders. Subsequently when rumors of possible problems began to circulate, he offered to resign. His offer, however, was not accepted."[11]

After dismissing Abrams from the organization, Cousins himself hurried to Washington to see Senator Dodd and to ask him to hold off the publicity on the matter until after the rally had taken place. Ironically, Dodd was a neighbor and friend of Cousins who had worked with him in the United World Federalists. Dodd had been Connecticut state chairman of UWF when Cousins was national chairman, and Dodd had defended that organization against charges of anti-Americanism by veteran's groups. Due to their relationship, Dodd agreed to hold off his attack "despite the fact that he told Cousins he was under considerable pressure from his own committee to issue a public statement immediately." Just what Cousins said to Dodd was at the time the subject of heated debate, but in a speech to the Senate on May 25, after Dodd called upon SANE "to purge their ranks ruthlessly of Communists," the senator announced that Cousins had expressed his eagerness to have his help in cleaning SANE's house of subversives:

I wish to pay my personal tribute to Mr. Norman Cousins, the chairman of the Committee for a Sane Nuclear Policy, for the manner in which he has reacted to the revelations of the subcommittee. . . . When he saw me in Washington he asked for the subcommittee's assistance in ridding SANE of whatever Communist infiltration did exist. He offered to open the books of the organization to the subcommittee and to cooperate with it in any way.[12]

Attacked for his complicity with the Dodd subcommittee after the Senate speech, Cousins denied this accusation and said the only thing he told Dodd was that SANE "was not hiding anything. . . . Our organization is an open book. . . . We keep no secrets." He went on to explain that "we were confident that we could demonstrate the unfairness of the general impression that would result from the Abrams case alone."[13]

To further complicate the issue, a story appeared in the conservative *New York Journal-American* on May 26, reporting that Cousins accused Abrams of plotting to have Communists take over the rally. Cousins denied to SANE supporters that he had made any such charges; and he asked the paper for a retraction of the story, but without success. Another newspaper, the *New York Times*, made it seem that the entire Dodd investigation had been undertaken at Cousins's request. Cousins contended that this statement was "absolutely untrue. The first intimation I had that Senator Dodd was investigating Abrams in particular or SANE in general came through Robert Gilmore, who informed me that Henry Abrams had been asked to appear."[14]

The same day, SANE's national board met to make a final decision on how to handle what was now a public controversy. Clarence Pickett, Robert Gilmore, and Stewart Meacham—all associated with the American Friends Service Committee and all pacifists—proposed a policy statement which said in part:

SANE has not and will not trim its sails to suit opponents of a sane nuclear policy whether they be members of congressional committees, private citizens, or anonymous accusers. . . . SANE has not and will not be controlled by the Communist Party nor any outside interest or organization.

This statement was considered too radical and was turned down by a majority vote of the board.[15]

Later that day, a statement was adopted which, on the one hand, expressed resentment at the intervention of the Senate Subcommittee in SANE's affairs and, on the other hand, welcomed into membership only those persons "whose support is not qualified by adherence to Communist or other totalitarian doctrine." This statement came to be known as "Standards for SANE Leadership" and was sent to all the local committees, accompanied by a letter of explanation which stated: "The public, as well as our Committee, has a right to know the pertinent background of spokesmen and leaders of our Committee and its chapters in our great struggle for peace." As for implementation of this new policy, members would be asked to exercise "self-judgement" as to the "best interests" of the organization; and in the event of any serious challenge as to their "good faith," they would be expected to discuss matters "fully and frankly" with the national board.[16]

According to Donald Keys, "Co-operation was put on a performance basis," and the committee would

not be stampeded into the establishment of divisive screening machinery which will violate the basic principles of democratic process in which a man is judged on the basis of his current allegiances and actions rather than those of the past, or on the beliefs that he may be alleged to hold.

To Cousins and Pickett the action that SANE had just taken was mandatory for its continued existence as a peace organization in the United States. "Our policy, in brief, is that membership in the Communist Party is incompatible with association with SANE," they explained in a letter to all the SANE local committee chairmen. "We do not think it is possible to mount a powerful peace movement in the United States if we take a contrary position on this issue."[17]

However, the issue was not so clear-cut to the local SANE committees. The problem was further complicated because many local SANE chapters, as in the case in New York City where there were more than fifty, were not directly chartered by the central office, as were other groups, but rather by an intermediate Greater New York Committee. These groups, in order to work with SANE and in order that the national committee would have more control over them, were now required to take out a charter with the national organization which included the provision that "persons who are not free because of party discipline or political allegiance to criticize the actions of totalitarian nations with the same standards by which they challenge other nations will not be welcome as members."[18]

The new chartering requirement for the New York groups was deeply resented and denounced as a witch-hunt and a loyalty test and put them, according to acting chairman Walter Lear, in an "untenable position." There is little doubt that its main purpose was to get rid of local affiliates which seemed to the national board to be dominated by actual or potential Communists or the Communist-minded. According to Lear, however, the group was composed largely of ex-party members who "would like to make SANE their new religion" and added significantly to the nuclear-pacifist movement. And even the Senate Internal Security Sub-committee, despite exhaustive efforts, could not provide recorded proof of Communist party membership in regards to Henry Abrams and other New York local committee members who were suspect in this regard. But despite strong protests, National SANE held fast and succeeded in the complete reorganization of the New York City SANE activities.[19]

The national board felt that this would be the single act necessary to establish in the public mind that the SANE movement was free of Communist ties. After bitter debates and resentment on both sides, the Greater New York Committee was recognized according to the SANE directive. About one-half the chapters in the New York metropolitan area, which comprised one-half the SANE chapters in the nation, refused to take out new charters and thus were expelled from the organization. Although many New Yorkers continued working for SANE more or less independently of the national board, their diminished numbers hurt the organization, for they were a highly committed and politically astute group which comprised an important part of the SANE program.[20]

Although SANE seemed to be carrying out what the subcommittee had requested, Senator Dodd was not through with his attack on the perceived Communist infiltration in the nuclear test ban movement. While all this was going on with SANE, the senator launched his assault on Dr. Linus Pauling—a SANE sponsor at the time and frequent speaker at SANE sponsored rallies—demanding that he name those who helped him obtain the 11,000 signatures of scientists on the 1958 atomic test ban petition to the United Nations. Pauling declared under oath that he was not and had never been a member of the Communist party. He answered the questions fully, refusing only when he was asked to iden-tify other persons who had helped him with his petition on the ground that "those names would be used for reprisals against idealistic, high-minded workers for peace" and because "it might dissuade others from advocating peace." Pauling was ordered to reappear August 9 and to give the names or risk contempt proceedings. SANE labeled the "pro-ceedings of the Senate Subcommittee in this matter outrageous in its contempt for civil liberty and sinister in its implications for peace." Cousins wrote to a board member that "SANE should support Dr. Pauling fully in his position," for "he is under no obligation to expose people who acted in good faith to the possible harassment of a Senate investigating committee." The national committee never did, however, answer to the public's critical attitude on the basis "that this would inevitably result in an interpretation of both attacks on Pauling and others working for a sane nuclear policy and consequently cause severe damage to the entire SANE movement."[21]

Later in the summer, Senator Dodd subpoenaed twenty-seven more SANE supporters who were members and local officers of the Greater New York Committees. The New York people wanted National SANE to run an advertisement in the *New York Times* in their defense, but the national board refused, claiming that it was working quietly and more effectively behind the scenes, obtaining assurances that would save the twenty-seven from harmful publicity and Pauling from a contempt citation. "A precarious equilibrium" was involved, the national board said in refusing to take a stronger stand against the Dodd subcommittee. As the pressure mounted for the SANE leaders to denounce Senator Dodd as another McCarthy, Cousins explained his actions by stating: "I do not believe Senator Dodd is a McCarthy; therefore I will make no such statement," and "I do not make the mistake of thinking he is not just as committed to the cause of peace as I am."[22]

At the same time no names or lists were turned over by the national committee or any local committee to the Dodd Senate Subcommittee or any investigating committee. The national board affirmed on September 29 that "those lists are confidential and will not be released" and that National SANE had retained counsel to represent without charge any members called by the Senate committee. It was the board's policy that using the Fifth Amendment before an investigating committee and thus refusing to answer questions "in itself will not be automatic cause for dismissal from SANE." Furthermore, the national committee "respects the right of private conscience concerning declarations of political belief to governmental agencies."[23]

Following the SANE National Conference in Chicago on October 24, the board voted to affirm the May 26 policy statement and the several subsequent memoranda pertaining to it, including that of implementation. Only Stewart Meacham voted in opposition. The board voted that the policy of SANE was such that

members of the Communist Party, fascists, or individuals who are not free because of party discipline or political allegiance to apply to the actions of the Soviet Union and the Chinese Government the same standards by which they challenge others are not welcome on any level of this organization.

Although there was extensive vocal grass-roots protest, the chapters around the nation upheld the board's policy by a single vote, 29 to 28.[24]

The following spring, Senator Dodd, in anticipation of the release of Part II on "Communist Infiltration in the Nuclear Test-Ban Movement," made a speech on the floor of the Senate about his committee's inquiry of the Greater New York SANE Committee. Dodd charged that the Communists were still attempting to infiltrate SANE and read in the *Congressional Record* the names of the SANE witnesses. He also talked about federal legislation to cope with "the problem of Communist infiltration" but added that if SANE continued the practices in which it was now engaged in dealing with this problem, legislation might not be needed.[25]

In response to press inquiries after the Dodd speech, Norman Cousins released a statement which said: "Senator Dodd has stated that the Communist Party has attempted to make the National Committee for a Sane Nuclear Policy a chief target of its infiltration efforts. He has also emphasized that this attempt has failed." A similar response was made to press inquiries when the Senate report was released on March 19.[26]

The SANE board meeting in April culminated with a declaration which read "that it deeply regretted the subpoenaing and public release of testimony of those who worked in New York SANE and continued strongly to resent the harassment of Professor Linus Pauling by the Senate Internal Security Subcommittee." The board also stated that it would continue "not to be intimidated and will continue its policy of noninvolvement with the Senate Internal Security Subcommittee, its representatives, and similar investigatory bodies." SANE believed that these assaults were primarily attacks on their program of world peace through disarmament and world law and therefore declared that the "National Committee will persevere in working for an inspected nuclear weapons test-ban and for comprehensive and controlled disarmament . . . and will not be diverted from its primary tasks by those who are basically opposed to these objectives."[27]

Although Senator Dodd and the Senate Internal Security Subcommittee in two massive reports never made final conclusions on SANE, the House Committee on Un-American Activities Report of 1961 did. Their annual report stated in part: "The Committee for a Sane Nuclear Policy (SANE) is not a Communist front. It is not controlled by the Communist Party. Its leaders are not Communists," the HUAC report concluded, "although a number of its national sponsors have extensive records of Communist-front activities." Even the FBI, who conducted intensive investigations of several local committees, did not find "any indication of any substantial Communist infiltration."[28]

By this time, however, the damage was done. The effects of the Communist infiltration issue on SANE and the American peace movement, according to some observers, were disastrous. Senator Dodd's attack upon SANE cut drastically into its membership, not merely because the leadership deliberately drove some people out but because large numbers resigned in protests against what they considered "McCarthyite" tactics among their key board members and sponsors within the organization. The way the national board handled the senator's accusations not only affected SANE as an organization but also its relationship with the rest of the peace movement within the United States.

The first protest appeared because the SANE board did not take a definite strong stand against Dodd and his committee. Sanford Gottlieb tried to explain the Committee's thinking by saying that "SANE was still proving credentials at this time. The McCarthy period was not over then." And Donald Keys pointed out that "the organization existed in a no man's land. . . . SANE occupied a large territory between two groups, close enough in to swing and hit something, but far enough out to exert some leadership." We were a "retreat bunker for liberals who couldn't find a place to take a stand in the structure of political parties," stated Keys, and thus the organization had to be careful in not offending people from both the Right and the Left.[29]

One major problem was the way SANE liberals chose to deal with the Communist issue. Norman Cousins knew from the very beginning there would be problems. As he wrote at one point, "I doubt that there is any single course of action before us that will be free of anguish and ordeal for the organization." The national board saw the handling of the issue as "an overwhelming, an obvious necessity." But certainly it cannot be said that these men did not care about civil liberties; they were, as they pointed out, "civil libertarians from way back." All had strong stands in that field. Norman Thomas, for example, had fought valiantly against the 1940 Smith Act which prohibited membership in any group advocating violent overthrow of the government, and Cousins wrote and spoke out against right-wing attacks of the World Federalists in the early 1950s. In the various memos they sent out, their "anguish" and "ordeal" were quite visible. They described over and over the way in which they wanted to think they could behave:

> If a valid question comes up, it will not be handled arbitrarily, but will be worked out . . . reasonably and carefully. . . . We will take the steps necessary to be able to guarantee these standards, but we will not stoop to methods that molest the dignity or the rights of the individual concerned. . . . We will deal with these charges soberly, quietly, and with common sense.[30]

There was no question that they would have liked to deal with it in this way. Nevertheless, because they felt the need to consider the image that they presented to the public, an impossible ambivalence ran through these same memos. Individuals would be judged "on a performance basis," it was declared, but everyone agreed that it was certainly not a judgment of performance that Abrams was asked to resign.

Communist infiltration of the nuclear test ban movement unfortunately became an issue that precluded rational behavior. The emotional impact that McCarthyism had was all too real for many of SANE's liberal leaders, and, as Sanford Gottlieb explained, this was not only an ideological or intellectual issue, as "many people were terribly emotional at best, hysterical at worst."[31]

To complicate matters further, there was also some dissension among SANE's leaders about Cousins's handling of Abrams. As Gottlieb explained, some members felt that Cousins with his initial action against Abrams "seemed to be throwing him to the Senate Committee wolves." "Norman should not have taken the action into his own hands," Donald Keys said later. "If we had been able to play as a team operation SANE would have handled it better." There also was a question about other committee actions taken without consensus from the board. These actions angered some of the members and prompted one in particular, Stewart Meacham, to resign. Finally, Cousins got Dodd to promise him that "if the people were going to be interrogated, there would be no circus like in the McCarthy period," but Dodd embarrassed Cousins before his fellow SANE workers when he made the whole thing into a public circus in order to discredit SANE and the nuclear test ban movement.[32]

Others felt that Cousins was entirely wrong. A.J. Muste, Bob Gilmore, and Stewart Meacham, all three pacifists who because of this issue resigned from the national committee, and Linus Pauling, who resigned as a national sponsor of SANE, were particularly critical of SANE's handling of the issue. These men, and others who resigned from SANE, felt strongly that the committee's role should have been to awaken the public to the irrationality of Dodd's claim. Gilmore, who had been SANE's chief administrator and in Norman Thomas's words, "its guiding hand and brain," argued that

SANE could have responded to Senator Dodd's attack with a ringing challenge to the Cold War strategem of discredit and divide, with clear affirmation of the right of everyone to debate and dissent. . . . The fact that SANE turned down this opportunity is, to my mind, a great tragedy.

Meacham, another American Friends Service Committee member on the national board, told Cousins, "We cannot afford to admit the Dodd Committee into our disciplinary procedures. . . . We dare not to allow ourselves to be bullied into giving it a place or a role which has no right to demand." One month later Meacham joined Gilmore in resigning from the national board, while Linus Pauling and Lord Bertrand Russell resigned as sponsors of the organization because of the way the board handled the whole issue.[33]

There was a curious reversal to Pauling's resignation. According to Cousins, Pauling telephoned him after the Abrams case in May 1960 and proposed that he become co-chairman of SANE along with Cousins and Pickett. He told Cousins that he realized the committee was faced with a situation that necessitated the action they took and, that as he himself had to face up to a similar situation some years ago, he felt his presence as co-chairman would help to close the breach then opening in the organization as a result of the Dodd attack. Cousins put his suggestion before the directors, but they felt that it would be impractical and possibly confusing to have three co-chairmen and offered him a place instead on the national board. After Pauling himself was subpoenaed by the Dodd committee, he not only refused to become a member of the board but resigned as a sponsor and wrote to Homer Jack that he could not accept the implementation policy described in the communication of July 29, 1960, from the two co-chairmen of the national committee. Pauling expressed the opinion that he "was willing to be subjected to interrogation about his political beliefs, memberships, etc. by any proper authority," but he "did not consider the two co-chairmen of SANE to have such a right to conduct such interrogation and expel from SANE a person who did not answer the questions in a full and frank manner."[34]

Although Pauling's protest certainly hurt the organization, the most persistent critic was the influential radical pacifist A.J. Muste, who resigned as a sponsor of the Greater New York SANE Committee over the issue. He wrote two lengthy articles in *Liberation*, entitled "The Crisis in SANE," to explain his position. Most radical pacifists sided with Muste and condemned what they, too, considered a capitulation to McCarthyism. Muste, along with Gilmore and Meacham, wrote a letter published in the *New York Times* on July 27, 1960, that stated: "We are now seeing the return of an evil which nine years ago pervaded much of American life. . . . This evil was known by the name of McCarthyism. Some time ago it was thoroughly discredited and routed— or so we thought. Today we wonder."[35]

According to Muste, Cousins "committed a grave . . . error in the way he dealt with Senator Dodd and his threat to expose SANE." Instead of firing Abrams and instituting "loyalty procedures," wrote Muste, "SANE should have told Dodd to do his worst." Muste acknowledged the problem caused by pro-Soviet elements in a peace organization in the United States and did not advocate a "united front," but he relied upon a "clear definition of aims as the basic means to sort out those who belong in an organization." He believed that had Dodd been put or kept in his place and the situation remained as it was, "SANE would have remained in control of non-Communists, it would have grown, and a lot of former pro-Saneites etc. would have been politically educated and would have provided a considerable amount of badly needed manpower to the peace movement."[36]

The position taken by Muste, Gilmore, Meacham, and Pauling was also the position taken by many of the local chapters of SANE and of the young people and students who had been so important in the various demonstrations that had brought the issue of nuclear war to the public. These people felt that the action of the national board reflected caution and conservatism. Local chapters in Washington, D.C., Boston, Brooklyn, Queens, Long Island, Forest Hills, Cleveland, Skokie, Jackson Heights, and other areas responded negatively to the board's policy. Typical of these responses were ones from the Washington Committee executive board which said: "We believe that the greatest internal danger of the last ten years has been the activities of investigating committees such as the Internal Security Subcommittee. . . . The goal is nothing less than thought-control."[37]

The Queens committee felt it was necessary to point out to the national committee that they were "strong enough now to stand up against the Dodd Committee." The local chapter explained that "SANE is in a position of power and respect throughout the country" and that "all the local chapters will support you, as will, without a doubt, the millions of Americans who are concerned with peace and the dignity of human beings." The local committee insisted that SANE "need not apologize" for its "magnificent peace stand, policies and activities. Rather it is the Dodd Committee that has much to answer for in reviving McCarthyite tactics in attempting to hamstring the people's peace movement." In his letter of resignation one of the board members from the Long Island committee, E. Russell Stabler, sadly added,

I look forward to a time when all of the original SANE workers can be reunited as part of a strong peace movement. This might happen if we could all be guided by the following remark by Albert Schweitzer in "An Obligation to Tomorrow: Now we must rediscover the fact that we—all together—are human beings, and that we must strive to concede to each other what moral capacity we have."[38]

Some chapters wanted a "peace movement which excluded no one from the work of survival." John W. Darr of the Brooklyn committee asked the national board to "look around the world and wherever you see a peace movement capable of influencing the course of events, as we are yet unable to do, you will find a movement free of screening, open to all who sincerely work for peace." Edmund C. Berkley of the Boston committee circulated a petition among several of the local committees urging a withdrawal from National SANE to start a "broad peace movement to be run democratically and open to everyone." But some local groups, like the one in Chicago, said they "deplored such suggestions" and extended to the national committee a "vote of confidence."[39]

A majority of students in SANE had the same sentiments on this issue as many of the local chapters. In a letter of protest to National SANE the Brooklyn student committee stated that "while we bemoan the Cold War and its effects upon the attitudes of our fellow Americans,

the resolution, and especially the proposed implementation, are themselves in the grand tradition of Cold War hysteria and McCarthyism.''
Furthermore, the Brooklyn students felt that SANE in keeping with its
democratic charter ''must be willing to accept anyone who has a contribution to be made in the struggle for peace.'' These students saw the
May 26 resolution and its implementation ''as irrevelant to the true
aims of SANE, and as being not in harmony with the feeling of the
major proportion of the rank and file.'' They expressed ''the hope''
that this ''inquisition'' which will ''only have a suicidal effect upon the
organization will not be attempted to be pursued any longer.'' When
the resolution was not withdrawn at the national meeting in October
1960 but only reaffirmed, many of the students quit SANE in disgust
and joined the Student Peace Union, which was becoming a fairly large
organization by that time, along with the fledgling Students for a Democratic Society. Despite national committee attempts to salvage the
campus student group, it was formally disbanded in 1962.[40]

With students, pacifists, and many grass-roots workers, especially in
New York, leaving SANE and with the organization being attacked in
the press, there was fear that the committee would collapse under the
weight of the internal conflict of opinion. The leadership of SANE,
however, remained steadfast that their course of action, though fraught
with difficulties, was the one that was necessary. Liberals in SANE
during this period were extremely sensitive about being ''tagged'' with
any label, especially that of ''Communist.'' Cousins, Jack, Thomas,
and others felt strongly that they had to protect SANE from such an
attack if they were going to keep their organization respectable.

Thomas, even after he took the Dodd committee to task for what he
called practicing a ''modified McCarthyism,'' stated that the vital issue
in the whole matter was that ''it is an absolute necessity in this country
that any drive for disarmament with hope of success shall not be, or
be thought to be, under Communist or near-Communist inspiration and
control.'' A peace organization ''open to all,'' as Linus Pauling called
for at the National SANE Conference in Chicago in 1960, would,
according to Cousins, be ''closed to most, since most Americans, even
most American liberals, would avoid an organization open to all fellow
travelers, Communists, etc.'' If SANE had adopted the Pauling position,
even if Dodd's subcommittee had not existed, the majority of the board
believed that the committee would have forfeited any possibility of
becoming a popular organization. As Gottlieb explained later, ''We

were a small minority in a very hostile country, so the quality of our people took on a great importance.'' To Gottlieb, quality obviously meant respectability, and it was equated with being anti-Communist or at least non-Communist. In Cold War America of 1960, their analysis certainly had some validity.[41]

Steve Allen, who was master of ceremonies at the Chicago National Conference and soon after became vice chairman of SANE, wrote that he and his Hollywood friends joined the organization because ''at last there was a center to coalesce around that was not extremist, not considered hopelessly idealistic, not denominational, not unrealistically radical . . . an organization to whose center flocked respectable people of all sorts.'' This scenario was repeated in many other professional communities all across the nation and certainly gave SANE an unmistakable credibility among the American people that since the McCarthy days was unprecedented. Allen and others like him were not overly sympathetic with the Dodd committee but were adamant on getting rid of and keeping Communists out of SANE, and the leadership of the organization certainly understood and sympathized with their position.[42]

''Some of our most valuable members,'' wrote Cousins, ''enjoyed national prominence in the entertainment field. They could be cut down in no time at all as a result of a public impression that etc., etc.'' He had given such people assurance, he went on to say, ''that joining SANE would not make them vulnerable to name calling.'' And when, for example, Allen was plagued by pickets carrying such signs as ''Steve wants to crawl on his knees to the Kremlin, you can have him, we don't want him,'' was pilloried in the media for being overly sympathetic to Communists, and was afraid of losing sponsors of his television show, Cousins and the SANE board evidently decided to eradicate the Communist taint as much as possible. Demanding Abrams's resignation was only the first step in this endeavor.[43]

Although the possible presence of Communists or Communist sympathizers in SANE was a definite problem, equally important was the threat to peace and civil liberties presented by the modified McCarthyism of the Senate committee. Muste argued that ''the Senate Committee was a much more appalling danger to a sound U.S. peace movement than what the Communists in this country are at this time able to do to such a movement.'' If the committee had acted intelligently, it would have first cleared itself of any sort of complicity or tolerance in relation to the Dodd committee's accusation; and then if there had been known

Communist party members, SANE should have discussed it with them and indicated that it did not believe it was possible to be responsible members of the Communist party and of SANE at the same time. SANE did not handle the problem effectively, for, to some extent, they let the Dodd committee handle it for them. By its expulsion of alleged Communists, SANE played into the hands of the enemies. As Homer Jack, then executive director, sadly explained: "Ironically, SANE helped continue what it was supposed to be fighting against: McCarthyism and the Cold War hysteria."[44]

Muste also questioned the liberal's cry of "political responsibility." He pointed out, and most of the SANE board agreed with him, that Dodd had sprung the whole thing on the eve of the Madison Square Garden Rally, presumably to torpedo it and, with it, SANE. Dodd's action appeared to be a case of political blackmail and came at a very critical time in the controversy about resuming nuclear tests. "How could any unafraid liberal, libertarian, any sensitive person whose political judgment was not blurred by personal friendship do anything *first* except cry to high heaven against it?" Muste concluded, "*That* was not done and that's my complaint."[45]

Cousins, the person to whom Muste referred, answered this criticism by saying that "he did stand up to Dodd, but not in the cliche sense, not in the way that's going to get cheap applause." Whether this was a valid defense against the critics or not, Cousins himself was deeply torn by the part he played in this whole incident, calling it years later "the most pulverizing experience of my life." But the most poignant part of this whole drama came out during one of Muste's frequent conversations with Cousins during the crisis. The two men admired each other tremendously; Muste was a frequent visitor at SANE's board meetings that year, and he and Cousins tried diligently to iron out their differences. Muste described one of their conversations this way:

I made the point that is stated toward the end of my second article, viz, that if SANE had stood up to Dodd in May, etc., etc., the result might have been a rallying of liberal forces to SANE, a serious blow to the "investigating" committees, and an immense lift to SANE, making it a formidable mass force. I added that this was, of course, a speculation and I could be wrong: Norman lowered his head, paused for an appreciable time, and then looked at me and said: "No, I think you are probably right, and this is what wrings my soul."[46]

Cousins denied making this comment but explained years later: "You always live in a state of anguish, always soul-searching. I don't know if I did the right thing then, and if this thing happened now I still would not know what else to do." His basic purpose in dealing with Dodd, he pointed out, was to protect a number of individuals against the kind of Star Chamber proceedings that could have destroyed or seriously hurt them; and as Norman Thomas and others realized, in quieting down the Dodd attack, he saved SANE from being destroyed in the process. "I have no remorse over the fact," he concluded, "nor any apologies to offer."[47]

In retrospect, it is clear that SANE lost some badly needed support from the way it handled this issue, but it may also have benefited from this experience. Sociologist Nathan Glazer pointed out that SANE alienated some of the more radical and certainly the youth, because its response to Dodd appeared to be "only a cowardly response to ignorant and evil pressures." But, on the other hand, "SANE is now capable of appealing effectively to the politically sophisticated who before simply refused to waste their time explaining why they could not work with Communists. . . . Indeed," he concluded, "SANE in general now seems to be overcoming the tradition of woolly-mindedness it inherited from the world federalist and pacifist background of its founders and is making a real attempt to think politically on all problems of arms control and disarmament. . . ."[48]

The "crisis in SANE" affected the organization and the peace movement tremendously, but all involved still believed that SANE had an important job to do and should continue doing it. At the height of the controversy, Norman Thomas wrote to Cousins that although it was "easy to think back with deep regret of what might have been done to arrest or minimize the present crisis, but the past is past and I still think the Committee for a Sane Nuclear Policy worth saving." Even Henry Abrams, who felt bitterly that he had been ill-used ("I should have been defended"), made it clear that SANE was doing a job that needed to be done and "shouldn't be hindered." Robert Gilmore seemed to put the whole situation into perspective when he stated: "No one quite thought it [SANE] would work . . . after thirteen years of cold stillness in the United States. But it did. It had the possibility of transforming itself into something like the British Campaign for Nuclear Disarmament. It lost that chance," he continued, "but it still has a lot of relevance."[49]

In fact, SANE's work for a nuclear test ban treaty was more relevant than ever. During 1960, while the committee was attending to its internal difficulties, President Eisenhower was becoming increasingly disenchanted with the testing moratorium, concerned that it was hurting the nuclear weapons program. Worried that cessation had placed the United States in a "disadvantageous position," he wrote in his memoirs that "prudence demanded a resumption of testing," yet he also thought that this decision should be left to his successor. Eisenhower felt he could not act during the fall campaign, but in his meeting with President-elect John F. Kennedy during the winter of 1960–1961, Eisenhower emphasized his conviction "that our nation should resume needed tests without delay."[50] Faced with this reality, SANE and other opponents of nuclear testing had no choice but to regroup and continue fighting to bring the arms race under control.

A Portal to a More Rational Future, 1961–1963

> The essential of my opinion is that the committees against nuclear arms exert an influence on governments so that they will take more seriously the danger which we may anticipate from nuclear arms. It is to be hoped that President Kennedy will have the courage to put forth much more in this direction.
> —Albert Schweitzer, 1960[1]

In January 1961, the "New Frontier" came to Washington, D.C., in the personification of a youthful and energetic president named John Fitzgerald Kennedy. Although Kennedy's inaugural address did not specifically refer to total or partial disarmament as a goal of U.S. policy, he did invite the Communist bloc to "begin anew the quest for peace before the dark powers of destruction unleashed by science engulf all humanity in planned or accidental self-destruction." To SANE, just beginning to recover from its internal difficulties, Kennedy's speech offered new hope and opportunities. The committee found the new administration "relatively open-minded" and one that could "be influenced by sober, concrete suggestions." SANE's liberal leadership agreed with Senator Humphrey when he suggested to them that as a voluntary organization they must continue to "encourage, support, and needle the administration" and remain "out front" with policy suggestions as often as they felt was necessary.[2]

Acting on these ideas National SANE sponsored a petition to President Kennedy, Prime Minister Harold Macmillan, and Premier Khrushchev urging them to continue the Geneva test ban talks until a treaty was achieved. "Time is running out for humanity, and you will have to hurry" read the SANE letter. "The differences which separate men must be submerged in renewed effort for survival and the common good." Unfortunately, the only response the committee received was from the Soviet premier who released a letter on St. Valentine's Day in Moscow to Cousins and Pickett assuring them that the Soviet government would in 1961 work tirelessly for a nuclear test ban treaty "to ensure stable peace on earth."[3]

At the same time, SANE began making plans for large demonstrations in Washington, Boston, Chicago, New York, New Jersey, and other communities, as part of the nationwide April Peace Mobilization patterned after and coinciding with the annual Aldermaston "Ban the Bomb" marches in England. With the theme "Security Through World Disarmament," this action marked SANE's first venture into large-scale national demonstrations. An estimated 25,000 Americans walked for peace on April 1 in the largest anti-war demonstration in the United States since World War II. In spite of uniformly bad weather from Seattle to New York, Americans walked, sang, prayed, and generally demonstrated their opposition to the current arms race. Sponsors were generally the local SANE committees and/or local American Friends Service Committee groups.[4]

The largest demonstration was at the United Nations Plaza in New York, which culminated an eight-day, 109-mile march from McGuire Air Force Base in New Jersey, sponsored by New Jersey SANE and Student SANE. More than 3,500 persons heard speeches by Clarence Pickett; Dr. John Bennett, Dean of Faculty, Union Theological Seminary; Dr. Hugh Wolfe, American Institute of Physics; Rev. Donald Harrington; and Councilman Stanley Isaacs of New York. Messages were read from Schweitzer, Russell, C. Rajagopalachari of India, Walter Reuther, Eleanor Roosevelt, Lord Boyd-Orr, Pablo Casals, Governor Robert Meyner and Senator Harrison Williams, both Democrats from New Jersey, and others. The ninety-minute rally ended after the crowd had roared its approval of a resolution urging the United States, Britain, and the USSR to negotiate an immediate cessation of nuclear bomb tests. There were also significant demonstrations in Los Angeles, San Francisco, Seattle, Chicago, Milwaukee, Washington, D.C., and Boston. Marchers sang a typical song of the time, "One, two, three, four, we don't want any war; five, six, seven, eight, let the world negotiate" and carried signs calling for the halt of bomb tests and balloons bearing the inscription "Security Through World Disarmament."[5]

All the rallies came off without incident and were very successful as the marchers were generally treated sympathetically by the American press. The *New York Post*, for example, editorialized:

> Call them impractical, unworldly, even irrelevant; they nevertheless represent a manifestation of what used to be called the Christian conscience. . . . We wince when we hear them described as eccentrics and fools by those who talk glibly of "atomic supremacy" and who tell us reassuringly that life will be rugged but quite bearable for the inhabitants of an atomic wasteland. If we are to apply sanity tests to politics, the Easter marchers may be in far better shape than many of the characters who demean them.[6]

Meanwhile, the thirty-two month negotiations in Geneva were reaching a climax over a Russian proposal for a three-person council to administer the inspection system and was very close to adjournment. Calling a special meeting of the national board at Cousins's home in New Canaan, Connecticut, SANE reaffirmed its previous policy towards the test ban and urged the Kennedy Administration to continue to negotiate at Geneva "with great patience" and not to resume nuclear tests except under UN control (or surveillance by the USSR and the United Kingdom). The national board also suggested that America continue to offer, as it had done in the past, opportunities to Russia for compromises which would meet their real or imagined fears and yet not jeopardize legitimate U.S. security. The attending board members agreed that "the US should not test nuclear weapons underground, under water, in the atmosphere, or in outer-space—whether or not the Geneva negotiations continue, are recessed, or are permanently adjourned."[7]

There was also general sentiment at this special meeting that SANE could no longer confine its program to the test ban and disarmament issues when a crisis in Berlin or elsewhere threatened nuclear war. On the other hand, there was wide hesitation about SANE's becoming another general foreign policy committee. As the Berlin crisis mounted that summer, as the Soviets prepared to seal off Communist East Berlin from its western counterpart, SANE's board realized the futility of working for a test ban or disarmament treaty if it did not concern itself with other flashpoints of East-West confrontation. Thus the board followed Norman Thomas's suggestion that there was "not much point to work on disarmament with the Berlin crisis overshading the whole situation . . . '' and asked him to write a comprehensive policy statement which he entitled "SANE alternatives to war over Berlin.''[8]

The completed statement was abbreviated into a full-page advertisement and was placed in twelve American newspapers on July 20 and 21. In the statement, National SANE called for the establishment of a Berlin Authority supervised by the Big Four and ultimately an arms-free Germany, as one alternative to nuclear war over Berlin. Asserting that the USSR and the United States are "now on an atomic collision course," the statement declared that "the unthinkables are no longer unthinkable" and Berlin could "touch off a nuclear war." Calling for "no extermination without representation," SANE urged the United States to "bring the Berlin issue before the United Nations." The statement pointed out the impossibility of reunifying the two separate and distinct German states on the basis of self-determination, suggesting that only under an international authority could East and West Germany work out means of cooperation and interchange that could lead to federation or reintegration.[9]

SANE's Berlin statement produced a tremendous response. Although most of it was favorable, some respondents believed that SANE was being too soft on the Communists. "There is no SANE way to deal with the Communists," one Afton, Missouri, resident wrote the committee, "except to wipe them off the face of the earth forever." Another person from Long Island City, New York, sent twenty-four postcards to SANE stating in big bold letters "BETTER DEAD THAN RED." Another letter questioned both the sanity and integrity of the committee as well as its "intelligence." "This isn't realism, it's moral bankruptcy in the name of self-preservation. . . . You had better pad your knees." The letter concluded, "It's a long crawl to Moscow."[10]

Meanwhile, President Kennedy moved toward a showdown with Russia. In a national broadcast on July 25, the president asked that large numbers of reserves be placed on active duty and announced a dramatic increase of nearly 25 percent in American military strength. On August 13, the Soviets built the Berlin Wall, and two weeks later Khrushchev broke the three-year Russian-American moratorium on the testing of nuclear bombs by beginning a series of tests which climaxed in November with a 58-megaton weapon 3,000 times more powerful than the bomb that had obliterated Hiroshima. SANE immediately released a statement condemning the move and called for a "mammoth protest throughout the world." "We believe the unwise action of the Soviet Union should not be imitated by the United States," the SANE statement declared. "Before any decision is made by the U.S. concerning resumption of tests, the U.S. should bring this issue before the United Nations, galvanizing a preponderance of world public opinion to urge the Soviet Union to put off its tests."[11]

On the day of the Russian announcement, SANE organized a protest in New York of some 2,000 people in front of the Russian Mission to the United Nations, and on the following day, one in Washington, D.C., before the U.S. Embassy. Unfortunately for SANE and other disarmament advocates, the United States almost immediately dissipated its moral advantage by announcing that it would resume tests, although, for the time being, underground only.[12]

The Soviet actions and America's hard-line response were severe blows to the cause of disarmament and undercut months of patient work on the part of SANE and other organizations which had worked to forestall testing by all nations and to bring the test ban negotiations to a successful conclusion. It appeared that the test ban talks were dead for the foreseeable future, although the meetings in Geneva were still being perfunctorily held.

Three weeks later, President Kennedy tried to regain the peace initiative when on September 25, in a dramatic address before the United Nations General Assembly, he challenged the Soviet Union to a "peace race" instead of an "arms race," coincidentally adopting the exact phrase that Seymour Melman, a SANE board member and Columbia University professor, had used three months earlier. In an important statement of foreign policy goals, Kennedy underscored the dangers of nuclear war, made the first major public U.S. commitment to total disarmament, and called for a strengthened United Nations and a negotiated settlement on Berlin. Declaring that "mankind must put an end to war," Kennedy's speech reduced the fever-pitch tensions centered around the Berlin question and slowed, temporarily at least, the rapid drift toward world war.[13]

SANE was quick to respond to the president's statement and joined with other peace and disarmament organizations in hailing it as a forward move. Declaring that Kennedy's speech provided "an anchor to windward in a rapidly deteriorating domestic and international situation reviving hope of a reorientation of United States policy along more moderate lines,'' National SANE sent telegrams to the chairman of all its local committees and to its sponsors and board members, asking for a deluge of wires commending the address.[14]

At the Fourth National Conference in New York on October 12–15, the board adopted Melman's, and now Kennedy's, concept of challenging the Soviet Union to a peace race instead of an arms race and made it a part of SANE's 1961–1962 Policy Statement. ''We call for the launching of a Peace Race,'' the adopted statement of the policy read, ''in which the two blocs join to end the arms race, contain their power struggle within constructive bounds, and encourage peaceful social change.'' The statement continued by declaring that this policy could best be implemented ''by understanding that there are competing groups with different approaches to international relations within each bloc, and by seeking to encourage and strengthen the most peace-minded among them.'' It concluded that ''the Peace Race must have the following elements: cessation of nuclear weapons tests, disarmament, strengthened U.N., negotiations for political settlements, economic aid, and reappraisal of civil defense.''[15]

At the same time, SANE assumed leadership in Washington and in local communities in pressing for the establishment of the U.S. Arms Control and Disarmament Agency. After its approval by Congress and the president in September 1961, SANE sought to build public support for the agency and worked to increase its budget. SANE also contributed to the formation of Turn Toward Peace, a joint national effort by peace, church, veterans, labor, and public affairs groups to develop alternatives to the threat of war as the basis of U.S. foreign policy. Robert Pickus of a peace organization called Acts for Peace in California and Sanford Gottlieb of SANE served as national staff for the joint effort, while Norman Thomas was its acting chairman. Later Robert Gilmore, who had resigned the previous year from the SANE board, took over this position.

Turn Toward Peace was an experimental, loosely federative effort designed to gain approval from the participating organizations only in its overall direction, while each organization remained free to promote its own program. Groups such as the Americans for Democratic Action, American Friends Service Committee, Committee for Non-Violent Action, SANE, American Veterans Committee, and the Division of Peace of the Methodist Church participated in a common search for initiatives which the United States could take, without prior Soviet approval, to elicit a positive response from the least belligerent groups in the Communist bloc and to improve the climate for future negotiated agreements.[16]

Meanwhile, the pressures on President Kennedy to resume testing in the atmosphere, as the Soviet Union had done, were increasing. While there were reports of genuine reluctance on the part of the administration, SANE's leaders believed that conservatives, the military, and weapons development groups would get the upper hand unless substantial public opinion was quickly brought to bear. Accordingly, the international sponsors of SANE, including Martin Buber, Pablo Casals, Francois Mauriac, Bertrand Russell, and Albert Schweitzer, joined Clarence Pickett, co-chairman, and Norman Thomas, program chairman of SANE, in an appeal to Kennedy not to resume atmospheric nuclear tests. The statement asked all nuclear powers, including France, "to refrain from further nuclear explosions pending an agreement for a test-ban treaty with adequate inspection and control."[17]

Kennedy restricted the American response to underground shots in 1961, but pressures from testing advocates, headed once more by Edward Teller, and the Pentagon contributed to his decision to announce the resumption of tests in the atmosphere in a televised speech to the nation on March 2, 1962. With the Geneva negotiations deadlocked and the United States ready to test unless an agreement was completed by April 1, Norman Cousins tried to put the moment into perspective in a letter to executive director Homer Jack stating that it was "clear that SANE played an essential part in bringing about a moratorium and prolonging it until last September." But now, he lamented,

Because of the resumption of tests by the Soviet Union and the United States, in that order, it is natural that many of us should have the most anguished sense of disappointment and foreboding. And we all wonder what should be done now that our principal objective has been shattered.

"It seems to me", Cousins warned, "that one thing we do *not* do is to become a committee of the defeated. Fatalism in the U.S. needs no help from us; it has flourished without our affection and will continue to do so."[18]

Undaunted, SANE and the American Friends Service Committee convened a small group of experts from several viewpoints, including Norman Thomas, Homer Jack, Erich Fromm, Seymour Melman, and

David Riesman, and issued a comprehensive statement, "Initiatives to Break the Geneva Impasse," which was released to the press on April 7. The forty-two point statement concluded by affirming, "the utility of continuous negotiations and their necessity at Geneva and elsewhere" because "the will to negotiate must never lessen, for the alternative is an ever-increasing arms race leading ultimately to nuclear war."[19]

Shortly before the resumption of American atmospheric tests, SANE placed three advertisements in U.S. newspapers. On April 10 a full-page SANE ad appeared in the *New York Times* asking "What are the risks of tests?" under a mushroom cloud giving numerous and persuasive reasons why there was more risk to mankind in resuming nuclear tests in the atmosphere than in not testing. One week later, another SANE ad was published with the headline "Mr. President, You Stopped the Steel Strike; You Can Still Stop Nuclear Tests." The ad pointed out to the public that just two days before eight nations made an important compromise proposal that called for the USSR accepting the principle of on-site inspection and the United States accepting in turn a nationally based detection system. If any country refused to admit inspections, the treaty would be abrogated. Calling it "a reasonable compromise," SANE urged the administration to accept the eight-nation suggestion as a basis for discussion and to postpone the series of atmospheric tests.[20]

Of the three advertisements, however, the most spectacular by far was entitled "Dr. Spock is worried." A few months before, after President Kennedy announced his decision to resume nuclear testing, Dr. Benjamin Spock, the famed pediatrician and author of one of the all-time best sellers, *Baby and Child Care*, had sent SANE a donation and was persuaded by Homer Jack at the third invitation to become a national sponsor. Spock stated that Jack's letter, quoting a passage from Albert Einstein's biography by Phillip Frank, made him realize his great responsibility as a public figure and that "there wouldn't be peace and disarmament unless the people demanded it. I thought of all the children who would die of leukemia and cancer, and of the ultimate possibility of nuclear war, and I joined SANE."[21]

SANE wasted no time in publicizing Spock's acceptance. William Bernbach, SANE board member and partner in Doyle, Dane, Bernbach, offered his advertising agency's services to place a full-page ad in the *New York Times* to proclaim Spock's views. Spock remembers this incident as an important turning point in his life. Having at his disposal

What are the risks of tests?

There is _more_ risk to mankind in resuming nuclear tests in the atmosphere than in not testing

■ If we and the Russians resume testing, tit for tat, other countries will be encouraged to join the deadly testing race. Each new country armed with nuclear weapons multiplies the chances of nuclear war.

■ More tests will mean a new round in an unlimited arms race, increasing the tensions and fears that lead to war.

■ Radioactive fallout will increase, endangering our lives and especially those of our children. Nobel Prize Geneticist Hermann J. Muller recently wrote that "as many as 300,000 may die early as a result of fallout from all the tests up until now . . . (and) the mutations produced . . . will probably result in even more deaths and deformities scattered widely through the next 2,000 years."

Let's not play Russia's game.

■ The Russians want us to test so they can begin another series of tests without further world criticism.

■ The Russians want us to test so we can share with them the blame for increased world-wide fallout during the spring rains.

President Kennedy and Secretary of Defense McNamara have repeatedly stated that the U. S. is ahead in nuclear technology and stockpiling. Physicist Hans A. Bethe has recently said that "the value of nuclear tests has been greatly exaggerated — we already know so much about atomic weapons that there is not much more to learn." Nor is there any need to add to an "overkill" capacity.

President Kennedy's statement on resuming atmospheric tests was provisional. There is _still_ time to call a halt to testing.

■ The Disarmament Conference at Geneva should be given a chance to succeed.

■ The progress which may be made on Berlin and Germany and on joint exploration of outer space should be safeguarded.

There is _still_ time to reach a compromise on a test-ban treaty.

President Kennedy told the United Nations: "In a spiraling arms race, a nation's security may well be shrinking even as its arms increase." A new test series will contribute to the spiraling arms race. On balance, American and world security will shrink through a further round of tests.

There is _still_ time for you to urge the President to call off atmospheric tests.

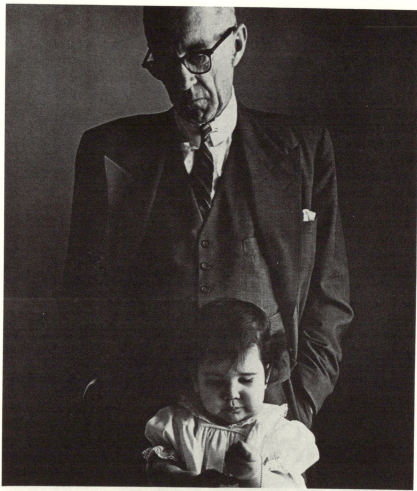

Dr. Spock is worried.

If you've been raising a family on Dr. Spock's book, you know that he doesn't get worried easily.

From the university in Ohio where he works, he sends you this message about the resumption of nuclear testing in the atmosphere:

"I am worried. Not so much about the effect of past tests but at the prospect of endless future ones. As the tests multiply, so will the damage to children—here and around the world.

Who gives us this right?

"Some citizens would leave all the thinking to the government. They forget the catastrophic blunders that governments have made throughout history.

"There are others who think that superior armaments will solve the problem. They scorn those who believe in the strength of a just cause. They have forgotten that a frail idealist in a loin cloth compelled the British to back out of India.

"There are dangers in any course. I would rather we took small risks today if there is hope of lessening the enormous risks which lie ahead.

"And if I am to be destroyed through some miscalculation I would prefer to be destroyed while we are showing leadership in the search for a cooperative world than while sitting in an illusory fortress blaming our opponents for the lack of a solution.

"In a moral issue, I believe that every citizen has not only the right but the responsibility to make his own feelings known and felt."

—*Benjamin Spock, M.D.*

Dr. Spock has become a sponsor of The National Committee for a SANE Nuclear Policy.

Other sponsors are listed below, with a brief description of what SANE stands for.

If you are worried too about the present series of nuclear tests in the atmosphere, telegraph or write President Kennedy and your Congressman.

If you would like to do still more, send a contribution to help us run advertisements like this one all over the country. The National Committee for a SANE Nuclear Policy, 17 East 45th Street, New York 17, N.Y.

a whole page of the *New York Times* to give a message to the world, Spock felt that he had to establish relatively unassailable reasons for becoming a peace activist and for persuading others to do so as well. After working for a month on numerous revisions, he finally ended up with a 4,000-word statement that he thought was pretty good and jokingly called it "The Manifesto." When Doyle, Dane, and Bernbach advised him that they would use fewer than 400 words for the ad, Spock said, "It was like an abortion to destroy the thing I had created, by reducing it to ten percent of its size." Later a young executive at the agency suggested leaving out the parts in which he was arguing with an imaginary adversary, and the ad was cut in half over again. "The further cut nearly killed me at the time," declared Spock. "The result was an almost purely moral statement."[22]

The advertisement included a three-fourths page picture of a sober, reflective Dr. Spock standing behind and looking down on a small girl, followed by a caption which stated in part: "I am worried not so much about the effects of past tests, but the prospects of future ones." Calling the tests damaging to children and therefore "a moral issue," Spock ended in a passionate plea: "I believe that every citizen has not only the right, but the responsibility to make his own feelings known and felt."[23]

A tremendous impact was created by recruiting Dr. Spock, for the advertisement was reprinted in 700 newspapers all over the world. *Time* and *Newsweek* both gave coverage to this famous advertisement. *Newsweek* did not make any editorial comment, but *Time* called it "Sane, but less than realistic." Posters of the ad went up in store windows, nurseries, doctors' offices, and even on baby carriages. More than 25,000 reprints were distributed throughout the nation, including at a Pediatrician's Convention in New York City; and more than 20,000 were addressed and sent to President Kennedy at the White House.[24]

Although Spock received some unfriendly responses and even had a few long used, dog-eared copies of *Baby and Child Care* returned to him, the overwhelming majority of Americans who wrote to him were grateful for his peace effort. One man from Toledo, Ohio, wrote that he and his wife had raised their first child with the determination never to read his book and had every intention of following the same procedure with their second child. However, after Spock became a SANE sponsor and they saw the ad, they decided they had better consult him and purchased his book "and read it from cover to cover." A SANE national board member from Connecticut, Stephanie May, wrote him that she had never felt "such a feeling of pride, gratitude, even love" as when she saw the ad the day before in the *New York Times*. May noted, "You have inspired me, and countless others, to keep trying, to continue with all the strength we have to make our voices heard."[25]

In spite of such protest, the U.S. atmospheric tests in the Pacific resumed on April 25. SANE's program chairman, Norman Thomas, responded by calling the test renewal "a political and moral disaster." "The United States has accepted a serious moral and political defeat by resuming nuclear tests in the atmosphere . . . ," a statement released by National SANE contended. "We of the National Committee for a Sane Nuclear Policy protest the new American series of nuclear tests just as strongly as last autumn we protested the new Russian series." Concluding that "now that the U.S. has started atmospheric tests, it is more imperative than ever to achieve agreement on a treaty ending all tests," SANE continued to urge the American citizens to ask Kennedy to call off further tests and to start round-the-clock talks in Geneva until a test ban treaty was signed.[26]

At the same time, Greater New York SANE held a series of protests in Times Square urging the United States and the Soviet Union to halt such tests and continue disarmament talks in Geneva. Delegates from SANE presented written and oral pleas to the U.S., Soviet, and British Missions to the United Nations, set up 150 pickets outside the U.S. Mission, and left copies calling nuclear tests "a declaration of war by the nuclear powers on the rest of the world without provocation and to the peril of all." New York SANE also manned an anti-testing vigil at Times Square. Beginning on April 25, the day the United States resumed atmospheric tests, a vigil was conducted each night until May 5, including one star night which included appearances by Shelley Winters, Mimi Benzell, Douglas Campbell, Julie Harris, and others.[27]

The resumption of atmospheric tests by the Soviet Union and the United States led to a renewed interest in the matter of fallout and its effects. A new study was prepared by SANE on this issue called "The Current Hazards of Fallout to Human Health." To bolster public support for their arguments, SANE published an ad in July 1962 showing a milk bottle with a poison label with the caption "Is this what it's coming to?" The controversial ad emphasized that threat to health by Iodine 131, a radioactive substance that comes from the fallout of nuclear explosions and is taken up by cows and appears in milk. This emphasis naturally brought a loud protest from the milk industry. Ernest Kellog of the Milk Industry Foundation chastized SANE "for scaring people into acting adversely to their own conscience" and suggested that danger from fallout from weapons testing was being used falsely as an "expedient in stirring up public opinion against the nuclear weapons race."[28]

The following month, Graphic Artists for SANE, a new chapter of the national committee which included such prominent artists as Jules Feiffer, Ben Shahn, and Edward Sorel, designed a poster with a pregnant mother and the caption "1¼ Million unborn children will be born dead or have some gross defect because of Nuclear Bomb Testing." The ad was so popular in appeal that it appeared on thousands of subways and train platforms in Greater New York and ended up in the United States Information Agency Graphic Arts exhibit in the Soviet Union in 1963 after a hurry-up request for some "peace posters" before the traveling exhibit was taken to Moscow.[29]

Nuclear testing and its effects became a secondary issue, however, when in late August 1962 an American U–2 reconnaissance plane flying fourteen miles above Cuba reported the first Soviet surface-to-air missile site. Although President Kennedy warned the Soviets and the Cubans against installing offensive, ground-to-ground missiles, on October 14 the first photographs were taken of a launch pad under construction which could fire ballistic missiles with a range of 1000 miles. Several days later a 2000-mile missile site was observed under construction. On the evening of October 22, the president broke the well-kept secret to the American people. Because the Soviets were building bases in Cuba "to provide a nuclear strike capability against the Western Hemisphere," Kennedy announced the United States was imposing "a strict quarantine on all offensive military equipment" being shipped into Cuba. American military forces, he added, were on full alert, and the United States would "regard any nuclear missile launched from Cuba against any nation in the Western Hemisphere as an attack by the Soviet Union on the United States, requiring a full retaliatory response upon the Soviet Union." He appealed to Khrushchev to remove the offensive weapons under United Nations supervision.[30]

The national board of SANE met during the President's speech and immediately issued a press statement commending him for taking the issue to the Organization of American States and to the United Nations. The board also urged the president to ask the UN Security Council "to form a commission to visit Cuba immediately for confirmation of the

Is this what it's coming to?

1¼ Million unborn children
l be born dead
or have some
gross defect
because of
Nuclear Bomb
testing

1¼ million is a maximum number indicated by the report of the Federal Radiation Council of May 1962. Other authorities regard this figure as a minimum. Of these, 250,000 children will be born with some gross defect. According to the report, this includes "such things as congenital malformations, idiocy, blindness, deafness, feeble-mindedness, traumatic atrophy, hemophilia, and mental diseases." The number of children who will die in infancy or be born dead, will be, the report states, "perhaps five times larger than the number of inherited defects of the type" mentioned above.

In addition, "there may be an unknown but probable a considerable larger number of mutations with less obvious effects such as minor physical abnormalities, mild diseases, impairment of physiological functions and reduced resistance to infection or other stresses of life." All this means the individual will have a lower chance of surviving after birth. The Federal Radiation Council report is entitled "Health Implications of Fallout from Nuclear Weapon Testing through 1961." As the title indicates, it makes no allowance for tests occurring since 1961, either now or in the future.

exact military situation" and asked him to "adhere to the previous vow not to take military action against Cuba." The following day, SANE cabled the Soviet Peace Committee in Moscow to urge their government to suspend its arms shipments to Cuba and asked the U. S. government to suspend the blockade of Cuba and to consider closing American missile bases in Turkey in exchange for the dismantling of Soviet bases in Cuba.[31]

On October 24, a full policy statement was issued by SANE which was published as an ad in the *New York Times* the following day. Stating that both the United States and the USSR must acknowledge guilt for this predicament—the USSR for recklessly extending the Cold War by setting up missile bases in Cuba and the United States for unilaterally instituting a quarantine on all offensive military equipment traditionally regarded as an act of war—SANE suggested an alternative course which could be pursued. The alternatives included immediate military disengagement by all the concerned parties with the USSR withholding its arms shipments to Cuba, the United States withdrawing its blockade, and Cuba halting work on missile installations; no military invasion of Cuba by the United States; acceptance of mediation by the United Nations; and the development of a long-range solution to American-Cuban differences. The national committee also played a key role in the then largest outdoor peace rally ever held in New York history when 10,000 persons gathered at the United Nations that "Cuba Sunday," October 28, to express their concern about the possibility of nuclear war.[32]

The same day the crisis was resolved when the superpowers agreed to removal of Soviet missiles in return for an American pledge not to invade Cuba. The easing of tensions following the dangerous major power confrontation at the brink of thermonuclear war offered renewed hope to the world of an early treaty banning nuclear weapons tests. As President Kennedy stated in his letter of October 28 to Premier Khrushchev: "I agree with you that we must devote urgent attention to the problem of disarmament, as it relates to the whole world and also to critical areas. Perhaps now, as we step back from danger, we can together make progress in this vital field." Following an exchange of letters between the president and the premier on the test ban, SANE felt that "this may be the best moment since the ill-fated Summit of May, 1960, for a genuine U.S.-U.S.S.R. detente, beginning with a test-ban agreement and continuing with a refusal to open the nuclear club any further."[33]

SANE's fifth anniversary was celebrated on November 15 at a dinner in New York City honoring Steve Allen, the committee's vice chairman. Mrs. Eleanor Roosevelt, who was honorary chairman of the affair, died on the eve of the dinner and, with the permission of her family, the Eleanor Roosevelt Peace Award was established to memorialize her dedicated work for a world at peace. The award consisted of a bronze plaque bearing the sculpted profile of Mrs. Roosevelt designed by SANE board member and artist, Stephanie May. First given to Steve Allen, subsequent recipients of this annual award have included former Ambassador James J. Wadsworth; Cousins; Pickett; Spock; Thomas; Max Youngstein, producer of the film "Fail Safe" and former national treasurer of SANE; former Representative George Brown (D-CA.), former Senators George McGovern and Eugene McCarthy; Wayne Morse of Oregon; Ernest Gruening of Alaska; Dr. Martin Luther King; the United Auto Workers; Allard Lowenstein, president of Americans for Democratic Action and head of the Dump Johnson Movement in 1968; Daniel Ellsberg; Soviet dissident Andrei Sakharov; journalist I.F. Stone; and Senator Edward Kennedy.[34]

As 1963 began and the test ban negotiations remained deadlocked with no agreement in sight, SANE continued to press on the fallout theme, encouraging a new group, Dentists for SANE, to publish the advertisement "*Your* children's teeth contain Strontium 90." The more than 200 dentists who signed the ad stated that they deplored the buildup of radioactive Strontium–90 in children's teeth and bones and declared that "as dentists our responsibility to promote life and health compels us to make this public appeal to all governments to cease nuclear weapons tests and to develop those international agreements which would eliminate the nuclear arms race." As Pope John XXIII issued his famous "Pacem in Terris" (Peace on Earth), SANE participated with the American Friends Service Committee, the Women's International League for Peace and Freedom, and Women's Strike for Peace in an Easter/Passover appeal to President Kennedy to negotiate an effective test ban treaty with the Soviet Union and pledged their support and signing of the treaty when it was necessary.[35]

It was at this point that Cousins, acting as unofficial liaison between President Kennedy and Soviet Premier Khrushchev, helped to break an

<u>Your</u> children's teeth contain Strontium-90

All children's teeth now contain radioactive Strontium-90 from nuclear weapons tests.

Radioactive Strontium is a potential cause of leukemia, as pointed out in the United Nations report on radiation. Early signs of leukemia appear in the mouth, and dentists are familiar with them.

Scientists can tell how much radioactive Strontium-90 is in children's bones by measuring the radioactive material in their teeth. A recent analysis of baby teeth shows a 16-fold increase in Strontium-90 over the past five years.* Unlike baby teeth, however, the permanent teeth and bones retain Strontium-90 throughout their existence.

As dentists, we deplore the buildup of radioactive Strontium-90

in children's teeth and bones. It is a measure of the sickness of our times. Even if nuclear weapons tests cease today, the accumulation of Strontium-90 will continue for years.

We oppose nuclear weapons testing by all nations not only because of the contamination of bones and teeth of our children and patients, but because it is a direct stimulus to the runaway arms race. The testing race only multiplies mistrust and tension, and increases the chances of nuclear war.

Therefore, as dentists, our responsibility to promote life and health compels us to make this public appeal to all governments to cease nuclear weapons tests and to develop those international agreements which would eliminate the nuclear arms race.

*Committee for Nuclear Information St. Louis Baby Tooth Survey

David Abramson, Norman E. Alderman, Seymour Algus, Maurice S. Atkin, Mark August, Morris Berger, Harold L. Berk, Meyer F. Berkelhammer, Milton Berman, Frank Bisk, Frank E. Beube, Carl Blacharsh, Milton Bloch, Daniel H. Bloom, Bertram Blum, Daniel W. Boykin, Leo Botwinick, Robert S. Breakstone, Raymond M. Bristol, Benjamin R. Bronstein, Louis J. Budner, Jack Budowsky, Harold J. Canter, Murray A. Canter, Andrew F. Catania, George Cohen, Louis M. Cohen, Maxwell B. Colton, Eugene M. Coven, Ralph S. Crapanzano, Stanley Darrow, Zalmen A. Dunn, Irving J. Eckman, Robert S. Eisenberg, Manasseh Elson, Sol Engel, Ulysses Erdreich, Sol Ewen, M. Marvin Fader, Alan Feinstein, Leon Feinstein, Samuel Feinstein, William B. Feldman, Stanley Feuer, Lester Fineman, Stanley Finkelstein, Julius Fox, H. William Frankel, Eugene Fried, Abraham Friedman, Charles Gargle, Philip Gold, Burton Goldberger, Sol M. Goldin, Irving Guldman, David Goldstein, Martin Goldwasser, Leonard Gorelick, Manuel Gottlieb, John Graziano, Albert Green, Lewis L. Greene, Howard Grindlinger, Paul Grindlinger, Henry Hack, Charles Handelman, Henry Hausen, Murray M. Hilton, George A. Hindes, Jack Hirsch, Robert Hoffman, Norman Horowitz, Irving Jaffee, Nathan Janiger, Ilse Janzen, Paul Jarmon, Herman Kasten, L. Paul Kaufman, Stanley L. Kent, Joseph M. Kessler, Nathan Kobrin, Benjamin S. Koplik, Ralph Krainin, Seymour Krauth, Louis Kroll, Paul A. Krooks, Morton Lauter, Nathan M. Leban, J. Lewis Leboy, Harold A. Leegant, Joseph M. Lieberman, Robert R. Lemkin, Emil W. Lentchner, Philip H. Levin, M. Robert Levine, Wilfred Levine, Frederick Levy, Jacob M. Levy, Benjamin Lieberman, Lawrence Lieberman, Victor O. Lucia, Alvin V. Lyons, Samuel Mamlet, Irwin D. Mandel, William I. Margalies, Ralph Margulies, John Oppie McCall, Mortimer Messing, Roger H. Miller, Solomon Mink, Richard M. Moudnik, Melvin L. Morris, Samuel D. Moskowitz, Sidney Moses, Abraham I. Mulson, Hursh Mullman, Seymour L. Nash, Bernard Nathanson, Samuel E. Neikrug, Leonard M. Nevins, Irving Nussenbaum, Benjamin Ogman, Judah M. Orkin, Jack C. Orrach, Herbert I. Oshrain, Eliot Oxenberg, Irving J. Panken, Leon Pentel, Irving Peress, Arthur L. Phillips, Eugene R. Pinto, Nathan Platt, William Rakower, Benjamin S. Recant, Robert M. Reiss, Lewis Rice, Leo H. Roper, Aaron Rosenbaum, Theodore Rosenbury, Emanuel Rosenberg, Martin Rosencrans, Harold Rosenman, Mitchell L. Rosenson, Withal Rossein, Ephraim A. Rothenberg, A. Allen Rothman, Bernard Rudin, Irving Rusnack, Robert W. Sabin, Alexander M. Samuels, Daniel Samuels, Harry Sardell, Donald Sasonkin, Solomon J. Satine, Harold Scheiten, Paul Scheman, Marvin Jay Schissel, Dan Jay Schlossman, Richard M. Schneer, Walter Z. Schuman, Elias Schwartz, Louis Schwartz, Louis Laszlo Schwartz, Samuel Schwartz, Ben Seidler, Martin Seiger, Paul W. Selden, Abbe J. Selman, A. J. Shapiro, Bernard Shapiro, Gerald I. Shapiro, Earl H. Shatskin, Alfred R. Shepard, Max Siegel, Samuel R. Siegel, Stanley Siegel, Sidney Silverman, Paul Singer, Simon Solovey, Nathan Somerman, Robert Spalten, Clifford N. Stern, Irwin Steuer, Arthur W. Stulbaum, Irving K. Tayner, Harold J. Tennen, Earl G. Thompson, Michael I. Uris, Maurice S. Varen, Allan Wallshein, Bernard Weber, Seymour R. Weinstein, Arthur Burton Weiss, Robert V. Weissman, Jacob J. Weksler, Bernard L. Winter, Louis Wolf, Harold Yachnes, Maurice Yarkow, Harry Zweig

SPACE FOR THIS STATEMENT HAS BEEN PAID FOR BY THE DENTISTS WHOSE NAMES APPEAR ABOVE. FOR FURTHER INFORMATION WRITE TO DENTISTS' COMMITTEE FOR A SANE NUCLEAR POLICY, 17 EAST 45TH STREET, NEW YORK 17, N. Y. GIFTS TO FURTHER THE AIMS OF THE ORGANIZATION ARE WELCOME.

impasse in the negotiations. In early 1963, with negotiations deadlocked over the question of inspections and Khrushchev doubtful that the United States really wanted a treaty, Secretary of State Dean Rusk asked Cousins if he could advise the Soviet leader that Kennedy was acting in good faith and genuinely wanted a treaty. Cousins stood high in the Russians' estimation as a result of his sponsorship of the Dartmouth Conferences between American and Russian intellectuals and scientists. In addition, Cousins had met with Khrushchev in Moscow in December 1962 on behalf of Pope John XXIII and successfully negotiated the release of Cardinal Josyph Slipyi of the Ukraine, a Roman Catholic prelate who had been interned under the Stalin regime.[36]

At a seven-hour meeting with Khrushchev at his Black Sea retreat in late April, Cousins told the premier how a number of citizens' organizations had come together in the United States to develop public support for the president's position in favor of a test ban treaty and how Kennedy encouraged this campaign from its inception. After discussing several misunderstandings that both countries were having with the other, the Soviet premier finally declared his acceptance of Kennedy's good faith in sincerely wanting a test ban treaty and agreed to join the United States in making a fresh start in order to get negotiations moving again.[37]

After Cousins's successful meeting with Khrushchev he met with Kennedy at the White House. A few days later he wrote Kennedy a letter that provided precious reinforcement to the president's plans to issue a breakthrough speech on the Cold War during his June commencement address at the American University in Washington, D.C. Urging a dramatic U.S. peace initiative, Cousins suggested that such a step might affect the course of Soviet policy and would certainly help the American image in the world. Responding positively to Cousins's thoughts, the president's American University commencement included a landmark policy statement in behalf of detente. He spoke movingly of peace "as the necessary rational end of rational men," and appealed to the Soviets to join him in seeking a relaxation of tension. Cousins was so pleased with the president's speech, stating "it met the demands of the situation brilliantly and inspiringly" and accordingly wrote to Kennedy the following day. "The faces that lit up before you at American University yesterday were only a reflection of the faces and feelings of countless people who were responding to your talk," Cousins told the president.

It was that rare event when a man speaks both to the moment and to the next generation. The first calls for courage; the second for vision. You had both. The infusion of hope and energy you gave the nation, and, I am sure, a large part of the world, puts us all in your debt.[38]

More importantly, Kennedy's speech elicited a positive response from the Kremlin and paved the way for the conclusion of the Partial Test Ban Treaty (underground testing was still allowed), which was signed in Moscow on July 25. In gratitude, President Kennedy sent Cousins the UPI newswire on the treaty, along with personal expression of appreciation. Later, the president gave him one of the original signed copies of the treaty document itself.[39]

With the conclusion of the test ban treaty, Kennedy and pro-treaty advocates confronted an obstacle nearly as formidable: the Constitutional requirement to secure a two-thirds vote of approval in the U.S. Senate. Fifty votes seemed certain, but another seventeen were needed. Cousins and SANE rightly worried that many senators feared a test ban treaty would appear in the public mind as a dangerous limitation on American nuclear capability and therefore injurious to the nation's military security. Private polling information indicated that the trend of public opinion was moving toward support of a test ban. But impressions garnered from congressional mailbag and visitors' tally sheets suggested popular opposition to the test ban was running at about 10 to 1. In some weeks, it appeared as high as 20 to 1.

To counter this opposition, SANE published a full-page advertisement in the *New York Times* on August 2 entitled "Now it's up to the Senate . . . and *You!*" After stating how important the treaty was to world peace and that the Senate should ratify this treaty unanimously and soon, the advertisement concluded: "Over five years ago, the National Committee: for a Sane Nuclear Policy was formed to seek these ends. A nuclear test-ban treaty was then, and is now, first on our list of national priorities." SANE congratulated the men who secured this vital agreement and stated: "We are proud of our role in its achievement. We look forward to redoubled efforts by our nation to achieve safe-guarded, worldwide disarmament. . . ."[40]

In Washington, Cousins discussed the politics of ratification with presidential press aide Pierre Salinger. Encouraged by Salinger, Cousins organized the Ad Hoc Committee for a Nuclear Test Treaty for the purpose of rallying public opinion behind a ratification drive. With this

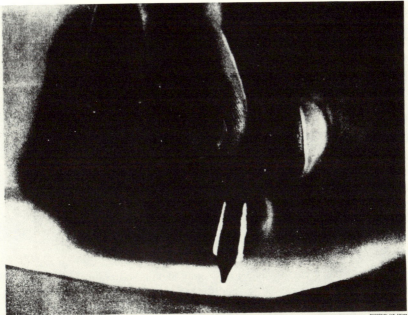

PHOTOGRAPH: CARL FISCHER

Now it's up to the Senate...and You!

A treaty ending nuclear weapons tests is now before the United States Senate for ratification. In their meetings in Moscow, the United States, the Soviet Union and Great Britain have agreed that a treaty outlawing nuclear tests in the atmosphere, under water and in outer space is in their interest and in the interest of world peace.

According to the laws of the land, a treaty does not become effective until ratified by a two-thirds majority of the U.S. Senate. There is every reason why the Senate should ratify this agreement unanimously and soon:

A test ban treaty will put an end to widespread radioactive fallout from nuclear testing. Present and future generations will be spared additional reproductive damage and bone cancer. Little can be done about what has already occurred.

The spread of nuclear weapons and their development by new nations will be slowed, reducing the chances of nuclear war.

But most important — the world will have taken the first step to end the suicidal nuclear arms race.

A test ban can signal an historic turning point. There is evidence that the test ban agreement represents a breakthrough of moderate and responsible opinion both within the United States and the Soviet Union. This development provides an opportunity to begin the real work of building

peace. The treaty opens wide the door to next steps — more important and far-reaching steps for lessening world tension and for achieving universal and controlled disarmament.

Only world security under a stronger United Nations can take the place of national insecurity, the arms race, and the rule of fear. The world will not be safe until "the war flags are furled in the Parliament of Man."

Five years ago, the National Committee for a Sane Nuclear Policy was formed to seek these ends. A nuclear test ban treaty was then, and is now, first on its list of national priorities.

We congratulate the men who have secured this vital agreement. We are proud of our role in its achievement. We look forward to redoubled efforts by our nation to achieve safeguarded, worldwide disarmament.

The moral leadership of the world belongs to the nation which shows the way, step by practical step, to build the edifice of peace. The first step is now up to the United States Senate. By ratifying the treaty, the Senate can make clear the will of the American people to seek a just and lasting peace under honorable and safeguarded agreements. The Senate will act with due caution and after careful review. It is necessary to the Senate's decision that the lawmakers know where the country stands and what its citizens will support.

This is where you come in. Write three letters and write them now. One each to your Senators, and one to President Kennedy, indicating in your own words, your support for the test ban agreement.

in mind, Cousins and other leaders met with Kennedy on August 7 and advised the president of their plans for a nationwide campaign of advertising and public discussion. For nearly two months in the summer of 1963 debate over testing dominated the news. Between the efforts of Cousins's ad hoc committee and groups like SANE and those of the administration the tide of Congressional mail began to turn. And public opinion polls showed a steady rise in popular support for the treaty and easing fear over any danger to the national security.[41]

The campaign for ratification of the test ban treaty culminated in hearings before the Senate Foreign Relations Committee. The two principal witnesses against ratification were Teller and General Thomas S. Powers, chief of the Strategic Air Command. Their opposition, however, was almost anticlimactic. Several other important figures, including Cousins and the chairman of the Joint Chief of Staff, testified in support of ratification, with gratifying effect.[42]

As the treaty came down to a vote in the Senate, the number of supporters increased, while public opinion polls showed that 80 percent of the American people favored the treaty. Finally, on September 24, 1963, the Senate approved the treaty by an 80 to 19 margin, the largest vote in favor of arms control recorded in the Senate since the 1921–1922 Washington Naval Treaties. Kennedy called the vote "a welcome culmination of this effort to lead the world once again to the path of peace" and stated that no other single accomplishment in the White House gave him greater satisfaction.[43] A few weeks later the president sent his personal appreciation to Cousins for his leadership with the committee on behalf of the treaty stating "the Committee made a real contribution in developing a better understanding of the purpose of the treaty and your initiative with the group was essential."[44]

SANE members rejoiced at word of Senate ratification. The Partial Test Ban Treaty capped a six-year battle against atmospheric testing; and SANE was singled out by national leaders like Jerome Wiesner, Kennedy's scientific advisor, as one of the key groups that had made the achievement possible. SANE leaders like Jack, Keys, and Cousins, however, were measured in their reaction. While Cousins, for example, praised the treaty as a welcome respite from "the long stretch of unremitting failure and almost constant despair," he cautioned against the temptation for activists to withdraw from the disarmament struggle. He contended:

The treaty is not an end in itself. It is a part of—or should be—a large delicate enterprise for making life less precarious for the humans who inhabit this planet. It is a portal to a more rational future. . . . Instead of ending the debate over nuclear testing, it has actually only begun.[45]

Maddeningly, however, the very success of the test ban treaty undercut the momentum of citizen disarmament activism. Concluding that their work was over, several nuclear pacifists grew more "respectable" and merged into the liberal wing of the Democratic party. SANE itself shifted its focus from demonstrations to lobbying and "responsible criticism," causing much of its grass-roots vitality to dry up. By the end of June 1964, SANE had unpaid bills totalling over $25,000. Some of the directors, like Norman Cousins, argued that SANE should cease functioning as a national organization because its original objective had been realized. But the majority of the directors wanted SANE to continue in order, as executive director Homer Jack wrote, "to take advantage of an international climate whereby other measures can be negotiated toward a major U.S.-U.S.S.R. detente."[46]

SANE leaders understood, however, how difficult it was to inspire commitment beyond crisis and tried to rekindle the organization with vitality and enthusiasm, bringing about an important organizational transition. Dr. Benjamin Spock and Harvard history professor and 1962 independent peace candidate H. Stuart Hughes became co-chairmen of SANE, succeeding Cousins and Pickett, and SANE's program director Donald Keys succeeded Jack as executive director. Cousins went back to the United World Federalists and became its honorary president; Jack became director of the Department of Social Responsibility of the Unitarian Universalist Association of the United States and Canada. Both he and Cousins remained on the SANE national board, however, and Pickett was made an honorary sponsor.

Understanding how detente brought new challenges to SANE and the nuclear protest movement, new executive director Keys set the tone for the post-treaty SANE when he wrote:

The initiatives for peace belong today in the hands of those groups which are now willing to do the difficult day-to-day job of public education and the slow task of building political power within the establishment in order to generate the necessary mandate to implement the policies which have now been accepted. The goal for SANE must remain the creation of a conscious public awareness of the only alternative which is open to mankind if it is to survive and the buildup of effective political power for its implementation.''[47]

Meeting in an atmosphere of detente, SANE observed its sixth anniversary at its annual conference in New York City in early November 1963. Much of the discussion centered on an examination of future priorities for the organization. The conference voted that local and national efforts on the economics of disarmament related to the overkill military budget and local efforts to eliminate civil defense programs were essential. It expressed concern about the stereotyped images held by both the United States and the Soviet Union of one another militating against continued negotiations. Efforts were also made to show that resources released from the defense budget could invigorate the economy, provide jobs, and help with the goals of civil rights. But everyone agreed that the two most important priorities that warranted comprehensive examination were a proposed merger of SANE with the United World Federalists and the peace issue as it related to the 1964 elections.[48]

Although the idea of merger with the United World Federalists had its roots in the special board meeting of June 1961, the movement gained substantial support when an editorial in the September 1963 issue of *War/Peace Report*, house organ of the War/Peace Institute in New York, stated that such a union "could give the American peace movement a much-needed backbone." The merger with the United World Federalists seemed a good possibility for numerous reasons, particularly since Norman Cousins had been and was still a leader in both organizations and other prominent mutual spokesmen included Rev. Donald Harrington, Oscar Hammerstein II, Walter Reuther, and Donald Keys. Moreover, the two organizations had many of the same policies, and both were suffering from declining local activity and increasing disinterest following the ratification of the test ban treaty in September 1963.[49]

There were, however, noteworthy differences between the two organizations. SANE had a much shorter history than had United World Federalists and was less democratic; it had used picketing and other forms of action protest, whereas United World Federalists had not; and it emphasized immediate goals, such as a complete nuclear test ban treaty, as contrasted to the United World Federalists' emphasis upon the more general and more distant goal of world federation. An even more important difference was the split over getting involved in world tension issues such as Berlin, Cuba, and Southeast Asia. In June 1961, SANE decided to state a policy regarding these crisis areas, but United World Federalists had not and did not propose to do so in the future. Erich Fromm voiced this concern in a letter he wrote to Homer Jack on November 15, 1963:

I want to express once more my deep conviction that it would be a great mistake to merge with the UWF, [for] just reading through a few issues of *SANE World*, I was again impressed by the combination of the two aspects on peace which are important, disarmament and foreign policy. There is no other organization which combines these two and has combined them increasingly in the last few years. . . . There is also, in my mind, no doubt that every statement of this kind we have been making would incur the resistance of the World Federalists.''[50]

While recognizing these problems, the majority of the SANE board was still in favor of the merger, and it was approved at the Seventh National Conference in November 1964. The framework for a new organization—policy, by-laws, budget, and staff recommendations—produced by the joint Consolidation Committee of the two organizations headed by Norman Cousins was presented to the delegates for their recommendation. After much discussion on the proposed policy statement of the new organization, an ''overwhelming Conference approval of merger'' was given the following day. All that was now needed was approval by the governing body of United World Federalists, and a positive decision was expected quickly. When the escalation of American involvement in the Vietnam War took place in early 1965, however, negotiations for merger were discontinued when it became apparent that strong opposition from some of the old guard United World Federalists board members and divergent views in the two organizations over the issue of protesting American military involvement in Vietnam would prevent a realistic merger.[51]

Gaining political power within the establishment had also long been of concern to SANE. Back in 1960, Sanford Gottlieb, who was the director of Washington, D.C., SANE, was appointed political action director by the national committee and was to be permanently located in Washington. Gottlieb was always interested in politics, had a Ph.D. in political science, and as early as June 1961 was trying to get SANE into that field. ''SANE will have to operate at two levels: as a pressure group, and as a force within at least one of the two major political parties,'' Gottlieb explained. "No pressure group operating solely as such can win a majority in the United States: the support of a political party is required." He maintained that SANE's members would have to get into precinct politics and generally develop into politically sophisticated leaders of their community.[52]

Gottlieb's recommendation touched off a spirited debate as to whether SANE should endorse political candidates in the 1962 congressional elections. Norman Thomas and William Butler were asked to write out their views for discussion at a national board meeting. Although Butler argued that "SANE could be more effective in bringing pressure upon all governments if it did not participate in public controversies," the group led by Thomas soon prevailed. Believing that, as Thomas stated, "the great decisions leading to war or peace must in the last analysis be taken in the political field," SANE decided to work in electing congressional candidates in 1962 "who came close to their reasoned position." A "Questionnaire for Candidates" was published which included questions on world disarmament, the World Court, nuclear test cessation, military intervention in Third World countries, disengagement in Europe, American initiatives for peace, American policy toward China, and civil defense. Concern that political endorsements might possibly create divisions within the organization was somewhat abated when a requirement of two-thirds approval for such endorsements by both the interested local committees and the national board was established.[53]

In 1963, a Peace Politics Clearing House was organized which linked representatives of peace organizations and groups interested in supporting candidates who emphasized alternatives to the arms race. Sanford Gottlieb represented SANE on the newly formed committee. The following year SANE began to get deeply involved in the presidential election. In June 1964 the organization came out with another questionnaire for the candidates, and in July Gottlieb proclaimed that "Peace is Good Politics in the 1964 Elections."[54]

In the fall, the national committee compared the 1964 Democratic and Republican platforms with "A SANE Standard" in regards to peace, negotiations, Communism, United Nations, NATO, multilateral force, Cuba, China, and Vietnam. Jack attended the Democratic National Convention as an observer for SANE. He considered "the convention's great achievement the nomination of Hubert H. Humphrey, for he is more informed about disarmament and detente than any Vice-President (or President) in living memory.'' On the other hand, the convention's "great disappointment has been the foreign policy planks of the platform, with Goldwaterism having influenced the Platform Committee far more than its parade of witnesses.'' Although officially SANE as an organization remained basically nonpartisan, it urged that Goldwater be forcefully opposed for "his election would raise immeasurably the chances of nuclear war—by accident—or calculation.'' SANE liberals worked for the election of Johnson but vowed to make clear the inadequacy of the Democratic foreign policy planks in comparison to foreign policy positions taken by some nongovernmental organizations, including SANE.[55]

In the November election, Lyndon Baines Johnson created around the Democratic party the widest coalition of groups, interests, and forces that had been assembled since Franklin Roosevelt's landslide victory in 1936. This coalition ranged from the moderate Americans for Democratic Action to a section of Students for a Democratic Society, whose slogan was "Part of the Way with LBJ.'' SANE hailed Johnson's campaign as a "Mandate for peace," stating that "Johnson concentrated on the twin aspects of the peace issue: nuclear responsibility and a patient search for lasting peace; playing an educational role which observers rarely understood or appreciated.''[56]

At SANE's Seventh Annual Conference in mid-November, a personal greeting from President Johnson was conveyed by Adrian S. Fisher, deputy director of the U.S. Arms Control and Disarmament Agency. Fisher told the audience that "President Johnson asked me personally to greet you and thank you for all the help you've been to me in my fight for peace.'' Relations between SANE and the White House had never been so cordial, and the national committee felt that substantial progress towards peace was certainly possible. What SANE did not know, however, is that while it seemed that peace was indeed becoming respectable, a firm consensus had emerged in the administration that the United States must soon undertake what General Maxwell Taylor described as a "carefully orchestrated bombing attack against North Vietnam.'' The only question was how soon and where it would take place.[57]

In early February 1965, a Vietcong attack on a U.S. military advisors' compound at Pleiku, South Vietnam, triggered a swift, though long-contemplated Presidential decision to give what the administration called an "appropriate and fitting response.'' Spokesmen from the president down justified the air strikes as a response to the Pleiku attack and emphatically denied that any basic change of policy had been initiated.[58] Despite the administration's disclaimers, the February decisions and resultant actions marked an important watershed in the war. For peace liberals in SANE, the watershed should be theirs as well. For if the partial nuclear test ban treaty had weakened SANE and the American peace movement, American involvement in the war in Southeast Asia brought both back to life.

5

Vietnam and the Politics of "Responsible" Protest, 1963–1973

Some people see me as a sort of absent-minded professor. My usefulness to the peace movement is in recruiting people from the middle of the road. I'm quite realistic about that.... But I'm willing to cooperate with anyone who's halfway responsible and wants to end this terrible war.... The peace movement must hold together and not quibble about who belongs to it. ... I'm willing to run for anything, including dogcatcher, for peace.

—Dr. Benjamin Spock, 1967[1]

One of the many ironies to emerge from the long and embittered war in Vietnam is a growing feeling that the antiwar movement in the United States, certainly the largest and most sustained in this country's history, had little or no impact on government policy. There are even a number of social scientists who make the claim that the movement was counterproductive, especially in regards to public opinion. That is, in the words of one critic, "The war might have been somewhat more unpopular if the protest had not existed." And George Ball, who served as under secretary of state under President Johnson, made an even more devastating comment when he wrote in 1973 that the antiwar protests only "dug us in more deeply" and intensified the administration's determination to win. He calculated, to the movement's retrospective dismay, that "only late in the day did widespread discontent. . . . appreciably slow the escalation of war."[2]

A central part of this problem, however, is that most of these writers, and apparently the American public, viewed the antiwar movement as one-dimensional—that is, that peace became identified as a "radical" cause and therefore turned off a significant majority of the American population and gave government leaders convenient scapegoats for their faltering policies. This stereotype is not surprising because it was precisely the radical wing of the antiwar movement that received the most publicity from the newspapers, wire services, television, and of course the White House. When, for example, SANE held its overwhelmingly middle-class, middle-aged, middle-of-the-road march in Washington in November 1965, what appeared on television news and in news photos were Viet Cong flags, interruptions by the tiny American Nazi Party, and the handful of marchers, out of several thousand, who were wearing beards and sandals. A few days later, the *New York Times* found it news to point out that the typical marcher was "a middle-class adult!"[3]

Although failing to assume the leadership role in this movement as they had in the test ban cause, SANE liberals certainly were important in working against the war and at the same time attempting to make peace a respectable endeavor. In attempting to balance these two goals, however, the organization suffered a severe internal division for the second time in the decade. This division, in turn, contributed to a fracture within the antiwar movement that diminished SANE's influence among more militant peaceseekers for many years to come. An examination of how peace liberals responded to the war in Vietnam, as well as the war taking place at home, provided not only a case study in understanding the liberal-radical rupture within the antiwar movement; but even more importantly it offered insight into what historian Allen Matusow recently called "the unravelling of America," due in large part to the failure of liberalism and the great uprising against it that convulsed this nation in the 1960s.[4]

SANE was an early critic of America's armed intervention in behalf of an anti-Communist regime in South Vietnam. It was one of the first organizations to call attention to the corrupt Diem regime in South Vietnam and in September 1963 urged the United States to dissociate itself from it as soon as possible. In early 1964 the national board sent an appeal to President Johnson calling for a neutralized North and South

Vietnam under international supervision. This policy statement of SANE's, signed by 5,000 educators, was the first major public statement on the issue. Professor Hans Morgenthau, the well-known political scientist and sometime advisor to the government, presented it on behalf of SANE to a surprised press. At their national conference in November 1964, Norman Thomas took issue with the prevailing mood of optimism and vigorously attacked American involvement in Vietnam, and SANE co-chairman H. Stuart Hughes charged that the Vietnam War was "becoming more and more immoral . . . must be ended . . . and almost any settlement is better than we have now." After a spirited debate, the conference called for "an immediate cease-fire" in Vietnam, an international conference to neutralize the area, and the "ultimate withdrawal of United States military personnel." A motion to express "moral indignation" over American conduct and maintenance of the war was adopted, with only two delegates in opposition.[5]

Peace liberals in SANE, however, were not overly concerned about Vietnam until the escalation decisions of early 1965. On the morning of February 7, Bernard Fall, the French-American journalist who became an expert on Vietnam, called his friend, SANE's political action director Sanford Gottlieb, at 7:00 in the morning and said, "They did it." Gottlieb quickly wrote a denunciatory telegram and asked SANE co-chairmen Dr. Benjamin Spock and H. Stuart Hughes to send it in their names. Spock recalled that "a commentator said the White House said the move is approved by all Americans except Dr. Spock and Professor Hughes."[6]

The depth of the disillusionment among peace liberals with President Johnson when he started bombing North Vietnam and the moral outrage that followed when the reelected president began the major escalation was perhaps best expressed by Spock, who had become SANE's most prominent and effective spokesman. Two days after the election in November 1964, President Johnson called Spock in New York to thank him for the work he had done on the Doctors for Johnson Committee during the campaign. "I hope I will be worthy of your trust," the President said. "I'm sure you will," Spock answered. When the United States started bombing Vietnam, Spock was outraged. He sent the president a series of letters, some of them stinging, in which he expressed shame of his country's actions. One letter was answered vaguely by the president, the rest by McGeorge Bundy, Walt Rostow, and other White House aides. When he saw that letter writing was not going to have any effect, he, like thousands of other peace liberals who felt personally betrayed by the war, began casting about for other means of protest.[7]

On February 19, 1965, SANE placed a full-page advertisement in the *New York Times* which read: "Vietnam: America Must Decide Between A Full-Scale War and A Negotiated Truce." The ad asked Americans to help mobilize public opinion to stop the widening of the war, to seek a cease-fire, and to negotiate an international settlement. In June 1965, SANE, with the help of other moderate peace organizations, sponsored an "Emergency Rally on Vietnam." The 18,000 people who packed New York's Madison Square Garden heard speaker after speaker including Spock, Thomas, Hans J. Morganthau, and Senator Wayne Morse, assail U.S. policy and call for negotiations with all concerned parties, including the Vietnamese National Liberation Front. Bayard Rustin, a longtime pacifist and civil rights activist who had organized the 1963 March on Washington, set the tone when he told the crowd that argument must give way to direct action. "We must stop meeting indoors and go into the streets," Rustin asserted; and following the rally many did just that as Spock, Thomas, Senator Morse, and Coretta Scott King led a group of 3,000 persons through the theatre district, Times Square, and across town to the United Nations Plaza. Peace liberals, who voted in 1964 for peace and got war, felt compelled to affirm their position through mass action.[8]

To put pressure on the administration, SANE began planning a march on Washington for the fall to protest what was happening in Vietnam, but within the confines of excluding radical groups and following a political line that specifically expressed concern over, rather than outright opposition to, the U.S. involvement in the war. In April, the committee chose not to endorse a Students for a Democratic Society (SDS) rally, for it was already convinced that the antiwar movement was antagonizing much of its potential support by inviting Communist participation and by its strong language and occasionally belligerent tone. Although hoping that radicals would not participate, Sanford Gottlieb, SANE's march coordinator, did not attempt to screen the participants. But there would be an attempt to screen the signs and to prohibit organizational literature. The committee even excluded radical historian Staughton Lynd, Robert Parris of the Student Nonviolent Coordinating Committee, and Nobel Prize winner Linus Pauling, a major figure in the movement to stop nuclear testing, from sponsorship of the SANE march. These men were excluded "for tactical reasons," Gottlieb later explained, because their past activities had apparently been too militant in the minds of some of the sponsors SANE was seeking.[9] Because of SANE's liberal credentials, however, the Americans for Democratic Action abandoned its resistance to antiwar protest and joined in the sponsorship, as did the newly formed Clergy and Laity Concerned About Vietnam and the National Student Association.

This coalition coincided with SANE's strategic perspective. It saw itself as working within the establishment, particularly among liberal Democratic politicians, to convince them that negotiations should begin in Vietnam and to strengthen the hand of those who adopted the "dove" position. In this respect the "immediate withdrawal" slogans were a liability. They would shut off the friendly ears of establishment figures and the protest would accomplish nothing. This perspective was clearly stated by the march's organizers. "The March on Washington has a detailed, carefully elaborated set of proposals designed to encourage a negotiated settlement," said the report.

This statement makes clear the distinct difference in approach between the administration and its critics. The former assumes that increased military pressure will bring the North Vietnamese to the conference table while the critics suggest that deescalation is the path.[10]

As sociologist Todd Gitlin pointed out in *The Whole World Is Watching*, SANE leaders worked assiduously "to present a reasoning, reasonable, moderate face to the government and the press." At the request of White House Asian Affairs advisor Chester Cooper and to avoid criticism that they were being one-sided in their protest, a message signed by thirty-one co-sponsors was sent to Hanoi which said that the marchers had no intention of supporting a military victory by the North Vietnamese or any other party to the war. The message concluded that all parties in Vietnam had the most urgent responsibility to come to an immediate political settlement of the war.[11]

SANE's march on Washington for peace in Vietnam occurred on November 27. Publicized as "A Call to Mobilize the Conscience of America," the action attracted an estimated crowd of 35,000 (most of them middle-class adults) and was, in the organization's words, "moderate and responsible." The committee acted as internal policemen and effectively isolated and controlled the extremists. SANE-approved signs dominated the picket lines and read: "Stop the Bombings," "Respect

1954 Geneva Accords,'' ''War Erodes the Great Society,'' and ''Self-Determination—Vietnam for the Vietnamese.'' In this way it strove to moderate both the demonstration's tone and to preserve the general atmosphere of dignity and restraint. SANE also loaded the speakers program with moderates who, SDS President Carl Oglesby observed later, were so eager ''to show their 'responsibleness' to criticize both sides equally that some of the speeches would hardly have been wrong for a pro-war rally.''[12]

Speakers at the rally included Norman Thomas; Spock; Coretta Scott King; Ronnie Drugger, editor of the *Texas Observer*; Representative George Brown, Jr., from California; Joseph M. Duffy, Jr., professor at Notre Dame University; Edwin T. Dahlberg, past president of the National Council of Churches; and Oglesby, whose speech attacking corporate liberalism and its constant element of imperialism ironically drew the greatest applause. Oglesby's speech became a classic in the New Left marking as it did a declaration of war against liberals, now irrevocably declared the enemy. In an exchange between Oglesby and Sanford Gottlieb following the march, Oglesby wrote that although one account of his speech said he ''all but read traditional liberals out of the movement'' (that is, SANE), he made it clear to Gottlieb that though we have our differences ''I think I need you—and that you need me.'' Gottlieb wrote back, ''I particularly agree with your statement of the mutual need of radicals and liberals.''[13] Although both agreed on this need, liberals and radicals in the peace movement increasingly went their separate ways.

Peace liberals, however, were much more concerned with the effect their march had on the news media and were encouraged when the *New York Times* coverage of the march emphasized the moderate tone and the respectable ''decorous'' throng. According to Gottlieb, the newsmen were ''victims of their own propaganda,'' for they ''expected a crowd of 'beats' and found middle-class America. One could almost hear the gasps of surprise in their reports.'' As a result, the news stories tended to concentrate on the marchers rather than on the content of the speeches. ''Yet,'' Gottlieb added, ''this had importance. In middle-class America, the neatly dressed, the well-groomed, and the restrained simply have greater acceptability, and their acceptability is 'transferable' to the realm of ideas.'' To recognize this, he concluded, ''is not to make value judgments about physical appearance, but to understand how to communicate.'' Although television coverage was highly biased in focusing on the small radical contingent, Gottlieb felt the demonstration was successful in that it made one important point: "This is that many serious, respectable people are looking for an alternative policy in Vietnam, despite efforts to blow this out of proportion."[14]

Most of the comments in the press reflected and supported SANE's position. Shana Alexander wrote in *Life*, for example, that "this march was not only the largest and the only professional demonstration I'd yet seen. . . . It was also the only reasoned and responsible one and therefore the first which might be at all effective." The *Christian Century* asserted that the "quality and character of the march conferred dignity on a movement which had been credited to a fringe of American society heretofore viewed as irresponsible. . . . " And Robert Sherrill in *The Nation* commented insightfully, "Middle-class Americans may not be any wiser than beatniks, but they mean a lot more to Johnson whose backbone to consensus is built right through the middle." These judgments were confirmed when only three days after the march Vice President Hubert Humphrey, at the suggestion of Norman Cousins, met with SANE leaders Spock, Gottlieb, and Jack to commend them on their "constructive and helpful" demonstration and to tell them he and other government officials were always available to listen and "to openly, responsibly, and frankly discuss their proposals."[15]

The Left developed a radically different, though equally salient, perspective. Even before 1965, the ideological and tactical thrust of the New Left led it to break decisively with the organized test ban and nuclear disarmament activism of the 1950s. SANE became the negative role model for the early New Left, and this animosity was carried over into the Vietnam protest movement.[16]

Morally revolted by the imperial war against the peasants of Vietnam, radical peace activists found traditional politics insufficient to express their opposition. To them, Vietnam utterly discredited Cold War liberalism, and their protest quickly developed into a relentless assault on liberal sensibilities. They also attacked what was considered the liberals facile call for negotiations. After commenting that the SANE march "helped to keep dialogue about peace alive in the country," Staughton Lynd in *Liberation* pointed out that there was a problem which the SANE march did not reach: "In asking for de-escalation leading to negotiations, SANE stayed away from the question of bringing American troops home." Robert Wolfe, writing in *Studies on the Left*, added: "It is already clear to everyone except SANE and its allies that one cannot protest the war in Vietnam in the name of a more sophisticated version of anti-Communism without lending credence to the very myth which has produced that war.''[17]

Nevertheless, peace liberals in SANE became progressively more skeptical of U.S. government policy. On December 25, 1965, President Johnson suspended bombing of North Vietnam in an attempt to induce the Communists to negotiate. Early the following month, Sanford Gottlieb met with representatives of North Vietnam and the National Liberation Front in Paris and Algiers. Upon his return, Gottlieb sent a letter to White House Press Secretary Bill Moyers which emphasized "the nationalistic motivations of those we fight" and stated that it was absolutely essential to continue the bombing pause. A week later, Spock wrote the President urging continuation of the bombing halt as "it might be our last chance for peace." "The alternative," declared Spock, was "to invite diaster in Vietnam, loss of world leadership, abandonment of the Great Society, and eventual revulsion by the American people." When Johnson resumed the bombing on January 30, Gottlieb immediately sent the president a statement adopted by the national conference and the board of SANE expressing regret and asserting that it "made a mockery of the U.S. government's professed pursuit of peace.''[18]

At the same time, the growing split between liberal and radical peace activists became more pronounced in the spring of 1966 when SANE initiated a "Voter's Peace Pledge Campaign," which was to culminate with a huge May rally to hand in pledges for the congressional candidates who had promised to work for a peaceful settlement in Vietnam. Rev. William Sloane Coffin, chaplain at Yale University, and Norman Thomas of SANE were co-chairmen of the campaign. One hundred Americans signed on as sponsors, including civil rights leader, Martin Luther King. Although the objectives of the project seemed so modest that a large segment of the peace movement, including most of the New Left, boycotted the event, an estimated 10,000 people, mostly neatly dressed adults, handed in 73,000 pledges signed by voters saying that they would work for candidates in the election who advocated a reduced military effort in Vietnam.[19]

SANE co-chairman Benjamin Spock paid his own way to fifteen states to campaign for peace candidates, all of whom lost in the Democratic primaries. Disappointed by the results, Gottlieb concluded that "the war has not bitten deeply enough into the American family, the American pocketbook, or the American conscience to produce many votes . . . but we will be able to look back at 1966 as the year the peace movement became political." According to Gottlieb, "Thousands of new people began to use the electoral process to bring about a change in government policy. They have gained invaluable experience, not the least of which is an understanding of the need for patient grass-roots organizing."[20]

Problems surfaced again for peace liberals when in 1967 the Spring Mobilization to End the War in Vietnam was being organized by a broad peace and civil rights coalition. The mobilization was coordinated by A.J. Muste, who stated that the goal of this new effort was the development of a "radical anti-war coalition" and that its cardinal principle would be "non-exclusion," that is, participation of any and all groups regardless of their goals, policies, or politics. Chosen largely for their prominence, Spock and King agreed to serve as co-chairmen. Thus it was within SANE itself that the lines between radical and liberal peace seekers were most sharply drawn.

Although Spock and his allies understood "non-exclusionism" would pose a major problem with SANE peace liberals, they strongly supported the demonstrations, while others on the SANE board were apprehensive. Cousins observed:

We didn't like the style of the thing. Some of the leaders had black racist tendencies streaked with violence. Some were Vietcong supporters. Some were opposed to negotiations. We couldn't control what those people would say or do, and we didn't want SANE to be taxed with ideas that most of us didn't share."

Seymour Melman, later co-chairman of SANE, stated that "the central issue was the prospect of violent behavior in marches that were not going to be politically effective." Spock, although deploring violence and supporting negotiations as the way to end American involvement in Vietnam, argued that only by participating in such protests could SANE exert any influence over them. He cautioned that disqualifying selected elements from the peace alliance would encourage dissension within the ranks: "I believe in going with other groups as long as their aims are roughly those of SANE," said Spock. "I believe in solidarity."[21]

Spock wanted SANE to "gradually create an image of being less self-righteous, less intolerant, less antagonistic to other segments of the peace movement," thereby winning over "some of the moderate radicals, some youths, and being accepted in a more brotherly spirit by some of the more radical groups.'' Thus his decision to become co-chairman of the April 15 march without seeking endorsement from the SANE national board increased tension within the organization. In what he called one of the "hard" decisions of his life, Norman Thomas symbolized the critical dilemma facing peace liberals in SANE. Thomas realized that not endorsing or participating in the Spring Mobilization might cause difficulties between the SANE board and the grass-roots membership but advocated staying away for "pragmatic reasons," mainly his feeling that

there should be some earnest organization of people who still try constructively to influence the government's actions rather than simply demonstrate against one side—our side—in terms of objections to mass murder which of itself would not be stopped simply by our withdrawal.

Swayed by such arguments the board passed a resolution by a vote of 22 to 4 stressing the need for SANE to concentrate on its own program and declared that the organization would remain in communication with the planners of the mobilization.[22] Therefore, despite very strong local committee sentiment to the contrary, SANE support for the march was not forthcoming.

Several local chapters were enraged, as were many of the SANE leaders who rallied around Dr. Spock. Many locals expressed their wholehearted support of Spock and followed the lead of the Washington SANE chapter which voted to support the April 15 Mobilization. Many of these people also played an active part in the mobilization, and Abe Bloom—vice-chairman of Washington SANE at that time—served as co-chairman of the Washington Area Committee for the Spring Mobilization. An article appeared on page one of the *Washington Post* on April 7, entitled "SANE is Split on Militancy of Dr. Spock," quoting one SANE board member who said that the organization feared that the protests in New York and San Francisco would erupt in "considerable confusion" and "extreme statements" and added that "the Spring Mobilization is going to be pullout-minded and we are negotiation-minded." The article also quoted Spock, who compared the difference between SANE and the Left Wing of the peace movement to the ideological battles of the 1930s among American Stalinists, Trotskyites, Socialists, and liberals. "I have always admired the way the five major civil rights organizations refrained from arguing in public," Spock commented, "and I think we [the peace groups] must bend every effort to stay together."[23]

The Northern California SANE chapter vehemently disagreed, however, and made its view public at a news conference at the Fairmont Hotel in San Francisco on April 12. The group issued a statement that said, "We believe a sound peace effort will recognize the presence of two armed ideologies in Vietnam, each seeking to impose its will by violence on the Vietnamese people." Robert Pickus, vice chairman of the Northern California SANE chapter, added, "Our concern is not to get the Communists out of the peace effort. We want to get them in, because the Communists also have to stop the killing." When asked about Spock's participation in a demonstration his organization did not support, Pickus answered: "We want to encourage him to rethink his position."[24]

Faced with published reports of a division in the organization regarding support for the mobilization, SANE felt it necessary "to make a public statement accurately reflecting its views." After presenting the resolution of February 12 and SANE's guidelines on demonstrations, the declaration read that the board "has made it clear that it could not officially support the demonstration. It has not, however, attacked the demonstration or in any way sought to obstruct its plans." The statement concluded that the board "respects the position of Dr. Spock in wishing to freely endorse as an individual action of groups other than SANE," and at the same time "also respects the position of executive director Donald Keys in implementing the majority view of the board." To the extent to which these two positions are in conflict, a committee of the board, composed of Norman Thomas, Lenore Marshall, Norman Cousins, and Robert Schwartz, "has under cognizance the task of review of the recommendation."[25]

Many SANE members took part in the mobilization, some marching under their chapter banners, and it proved to be a great success. With an enormous turnout and little disorder, the press reports were overwhelmingly positive; and in many peoples' eyes Spock's stand was vindicated. H. Stuart Hughes, who was out of the country teaching at the time, wrote to Spock from Paris that reports on the march "confirm the wisdom of your stand," and both Thomas and Cousins publicly acknowledged that Spock's participation in the march "had proved the right course."[26]

Following the march, however, SANE became more and more polarized. At the April 27 national board meeting, Dr. Spock and his supporters admonished Keys for his opposition to cooperation with other organizations and questioned his administrative relationships with other members of the staff and New York SANE. They then asked for Keys's resignation as executive director, which threw the organization into bitter turmoil. Although the discussion was quite heated, two important resolutions did result from this meeting. The first, which was adopted unanimously by the board, read that SANE would maintain cordial relations with all groups and individuals seeking world peace and where possible SANE would participate with other organizations in the formulation and execution of peace policies and joint projects. "SANE will not try to police the peace movement any more than the U.S. should try to police the world," the resolution continued. "National officers and staff members of SANE shall abide by the decisions of the board. They will not take action contravening SANE's policies nor publicly endorsing new movements and programs without prior consultation with SANE's board or the policy committee."[27]

The second resolution passed by the national board declared that "the national board be enlarged so that at least 50% of its members be elected from the chapters and the members at large" and that "provisions be made for representative voting from the members." Although Dr. Spock was undoubtedly reprimanded by the first resolution, he and his backers were happy to get the second resolution passed because they believed that the organization needed more democratization. The national board needed to see the local membership which was known to be more radical than most of the existing board members.[28]

Although these two resolutions were supposed to have a conciliatory effect, the following month the internal dissension became even more intense. At this point Lenore Marshall and Norman Thomas were asked by the board to play a mediating role, and Homer Jack tried to reconcile the opposing forces by "inducing Martin Luther King Jr. and Norman Cousins to become co-chairmen along with Ben Spock," creating "a new steering committee under the presidency of H. Stuart Hughes," and "retaining Donald Keys as executive director, with an enlarged staff." Jack concluded his suggestion with a plea:

At this moment in SANE's history, let us think and act generously and expansively, not legalistically or vituperatively. Above all, let us not retreat. Ours is a legacy of a ten-year effort. While we must not throw these cumulative assets away, let us not turn inward when the moment is surely to turn outward."[29]

In May, members of the corporation came out with a ten-page statement on "SANE Policy and Strategy For Peace," which, after analyzing policy choices between what they labeled the "social protest" and the "policy change" approaches, decided that SANE fit into the policy change or the more moderate approach, as opposed to the social protest approach carried on by the mobilization committee. The statement concluded that "National SANE clearly adheres to the 'policy change' orientation" and that because the

extended conflict between the supporters of "policy change" and "social protest" strategies would result in fragmenting SANE, both locally and nationally . . . it is difficult to avoid the judgment that those in the national board of SANE who adhere to the "social protest" viewpoint must stand aside so that work can continue."[30]

With this direction in mind, SANE's main activity during 1967 was the "Negotiations Now" campaign, an effort to locate "millions of as-yet uncommitted citizens to join with the leaders who have broken with the President over Vietnam." "Negotiations Now" was initiated by the most cautious wing of the peace movement, the wing that had usually opposed mass actions against government policy and had been hostile to both the nonexclusion and immediate withdrawal thrusts of the rest of the antiwar movement. It had enough financial backing to place large ads in daily newspapers, and its program was contained in a petition for which it sought signatures nationally. The petition requested the United States to take the first step and halt the bombing of North Vietnam, asked Hanoi and the National Liberation Front to respond affirmatively and join the United States in a standstill cease-fire, and called on America to be willing to enter into discussions with those who were actually doing the fighting, including the National Liberation Front.[31]

The statement accompanying this petition in advertisements rejected immediate withdrawal, which it said would mean "abandoning the responsibility for establishing conditions for a stable peace." The efforts of this group were aimed directly at bolstering the "doves" in Congress and the critics of Johnson's war policy within the administration. The

initial signers of the petition included Norman Cousins of SANE; economist John Kenneth Galbraith; Joseph L. Rauh, Jr., the leading spokesman of Americans for Democratic Action; Victor Reuther of the United
Auto Workers international affairs office; and historian Arthur Schlesinger, Jr.[32]

On Labor Day weekend, the National Conference for New Politics
met at Chicago's Palmer House, and Spock (who by this time was
widely advertised as a possible vice presidential candidate on a peace
ticket, with Martin Luther King for president) emerged from the national
conference as an officer of the New Left body. At the September meeting
of the SANE national board, Seymour Melman offered a resolution
reaffirming SANE's position on the range of issues discussed in Chicago, the significance being to point out the incompatibility of SANE's
position on certain issues and those of the National Conference for New
Politics, but the resolution was tabled 13 to 8, whereupon Norman
Cousins threatened to resign from the board. Irving Howe, a longtime
Socialist and editor of *Dissent*, offered a resolution declaring that since
SANE and the National Conference for New Politics policies conflicted,
officers of SANE should not serve as members of the National Conference for New Politics board. This would have effectively forced
Spock to resign as co-chairman of SANE, and the SANE board ruled
that the resolution was out of order. However, after a meeting of his
supporters at Robert Schwartz's home in New York City where all but
two told him their feelings that he could not be an officer of both
organizations, Spock resigned as co-chairman of SANE anyway, stating
that he "did not think he could do justice to both jobs, especially in
view of all the controversy involving the National Conference for New
Politics."[33]

While internal difficulties were splitting SANE, the peace movement
itself was becoming increasingly radicalized. Radical peace activists
were obsessed by the war and frustrated by their impotence to affect
its course. Accordingly, there was talk in peace movement circles of
moving from "dissent to resistance" and moving the antiwar movement
into attacks not only against the war but, increasingly, against the entire
apparatus of military-corporate domination both at home and abroad.
In fall 1967, the National Mobilization to End the War in Vietnam
issued a call for a March on the Pentagon. This action intensified the
dispute among peace liberals and within SANE in particular. Sidney
Peck, one of the coordinators of the march, emphasized a "three-

pronged approach" to the event. He promised a rally for those who wished to rally, a march for those who wished to march, and "direct-action" at the Pentagon for those who wished "to risk arrest if that is necessary to disrupt the war machine."[34] Again peace liberals on the SANE board were skeptical but decided to take no definitive action on this march, leaving the decision to the local chapters. However, the more conservative members of the board were still dissatisfied. Even though Spock was no longer co-chairman, these people believed that the organization was still following his radicalizing leadership.

On October 20, 1967, a story leaked to the *New York Times* appeared on its front page and shocked the entire organization. The article stated that on the afternoon of October 19 SANE's board of directors met in New York with the resignation of fourteen members of the board, staff, and sponsors on the table before them. In a covering letter these members said that "the resignation will not be tendered or made public until it is clear that the conditions which have brought us to this decision cannot be remedied." The letter laid out "the conditions" they would no longer tolerate. They said there was a basic division in the board of directors that reflected the split in the "peace movement" and that this division was "between those groups and people who support the use of dem-ocratic means to bring about change in the policy and those who believe the society must be overturned before peace is possible."[35]

This leaked letter, according to one observer, "had a sobering effect" as two of the fourteen members who threatened to resign, Seymour Melman and Irving Howe, came out the same day with their own statement, which was also printed in the paper. It read:

A private, internal discussion has been proceeding in SANE concerning strategy for stopping the Vietnam war. This discussion continues and there have been no resignations from the national board. Our hope is that the differences within SANE will be resolved amicably and constructively. . . . The *New York Times* article described the discussion within SANE as between "Left" and "Right." In reality, differentiations of "Right-Left conservative-radical" have lost their usual meaning in the face of the extremism of the Johnson administration and the frustration this engenders among millions of Americans. Insofar as "extre-mism" seizes some Americans it is generated by the tenacity of the Johnson administration in escalating the war.[36]

Given the intensified level of frustration among peace liberals at this time, these differences were not so easily resolved. Thus, the turbulent events of 1967 prompted the resignations of key SANE officials. Norman Cousins and executive director Donald Keys, for example, resigned because they feared that the committee had strayed too far to the left and was not willing to antagonize the militants within the movement. Benjamin Spock, on the other hand, resigned urging that SANE "try always to cooperate cordially with other responsible peace organizations and thereby enhance SANE's efforts." One thing was clear, however: SANE had lost badly needed support and leadership from both sides of the political spectrum. It became evident to those like chairman H. Stuart Hughes who remained within SANE that the organization's "middle-of-the-road position was being eroded on both sides. . . . We had no choice but to stay in the middle."[37]

Sanford Gottlieb, who became the new executive director, summed up the year quite accurately when he stated, "In 1967 frustration was at an absolute high. It was a mistake not to endorse the April march for the emotions were too high and no one could see reasons for not endorsing it." According to Gottlieb, the board of SANE was operating on two levels: the first dealing with analysis, strategy, and tactics; and the second with the very deep emotions which almost precluded any kind of real dialogue. "Polarization kept getting worse," Gottlieb added. "The Right didn't know what the radicals thought and more importantly felt, and the Left was so busy emoting that they stopped thinking in this period. Ultimately, SANE's middle position triumphed."[38]

Although SANE was badly divided, peace liberals in the Committee came through this period with a new consensus favoring electoral efforts to end the war and establish a new foreign policy. As early as July 1967, SANE for the first time in its ten-year history took a position on a presidential candidate. After contrasting President Johnson's 1964 campaign with his latest actions of "Americanizing the war, repeatedly distorting the reality of the Vietnamese conflict before the American public," and "strewing the path to a negotiated settlement with specious obstacles," SANE stated it would energetically support a presidential candidate in either party who would commit himself to undertake fresh initiatives to achieve a negotiated settlement in Vietnam. In October 1967, SANE became the first national organization to advocate removing Johnson from office and three months later the first nonpartisan organization to support Senator Eugene McCarthy of Minnesota to replace him.[39]

In a sense, however, SANE's work for McCarthy really went back to 1965. In his book on the McCarthy campaign, Richard T. Stout describes the 1965 SANE-sponsored March on Washington as "a milestone in the development of the force that ultimately rallied to the presidential candidacy of Eugene McCarthy." He quotes SANE organizer Jack Gore as saying, "A lot of contacts and acquaintances grew out of that march and were useful later." Most of the marchers were "neatly dressed, educated, middle-class Americans." That was an important political fact in those lonely days when Congress was mute, protest was rare, some of it was already disruptive, and J. Edgar Hoover was stating: "This small, but highly vocal minority which is staging these anti-Vietnam demonstrations is, for the most part, composed of halfway citizens who are neither morally, mentally, nor emotionally mature." According to Stout, "Orderliness for this middle-class throng was a way of life," but that day it was also a political tactic. In 1968, the same kind of thing would be called going "Clean for Gene." In both instances, it was the thing to do for the cause. In a sense, Stout wrote, the SANE march was the first meeting of what McCarthy came to call the "government in exile."[40]

Nineteen months later, in June 1967, "a number of anti-war leaders who had been conversing informally through the year," wrote Stout, "met in Washington, D.C. in the conference room of the Friends Committee on National Legislation, and what came to be known as the Dump Johnson movement was born." Those present included Allard Lowenstein, who would head the campaign and later become a board member of SANE; Sanford Gottlieb of SANE; Arnold Kaufman, chairman of the Political Action Committee for SANE; Curtis Gans; Bella Abzug of Women Strike for Peace; Jack Gore; Paul Gorman; David Hartsough of the Friends Committee on National Legislation; and Ed Schwartz of the National Student Association. These people played key roles in the Dump Johnson movement and ultimately McCarthy's presidential campaign.[41]

Following this meeting, the national board of SANE met on June 27 and took its first step toward support of a presidential candidate in 1968. The national board unanimously adopted a statement, "Political Policy for 1968," pledging that the organization "will energetically support a presidential candidate—in either party—who will commit himself to undertake fresh initiatives to achieve a negotiated settlement in Vietnam." The statement also asserted: "If the American people are given no choice" on the overriding issue of Vietnam "by either of the major parties, the emergence of an independent candidacy is virtually certain. SANE, while not taking a position, at present, on the desirability of such a development, will make a judgment on this question at the proper time.'' This was the first time in the organization's ten-year history that it officially decided to support a presidential candidate, and Benjamin Spock, in reading this statement to the press on July 17, announced that if he were asked he would consider running on a third party ticket (preferably as vice presidential candidate with Martin Luther King), if none of the major candidates offered any choice in regards to Vietnam.[42]

In October, SANE began its campaign to remove Johnson from office and devised its political strategy. It recommended techniques for building support for pro-peace presidential and congressional candidates and at the same time established three criteria for judging all candidates: advocacy of the quickest possible political settlement in Vietnam, support for measures to reverse the arms race and to find nonmilitary alternatives, and advocacy of a shift from military to civilian priorities in the use of this nation's resources.[43]

When Eugene McCarthy threw his hat into the presidential ring in November opposing unilateral withdrawal and advocating a negotiated settlement, SANE was openly enthusiastic and published his record on foreign policy in the January issue of *SANE World*. Debate began within the organization on whether to endorse McCarthy. The views of SANE board members, sponsors, chapters, and congressional district contacts were solicited by mail and presented at the December board meeting.

Some of the members felt that SANE should not get involved in partisan politics by backing a specific presidential candidate but should deal with issues rather than personalities. Some considered McCarthy too radical, and others not radical enough. The majority, however, were well satisfied with the Minnesota senator and thought it was an excellent idea to give him an early endorsement. Thus, at the national board meeting of January 27, 1968, by a vote of 36 to 0 SANE became the first nonpartisan organization to support McCarthy. The board statement read: "While it is still too early to determine whether there will be more than one candidate who generally meets SANE's criteria, at the present time only one candidate offers the voters a clear alternative to administration policies. He is Senator Eugene McCarthy." Allen Matusow has pointed out that McCarthy understood the mounting frustration within the antiwar movement and was offering his candidacy as an alternative to radicalism. Peace liberals in SANE and other organizations jumped at the opportunity to make political liberalism viable once again and restore to many people a belief in the American political process.[44]

Their confidence was reinforced when on the evening of March 31 Lyndon Johnson went on television to announce that he was halting the bombing of most of North Vietnam and initiating negotiations with Hanoi and stunned the American people with his announcement that he "would not seek, nor accept the nomination of his party for another term as president." The North Vietnamese Tet offensive and the antiwar movement in America had succeeded in toppling one of the most powerful presidents in American history. Calling this decision "a monumental victory for the American peace movement," SANE chairman H. Stuart Hughes congratulated its members and stated his hope that this development "would lead to its logical conclusion: de-escalation of the conflict in South Vietnam and an end to this senseless, tragic war."[45]

During the summer of 1968 SANE engaged in an all out effort for Senator McCarthy and the Vietnam peace plank which he supported. The committee testified at the platform hearings of the Republican National Convention in July. Convening in Chicago the following month in the wake of the tumultuous Democratic Convention, a special meeting of SANE's board reaffirmed earlier evaluations of Hubert Humphrey and Richard Nixon as "unacceptable" candidates. With the defeat of McCarthy and the narrower defeat of the peace plank, SANE helped to inaugurate the New Democratic Coalition which did not take a position on the 1968 presidential race but concentrated instead on helping selected congressional candidates and building insurgent organizations for a long-term campaign to win control of the Democratic party. An alliance of supporters of Senators McCarthy, Robert Kennedy, and George McGovern, radical liberals, and peace and civil rights activists, the New Democratic Coalition established a temporary steering committee which included Jack Gore as chairman, Julian Bond, SANE board members Allard Lowenstein, Arnold Kaufman, and Milton Rosenberg, and executive director Sanford Gottlieb.[46]

Coinciding with the McCarthy campaign and the presidential election was a growing feeling among the local SANE committees, especially after the Tet offensive of spring 1968, that the organization should change its policy on Vietnam. "Indeed on close inspection," Matusow later commented, "it turned out liberals were waist deep in Big Muddy along with LBJ and were no more certain then he of getting back to shore.'' On September 20, 1968, the Philadelphia SANE chapter asked the national board to adopt a resolution supporting a position of unilateral withdrawal from Vietnam; and, at the same time, the Washington Area SANE, by a vote of fifteen members attending an executive board meeting, also expressed its support for the unilateral withdrawal position. Roy Bennett, who was chairman of the National SANE Policy Committee, asked the members of his committee to make a recommendation before the national conference in December.[47]

As in 1967 the grass-roots membership favored a more radical position; the national board, a more conservative approach. The resolution that was passed ''urged the U.S. to begin the immediate withdrawal of substantial numbers of troops and weapons from South Vietnam as the first step toward the goal of withdrawal of all foreign troops in 1969.'' At the same time, the national board restated its support for a negotiated settlement which provided international guarantees for self-determination in South Vietnam and spelled out the conditions under which all foreign troops were to be withdrawn.[48]

In June 1969, 542,000 American troops still remained in South Vietnam. Because of the growing frustration with the war and their inability to affect its course, the SANE national board passed a stronger Vietnam resolution on June 7 that ''urged the U.S. to withdraw immediately and unilaterally 250,000 troops from South Vietnam.'' The board reiterated its support for the withdrawal of all external forces as part of a political settlement. ''However, if agreement on free elections and a cease-fire is not achieved by September 1969,'' SANE declared, ''the complete, unilateral withdrawal of United States forces is preferable to a continuation of this tragic and immoral intervention.''[49]

The following day, President Nixon made his first announcement of a troop withdrawal from South Vietnam. He pledged 25,000 American troops would be removed from Vietnam by the end of August, and on September 16 announced that another 35,000 would leave Vietnam by the end of the year. But SANE was not satisfied with his ''rather timid'' announcements of ''token'' withdrawal, and at its national board meeting of September 20 another Vietnam policy statement was adopted which read:

After five years of work for peace in Vietnam and in the absence of the likelihood of a negotiated settlement, we are initiating a program to help achieve the withdrawal of support for the Thieu-Ky regime and the rapid, complete and unilateral withdrawal of all U.S. forces from South Vietnam.

In the event such a withdrawal would create fears for their safety among the residents of South Vietnam, the resolution proposed that the Vietnamese who wished to leave be assisted in going to the country of their choice. U.S. immigration rules should be liberalized to facilitate this policy and foreign countries should be urged to liberalize theirs. "Finally," the resolution suggested "the U.S. government and U.S. nongovernmental organizations should offer immediate, massive economic resources, under indigenous invitation and control, for the reconstruction of all of Vietnam through international organizations, including the United Nations."[50]

National chairman Hughes conceded that the organization's five-year campaign to end the war obviously had not succeeded but insisted that SANE and other pro-peace organizations had been successful in discrediting the Vietnam War. "Virtually no one in a responsible position, now, not even Nixon, will try to justify this war," declared Hughes. Former co-chairman Spock, who the previous year was convicted of encouraging young men to evade the draft, hailed the resolution as "flat-footed and courageous" and promised to press for its objectives in demonstrations despite the risk of being arrested again.[51]

The demonstrations to which Spock referred were the Vietnam Moratorium on October 15 and the November 15, 1969, March on Washington by the New Mobilization Committee to End the War in Vietnam. The Vietnam Moratorium was organized by some of the young leaders who had been active in the McCarthy campaign, notably Sam Brown, the main organizer of the student volunteers for McCarthy in 1968. The November March on Washington was organized by a coalition extending from radical pacifists through more moderate antiwar groups and religious pacifist organizations. Stewart Meacham of the American Friends Service Committee and Sidney Peck of the mobilization committee were co-chairmen of the march, and program directors were Ron Young of the Fellowship of Reconciliation and Abe Bloom, former chairman of Washington area SANE.

The SANE board decided to support the Vietnam Moratorium and March on Washington, noting that the New Mobilization represented a broader spectrum than the mobilization committee which had sponsored the demonstrations in 1967 and that the policy of total unilateral withdrawal did not present a problem for the peace liberals now as it had two years earlier. SANE's support was based on the condition that the action be organized as "a peaceful and legal demonstration, designed to achieve maximum public participation."[52] SANE played an active part in both the Moratorium and March on Washington, both of which were hailed by the participants as huge successes. In October, the Moratorium was observed all across the nation, and on November 15 over 250,000 people assembled at the mall of the capitol building joining together in a common plea for peace. But President Nixon appeared no more moved by protest than Johnson had been.

Herbert C. Klein, Nixon's spokesman, said the one-quarter million or more who took to the streets to end the war were a small number compared to those who stayed at home to support the president's policy of gradual withdrawal. By watching a football game on television Nixon signaled that he had sealed himself off from public protest. His reaction made the Moratorium look to many Americans like a meaningless gesture. The polls indicated solid support for his Vietnamization policy, and in late November Nixon rallies were held in a number of cities. "We've got those liberal bastards on the run now," the president exalted, "and we're going to keep them on the run."[53]

Amid mounting frustration, peace liberals, like the movement in general, continued their protest. When the war in Laos heated up early in March 1970, SANE called the conflict in that country "a spillover of the war in South Vietnam" and said the war will end only when the United States ends its support for "a regime which despotically represses the non-Communist opposition." In a letter to Nixon on March 6, SANE chairman Hughes indicated a clear pattern of repression by the Saigon regime and said:

A political process should begin in South Vietnam when the United States begins to withdraw its support of the Thieu-Ky regime, thus signaling to the non-Communist nationalists that it is safe for them to function in the open. . . . The situation is intolerable not only because of the continuing dangers of escalation in Laos, but because a nation born of anti-colonialism continues to thwart self-determination in Southeast Asia nearly two centuries after its own promising birth.[54]

The focus of attention was changed to Cambodia when South Vietnamese and American troops invaded that country on April 30. SANE predicted that "Cambodia could become Nixon's Tet" and "erode the tacit support for Nixon and swell the ranks of the peace movement." Their prediction proved correct as college campuses erupted all across the nation to protest against this new invasion and the widening of the war. The culmination came on May 4 with the killings of students at Kent State and Jackson State Universities by National Guard forces and State Troopers. Campuses were closed throughout the nation, and on May 17 the organization placed a three-quarter-page advertisement in the Sunday *New York Times* with a petition in support of the "End the War Amendment" that brought forth an outpouring of antiwar sentiment plus a sizeable number of abusive responses.[55]

Even before these latest rounds of demonstrations began to subside and the students left the campuses, some of the leaders in the peace movement felt that the time for large demonstrations was over because of their ineffectiveness in influencing policy. Sam Brown, the coordinator of the Vietnam Moratorium Committee, issued a statement on April 19 that the committee was disbanding because it had run out of money and the time for large demonstrations had run its course. Sanford Gottlieb of SANE went along with Brown's assessment and later persuaded Brown to become a member of the national board of SANE. "National demonstrations under the present circumstances," Gottlieb said, are "at best a shot in the arm to participants, and it is obvious that they have no impact on policy. Also, of course, you run the risks of disruption," he added. "That isn't sufficient reason in itself to discard them, but in the absence of evidence that they influence policy, it is a compelling reason to consider what else you might do."[56]

During the summer, Brown wrote a long article in the *Washington Monthly* explaining his strategy for the peace movement. "Most American voters," Brown stated, "make political decisions largely on issues of tone and style rather than on the basis of rigorous foreign policy analysis.... They don't like long hair, campus protest, or, in short, anything which irritates the nerve endings of middle class values. They may dislike the war," he added, "but they dislike radicals even more." Gottlieb made the identical point in a companion piece, "Probing the Silent Majority," in the July issue of *SANE World*.

Middle America's view of the peace movement is highly colored by the notion—transmitted in part by the news media and filtered by a polarized public—that dissent against the war is led by flag-burning, pot-smoking, long-haired hippies.

And they don't like it. Apparently they dislike it even more than they dislike the war . . . although a majority of Americans today oppose the war in Indo-China, the pro-peace forces are not strong enough to bring the war to an end. This paradox stems from the cross-currents which buffer the "silent majority." Clearly those of us in the wing of the peace movement which is interested in changing the attitude of fellow Americans need some new approaches. To end the war, we need a broader base of support, a base which must be augmented by detaching parts of this "silent majority." Without such realignment, the decision-makers in Washington can manage to ignore opposition for the duration of this administration.[57]

The June meeting of the national board of SANE decided to attempt coming to terms with this issue and concentrate on reaching new constituencies. SANE began working with a top group of public opinion specialists who were in the process of producing an analysis of the silent majority. When the book *Vietnam and the Silent Majority: A Dove's Guide* by Milton J. Rosenberg, Sidney Verba, and Phillip Converse came out in August with SANE's assistance, Gottlieb reviewed it in *SANE World* declaring "this analysis could become the single most important tool in the non-violent arsenal." SANE distributed this book to its members and worked on trying to implement its strategy for peace. Gottlieb concluded his review by saying that this book "is not designed for those who have abandoned hope or have sought refuge in a sectarian stance. It is a primer for those who, as Norman Thomas used to say, are still willing 'to strain their minds and think. . . . ' "[58]

In the fall of 1970, SANE became a member of the National Coalition for a Responsible Congress—a post-Cambodia grouping of five campus-oriented organizations—in a two-pronged campaign designed to help peace candidates and raise funds to support a media campaign against U.S. involvement in Indo-China and to help educate the public, especially Middle America, to the crucial issues of the war and national priorities. The National Coalition for a Responsible Congress assumed responsibility for the electoral and fund-raising activities, and SANE and other peace organizations assumed responsibility for the nonpartisan educational activities. The SANE board also selected key congressional races in which the national membership helped to select a more peace-oriented 92nd Congress.[59] In February 1971, when Nixon again expanded the war by approving major ground operations at Laos, the antiwar movement called for a massive March on Washington on April

24 followed by acts of civil disobedience that became known as the "May Day" protests.

Although SANE had stated the preceding year that the time for demonstrations was over, the organization was swept up by the flood of antiwar sentiment supporting these actions. On April 6, 1971, the national board released a statement in support of the April 24 action, though not the acts of civil disobedience to follow in May. The statement read: "Our board was very favorably impressed by the unprecedented labor support and the Congressional endorsements of the demonstration, and by the organizer's unambiguous position in favor of a peaceful and legal action." Executive director Gottlieb explained in releasing the statement that "antiwar sentiment is running so strongly that many people who have never demonstrated can be expected to participate on April 24."[60]

Gottlieb was correct, for on a warm, sunny Saturday afternoon of April 24, a massive outpouring of marchers equaled or surpassed the estimates of 200,000 to 500,000 that attended the Vietnam Moratorium March on Washington in November 1969. Many of the participants took part in their first demonstration against the war. The demonstration drew more congressional support—endorsements from ten senators and at least twenty-nine representatives—than any past demonstration, and speakers were more insistent, more specific in their demands for an immediate end to the war. The demonstration also drew a broader cross section of rank-and-file union members, veterans, and active-duty GIs in addition to the now traditional population of students, professional antiwar activists, assorted radicals, and the disgruntled liberals from the past demonstrations. This antiwar action and corresponding polls showed beyond a doubt that the majority of Americans were in favor of extricating the nation from the tragedy in Southeast Asia.[61]

After the last protester had left Washington in May, the cry arose again that the time for these massive demonstrations had ended. Michael Harrington, who was chairman of the Socialist party in the United States and who served briefly as a member of the national board of SANE, wrote an article in the *New York Times Magazine* entitled "The Peace Movement is Using the Wrong Strategy." Harrington stated that

despite the most welcome success of the April 24 demonstration . . . I do not think that mass marches are an effective instrument for ending our Vietnam involvement. When they are non-violent and oriented toward political action, as the April rally was, they can have a certain positive effect, but neither that, nor the solidarity and good feelings which they evoke in the participants, justify the expenditure of time and money, which could be much better spent on political organizations. . . . In the absence of a continuing political campaign for the McGovern-Hatfield amendment to cut off funds for the war, the hundreds of thousands who marched on April 24 will have changed little in American life. What therefore needs to be done is to organize politically around the McGovern-Hatfield demand for ending the United States participation in the war this year. That is the kind of democratic militance the President of the United States cannot ignore.[62]

Harrington's idea of peace politics paralleled SANE's approach, and the organization worked to promote this strategy within the peace movement. A "Resolution of Peace Politics 1972" was adopted by the executive committee of SANE in November 1971 and was presented to the national antiwar convention sponsored by the National Peace Action Coalition in Cleveland, Ohio, on December 3–5. The resolution urged SANE members to concentrate their energies in 1972 on "influencing those specific decision-makers who make the decisions about the war in Indo-China" rather than participating in mass demonstrations. The executive committee called for effective "locally-based organizing efforts designed to generate pressure on specific members of Congress and to elect alternative candidates to Congress, and the Presidency." While praising the role of past antiwar demonstrations "in convincing the public and the decision-makers that opposition to the war was widespread, in sustaining the growth and morale of the peace movement, and in showing GI's in Vietnam that some Americans favored bringing them home," the resolution added that "there is little evidence that the enormous energies put into mass demonstrations have influenced the decision-makers in the Executive Branch and Congress as much as locally based organizing efforts to generate pressures on specific members of Congress and to elect alternative candidates to Congress and the Presidency." Therefore, the resolution urged all peace organizations to forget massive demonstrations and to join in electing peace candidates to office during 1972.[63]

The resolution was soundly defeated by the Convention, receiving only eight votes from the almost 1,000 delegates in attendance. Obviously, SANE and the rest of the peace movement had major differences in regard to strategy. The great uprising against liberalism that convulsed the nation during the previous six years had left peace liberals nearly impotent in affecting change within the antiwar movement. SANE continued, however, to endorse some of the widespread demonstrations in 1972, but "peace politics" became its main concern.

After months of research into the records of thirteen potential presidential candidates for the 1972 elections, the SANE board chose longtime peace advocate Senator George McGovern of South Dakota and stated that he was "the only candidate of either party who, since 1963, has consistently opposed the Indo-China war, called for reductions in nuclear overkill, and proposed both new priorities and plans for conversion of the arms industry to peaceful uses." On the issues of foreign and military power of greatest concern to SANE, George McGovern, the committee felt, had "both the longest and best track record."[64] SANE urged its members to actively campaign and run as state delegates on his behalf, and several of them did, including Gottlieb who ran and won in Maryland.

Following the Nixon landslide in the November elections and two days before the announcement by top National Security Advisor Henry Kissinger on December 16 that peace was not yet quite "at hand," SANE co-chairmen Edward Condon and Seymour Melman sent the following wire to President Nixon: "We urge you to terminate the U.S. role in Indo-China with or without the approval of the Saigon government. Only actions with such an approach can fulfill the promise that 'peace is at hand.' " On December 21, in response to a negotiating deadlock and stepped-up bombings over North Vietnam, the most intense and devastating attacks of the war, SANE issued a statement that "Congress Must Cut Off The Money," and placed the following advertisement in the *New York Times*, December 22 and 24 (with appropriate change): "Only 3 More Bombing Days To Christmas: If you think it is time to end the killing and heal the wounds, please wire your members of Congress and ask them to support end-the-war legislation. Congress has the power to halt the funds." Finally, the administration, caught between what Kissinger later conceded "was the hammer of antiwar pressure and the anvil of Hanoi," moved for peace.[65] The bombing raids culminated on December 30, and the talks were resumed with North Vietnam in Paris on January 2. The peace accords were then finalized and initiated on January 23, 1973, and a cease-fire went into effect throughout Vietman on January 27. Within sixty days the total withdrawal of American troops was completed.

Peace liberals in SANE along with the rest of the peace movement greeted the Paris peace accords with what historian Charles DeBenedetti called "wary satisfaction." They welcomed the military cease-fire and Washington's recognition of "the independence, sovereignty, unity and territorial integrity" of Vietnam as established in the 1954 Geneva Agreements, but they worried that the struggle was far from over. Antiwar spokesmen of all persuasions held that the fundamental question of who ruled in Saigon had only been raised from the military to a more complex political level on which the United States remained deeply involved: and they knew that the uninterrupted U.S. bombing of Cambodia on behalf of the Lon Nol regime, the fate of anti-government political prisoners in South Vietnam, and continued U.S. financing of the Thieu regime together pointed to an open-ended American presence in Indo-China.[66] Undeterred by flagging public interest, peace liberals never let up in their defense of the peace settlement. In August 1973, they organized to pressure Congress into legislating the ending of U.S. bombing of Cambodia; in November, to pass the War Powers Act; and in May 1974, to reject an administration request for supplemental aid to the Thieu and Lon Nol governments. It was the first time that Congress had taken decisive steps to curtail American involvement in the war and had rejected funds for the war since its inception.

When the South Vietnamese government collapsed in April 1975, peace liberals were grateful the war was finally over, but had no illusions that the Communist victory would bring peace with freedom to a country that had long known neither. SANE, along with other antiwar activists, protested to the leaders of unified Vietnam about reports of repressive acts carried out since the capture of Saigon. Peace liberals called upon the government of Vietnam to facilitate on-the-spot inspection by the United States, Amnesty International, or other independent international agencies in order to assure that those in the government's charge were treated in accord with international covenants regarding human rights and to release any individual held purely because of their religious or political convictions. And they wrote and spoke about the work yet to be done: issuing an amnesty for all military deserters, draft evaders, and resisters; the normalization of relations with the nations of Indo-China; U.S. support for the admission of Vietnam to the United Nations; and American reconstruction aid to Vietnam to heal the wounds of war.[67]

Peace liberals in SANE, like the antiwar movement in general, had a modest though important impact on American involvement in Vietnam. In tending toward a pragmatic and popular politics, groups like

SANE carried the antiwar movement off the campuses and reached out to a larger middle-class constituency. Besides helping to organize massive demonstrations in New York and Washington, D.C., these peace workers also organized in their home communities, raised money for newspaper ads, signed their names, and contributed to presidential and congressional peace candidates throughout the war's long ordeal. As political scientist Michael Walzer noted,

> Theirs was largely a politics of demonstration. They sought to create and then to express antiwar sentiment, leaving it to conventional politicians to respond to these expressions, to seek the support of the movement, by directly challenging or changing government policy.

Their real task was to generate a mood of hostility to the war, or at least of doubt and anxiety about it. That is why it was so important that the crowds be large, look respectable, and therefore elicit the best publicity possible. By doing it this way, they legitimized the protest, gave it political scope and meaning, and thereby certainly enlarged the area of accepted political action. Peace liberals, like their counterparts on the Left, plagued both Presidents Johnson and Nixon by their unrelenting opposition and limited the respective administrations' military options at least to some degree. And there is considerable evidence that the antiwar movement, despite its many internecine quarrels, was an important factor in the making of American foreign policy. "The dissidents did not stop the war," historian Charles DeBenedetti has written, "but they made it stoppable."[68]

That they were largely unsuccessful in convincing the American public, and most importantly, the decision makers was something that troubled them throughout. Although they tried desperately to remain respectable and to ride a fine line between advocacy and acceptability, a signficant part of the problem can be attributed to faulty communication. As sociologist Howard Schuman noted in his article, "Two Sources of Antiwar Sentiment," the antiwar movement largely reacted to the war on moral grounds while the public saw things in very pragmatic fashion and as such was not much interested in, or impressed by, arguments and information based on moral criteria. Hence, because protestors and the public by and large evaluated the war using different frames of reference, anti–Vietnam War demonstrations did not communicate about the war to most Americans.[69]

Susan Sontag put the same problem a little differently. In her response to "The Meaning of Vietnam" for the *New York Review of Books* she wrote: "The movement was never significantly political, its understanding was primarily moral, and it took considerable moral vanity to expect that one could defeat the considerations of 'Real-politik' mainly by appealing to considerations of 'right' and 'wrong.' "[70] The whole antiwar movement is subject to these criticisms, but peace liberals understood these dilemmas better than most and attempted to cope with them in a number of ways.

There was a growing feeling among peace liberals around 1970 that instead of large-scale street demonstrations they should have spent their time getting people into congressional campaigns and issue-oriented, grass-roots politics. Perhaps then they could have changed minds in Congress or changed the congressmen and therefore changed the will of Congress to stop funding the war. But there was so much understandable mounting emotionalism that came from the frustration of fighting to stop what seemed like an endless war that the movement did not analyze sufficiently what they were doing and the effect, or lack of it, they were having and act accordingly. When SANE did make the suggestion to work for election of peace candidates to the antiwar conference in Cleveland in 1971, the rest of the movement soundly rejected the idea.

Peace liberals in SANE also worked tirelessly to try to persuade the "Silent Majority" that they must reject American involvement in the war and call for its rapid termination through political settlement. These centrist liberals were among the few who realized what a potent force patriotism is among the American people and that it should have been used to the peace movement's advantage. "The greatest mistake of the peace movement has been to let go of all symbols of patriotism—particularly the American flag," stated Gottlieb in 1970. "If we want more of the unconvinced in the peace movement, we have to recapture the flag."[71]

In order to communicate pragmatic reasons for opposing the war in early 1970 SANE helped to inaugurate a Coalition of National Priorities and Military Policy which held town meetings on local needs and military spending in numerous cities throughout the country. By raising the related questions of local needs, the costs of new programs to meet them, and current military spending, the coalition hoped to involve many more groups and individuals than could be recruited through conventional antiwar arguments.[72]

Peace liberals in SANE can certainly be criticized by what at times seemed an obsessive concern with respectability and for excluding specific groups from coalition activity, both of which contributed to the fracture in the antiwar movement. And although they continued for so long to call for negotiations to end the war, feeling it was politically expedient and a face-saving device for the United States, they should have confronted the depths of Washington's determination to win its way in Indo-China and realized America really had no moral right to negotiate anything except, perhaps, as David McReynolds said in an exchange with Michael Harrington, "the routes our troops will take getting to the ports of embarkation."[73]

As historian Robert Schulzinger pointed out, "SANE offered concrete proof of how widespread were some of of the liberal assumptions about how American politics worked." According to these assumptions, government ultimately was responsive to reasoned "sane" arguments. The government did respond. President Johnson was forced out of office. President Nixon commenced American ground troop withdrawal thereby Vietnamizing the war, and still the war went on. Peace liberals stand indicted, wrote Schulzinger, for not recognizing the limit of their tactics' effectiveness. They also failed to take full advantage of calling attention to the relationship between the conventional warfare in Vietnam and the question of nuclear weapons. "On the other hand," concluded Schulzinger, "they had a sense of their own efficacy for they believed what they said and did mattered which kept them from defeatism, despair, or infantile rage." Amidst mounting frustration, peace liberals kept their battle an ongoing process, while most of the radicals, especially the student component, gave up in resignation, convinced of their ultimate failure to stop the war.[74] To a large degree what kept SANE going was a recognition that America's war in Vietnam was only part of a much larger problem.

When antiwar leaders were asked in February 1973 what was going to happen to the movement now that North Vietnam and the United States finally came to terms in Paris, Gottlieb explained that SANE had been planning for the post-Vietnam period for two years. "We have an unprecedented situation," he said. "It's the end of a shooting war, a time of warming relations with China and the Soviet Union, and the

President is asking a record $81.8 billion for a combined defense budget." He then added, "I didn't think people are so naive as to believe the world situation can change but the defense budget must stay the same. The defense budget is the next critical battle."[75]

Gottlieb understood that, although fighting the military-industrial complex was not as exciting as demonstrating against the Vietnam War, people were "ready to listen to solid analysis and good sense. . . . they were tired of just rhetoric." In order to meet this need the national board of SANE had earlier adopted a comprehensive five-year strategy statement. Largely written by Seymour Melman, "A Sane World Begins At Home: Demilitarizing American Society" laid out how and why "the power of an oppressive military machine must give way to the purpose of a humane society." To illustrate this problem, the committee placed a striking advertisement in the *New York Times* called "America has a tapeworm," which pointed out that because of excessive military spending "we are armed to the teeth and rotting to the core."[76]

Unfortunately for SANE and other peace organizations, the public was not very responsive to their message. After eight agonizing years of American military involvement in Vietnam and the resultant social disorder at home, the American people turned inward and were more concerned about the energy crisis following the Arab oil embargo of 1973–1974 than they were about curbing the power of the military-industrial complex. Resembling the period after the signing of the 1963 partial test ban treaty, the end of our war in Vietnam brought another plateau to the American peace movement. Accordingly, SANE's membership, power, and influence would decline rapidly until a new issue could be found to revitalize the American people into action.

6

The Nightmare That Won't Go Away, 1973–1982

I was happy. I could whistle
Till he got his anti-missile.
I felt better when I read
Anti-antis were ahead.
Now I'm safe again but can't he
Make an anti-anti-anti?

—Lenore Marshall, 1969[1]

A frequent criticism of the anti-nuclear weapons movement is that after the partial test ban treaty was signed in 1963 the individuals and organizations involved either disbanded, turned to other issues like the war in Vietnam, or faded from public view. As historian Paul Boyer observed in a 1984 article in the *Journal of American History*, "The historical record is full of evidence that the era from 1963 through much of the 1970s was one of quiescence and passivity on matters related to nuclear war and the nuclear arms race."[2]

Despite the fact that the United States conducted more nuclear tests in the five years after 1963 than in the five years before and that during the 1970s both the U.S. and the U.S.S.R. more than doubled their arsenals of strategic nuclear warheads and new weapons sprouted up much faster than the agreements that could control them, fewer and fewer people seemed to care. In a 1976 editorial, "The Nightmare That Won't Go Away," Norman Cousins deplored the fact that

hardly anyone talks anymore about nuclear stockpiles as the world's number one problem. An entire generation has come of age with only a theoretical idea of the nature of atomic destructive force. The anti-testing clamor of the early 60s now seems far off and unreal. Yet, like it or not, the nuclear threat is still alive, ugly, more menacing than ever.[3]

Although there are several reasons anti-nuclear activists turned from their primary preoccupation to other issues, the one having the most impact was American involvement in the war in Vietnam which became the almost exclusive focus of massive waves of political activism. As Boyer pointed out, the effect of Vietnam on the anti-nuclear weapons movement is well illustrated in the evolution of SANE, the organization that had symbolized the nuclear activism of the pre–1963 years.

While some SANE directors, including co-chairman Benjamin Spock and most of the grass-roots membership, shifted their energies entirely to opposing the Vietnam War, others tried to keep the nuclear issue paramount. After SANE's May 1965 Madison Square Garden Rally on Vietnam, a board member, Dr. Jerome Frank, wrote to executive director Donald Keys reminding him that "the central reason for SANE's existence is to campaign for the abolition of nuclear weapons." Although he deplored U.S. policy in the Dominican Republic and Vietnam, Frank expressed the view that SANE was an anti-nuclear testing or anti-nuclear bomb organization and that it had no business getting mixed up in the Vietnam War. "Every time SANE gets involved in side issues it diverts its energies from the main task," Frank asserted, "and at the same time may alienate potential supporters who agree on the nuclear issue but can't go along with the other one."[4]

In response to such criticism, Keys pointed out that SANE's concern with Vietnam or the Dominican Republic was consistent with the overall guiding policies it had held from its beginning. From its inception, SANE had recognized that war must be abolished as an instrument of national policy and that the organization must concern itself not only with testing but with control of developed weapons—with disarmament. SANE also had long realized that it could not be silent on crises that threatened general war and, therefore, could not ignore areas of tension and confrontation. The committee thus adopted a "watchdog" role over areas where war appeared likely; and when administration policy escalated the war in Vietnam, SANE had no choice but to react accordingly.[5]

As Keys noted: "SANE would so much rather spend time and effort on the greater question of disarmament and in support of positive measures leading to world community and world peace." He declared, however, that "until the current national aberration is terminated, no major progess in other areas is realistic." Although the SANE board continued to discuss and produce policy statements concerning nuclear testing, disarmament, and nonproliferation and recognized the necessity of continued attention and action, most members agreed that "the Vietnam issue must receive the major emphasis until the war is ended."[6] Reflecting this change from its original purpose, SANE in 1969 dropped the word "nuclear" from its name and officially became SANE: A Citizen's Organization for a Sane World.

It is a misconception, however, to assume that SANE remained unconcerned and inactive in opposing the spiraling nuclear arms race after 1963. Concern that America's bombing of Vietnam could escalate into nuclear war, SANE placed an advertisement in the *New York Times* in July 1965, which displayed a stark picture of a cockroach with the caption: "The winner of World War III." A nuclear war, if it comes, would not be won by the Americans, the Russians, or the Chinese, the ad stated, but by the cockroach, "a venerable and hardy species, that will take over the habitations of the foolish humans, and compete only with other insects or bacteria." In early 1968, David Inglis, senior physicist at the Argonne National Laboratory, pressed the SANE board to devote more time to its original interest in disarmament by opposing the installation of anti-ballistic missiles. SANE leaders set up a subcommittee which drafted a statement on this issue that could be adopted as SANE policy and released it with the signatures of leading scientists. The result was the famous SANE ad and poster, "From the people who brought you Vietnam: The anti ballistic missile system." Edward Sorel's satirical drawing of four generals and one Pentagon official in the War Room in Washington lighting an ABM quickly became the most successful advertisement in recent history for a political cause.[7]

The ad first appeared in the *New York Times* on March 24, 1969. It was repeated in the *Times* Sunday edition and appeared eleven times in selected newspapers in strategic cities in attempts to pressure influential or uncommitted senators. The ad was also reproduced by other groups in additional communities, and was used to illustrate articles in

The winner of World War III

A nuclear war, if it comes, will not be won by the Americans. It will not be won by the Russians. And although it has been so ordained by Mao Tse-tung, it will not be won by the Chinese.

The winner of World War III will be the cockroach.

"Let a man absorb 600 roentgens [of radiation] and he perishes soon and miserably," says Dr. H. Bentley Glass, a leading biologist, "but 100,000 roentgens may not discomfort an insect in the least."

"The cockroach, a venerable and hardy species, will take over the habitations of the foolish humans and compete only with other insects or bacteria."

If the cockroaches knew what was going on in Vietnam, if they realized how close to nuclear war the foolish humans have got themselves, they would be descending on the better neighborhoods to choose from the homes that may soon become available. In the United States. In the Soviet Union. In China. In Europe.

A few observations about Vietnam:

1. It has become a war that nobody can win.

2. The South Vietnamese, whom everybody is so anxious to save, are being destroyed in the process. (With friends like that, they don't need enemies.)

3. It has become quite apparent, in Santo Domingo as well as in South Vietnam, that the United States cannot be the world's self-appointed policeman. It just doesn't work.

There is no easy way out of the mess in Vietnam. But we think there is still time to take constructive steps:

We ask the President to stop the bombing of North Vietnam, and to negotiate with all the parties concerned, *including the people we are fighting—the Vietcong*. The negotiations must provide that the people of Vietnam be free to determine their own future.

We realize of course that the United States cannot just talk to itself in Vietnam. We have urged, and will continue to urge the Vietcong and North Vietnam to show a willingness to negotiate under neutral auspices.

If you think this makes sense, if you think this is closer to what you voted for in the last election, then do something about it.

Write or wire the President today, and send copies to your Senators. (Many of them are more worried than they are admitting in public.)

And if you can't stand the thought of the cockroach taking over the world, send a contribution to SANE so that we can afford to run this advertisement in other cities.

Nat'l Committee for a SANE Nuclear Policy
17 East 45th Street, New York, N.Y. 10017
__Here is $____ for your work.
__Please send me more information on SANE.
Name_____
Address_____
City_____ State_____

From the people who brought you Vietnam:

The anti ballistic missile system.

They're mad.
They're absolutely mad.
Everyone can see that things at home are getting worse all the time, and that little or nothing is being done about it.

The last thing in the world we need is to spend six or seven thousand million dollars for the down payment on an anti ballistic missile system.

But what can you expect from the type of mind that got us into Vietnam in the first place, and that keeps plunging us back in for one-last-victory-try every time it looks as though we might finally extricate ourselves.

Mr. Nixon and Secretary Laird and their advisors in the Pentagon seem to have lost touch with reality.

There are bombs going off in our cities, but they're not coming from China or the U.S.S.R.

The air we breathe is being poisoned, but it's not being done by enemy agents.

Many Americans no longer believe what the Government tells them, but it's not because they listen to Radio Moscow.

The gold in Fort Knox is, for all practical purposes, no longer our own—but the job wasn't done by Goldfinger or Smersh.

The war and weapons people have become so obsessed with International Communism, they fail to see that they themselves are laying the groundwork for a state of home-grown anarchy.

A few observations on the A.B.M.

The figure they use is six or seven billion dollars. But this is just the well-known foot in the door.

Experience with Pentagon procurement in the past indicates that actual costs run two or three times the original estimate.

Furthermore, there is every likelihood that the "light" ABM system will get heavier and heavier as it goes along, and would ultimately cost over fifty thousand million dollars.

All this for a "Maginot Line in the Sky" (as the N.Y. Times described it in a recent editorial), that would most likely be obsolete by the time it is operative, and wind up as surplus electronic junk on Canal Street.

Meanwhile, back in the U.S.S.R., do you think "their" hawks would be standing still for this?

What can we do about it?

Unfortunately, the Pentagon doesn't seem to be able to learn from experience, but we wouldn't give up hope for the U.S. Senate.

There are a lot of Senators—including conservative Republicans—who feel they were "had" by the infamous Gulf of Tonkin resolution, and this time they don't seem to be buying the Pentagon's big public relations campaign on the A.B.M.

This thing can be stopped in the Senate. But it will take the kind of grass roots' effort that did so much to change the political climate on Vietnam last year.

Our marching song has come again.

Time magazine on the military-industrial complex; and it became one of the rare illustrations used by the *Wall Street Journal* in a front-page article entitled "People With A Cause (and Money) Now Find It Pays To Advertise." SANE distributed some 250,000 handbill-sized reprints and 5,000 large posters of the ad; and ultimately they decorated the walls of thousands of college dormitories, private homes, and even congressional offices. Two Democratic California congressmen, Jeffrey Cohelan and Robert Leggett, used the SANE drawing to spice up their respective newsletters dealing with the military budget and the military-industrial complex.[8]

Using this resource, SANE members lobbied their senators in an effort to defeat the ABM authorization bill and in May 1969 sponsored a national conference in Washington for academics on ABM and the militarization of American society. At this conference, former officials of the Kennedy and Johnson Administrations joined university experts and congressional staff members to suggest that the power of the military-industrial complex should be reduced by tightening its purse strings. Notable participants included Nobel Prize winner in biology and medicine George Wald, Hans Morganthau, Yale psychiatrist Robert J. Lifton, Richard Kaufman of the Joint Congressional Economic Committee, two ex-Defense Department officials Robert Benson and Arthur Barber, Representative George Brown, Jr., of California, and Seymour Melman, chairman of SANE's program committee.[9]

The following month SANE called for a unilateral moratorium on the deployment of ABMs and the testing of MIRVs (multiple independently targetable reentry vehicles), a new weapon that would enable the United States to multiply the number of nuclear warheads on its missiles several times over. In a statement adopted by the national board on June 7, the committee urged that a bilateral moratorium on both weapons systems be at the top of the agenda in U.S.-Soviet negotiations. Pointing to the standoff which existed because both major nuclear powers believed that they had an assured retaliatory capacity, SANE declared that the development of ABMs or MIRVs "would seriously threaten to destroy this balance" and would "increase mutual suspicion and fear which are inimical to negotiations."[10]

Acting with the Coalition on National Priorities and Military Policy, SANE tried to spur the Strategic Arms Limitation (SALT) negotiations which opened in February 1969 and garner support for a Senate resolution calling for an immediate agreement with the Soviet Union to halt, on an interim basis, the deployment of strategic offensive and defensive weapons systems. Stating that the SALT talks may be the last chance to end the "mad momentum" of the arms race, SANE liberals grew increasingly frustrated during the next three years as the talks continued on a rotating basis between Helsinki and Vienna with little or nothing accomplished. When the ABM Treaty and the SALT agreement were finally signed in early summer 1972, many hailed the documents as the beginning of effective arms control. SANE, however, was critical, for although the agreement limited the deployment of ABMs, it left open the more crucial issue of offensive strategic weapons.[11]

"The best we can say about the ABM Treaty and the Interim Agreement on Strategic Offensive Arms is that the situation would be worse without them," SANE executive director Sanford Gottlieb told the Senate Foreign Relations Committee on June 29. Gottlieb's testimony followed an earlier statement released to the press on May 30, presenting SANE's initial analysis of the Moscow agreements, which regarded the new accords as "a lost opportunity because they allow the continued deployment of intercontinental bombers and the placement of multiple warheads on missile launchers." According to SANE, the Moscow accords represented "only the tiniest step towards ending the nuclear arms race." As Gottlieb added, emphatically, in his testimony before the Senate Foreign Relations Committee, "An unrestricted nuclear arms race has been replaced by a nuclear arms race with a small measure of mutual restraint."[12]

Gottlieb urged the Foreign Relations Committee to vote for the ABM Treaty, but he expressed reservations about the Interim Agreement on Strategic Offensive Arms. He feared that this agreement must not be allowed to serve as the basis for a new round in the arms spiral. Specifically, Gottlieb called for restraint in the further development and deployment of the B–1 bomber and the Trident submarine system, as well as other new American offensive nuclear weapons systems. In addition, he urged vigorous pursuit of further arms control agreements such as comprehensive nuclear test ban, limitations on strategic bombers and on anti-submarine warfare, a reduction in the number of offensive missile-launchers, mutual force reductions in Central Europe, and limitation on military aid to other nations.[13]

SANE's fears proved to be well founded, for instead of an immediate reduction in defense spending, SALT I led to a new round of strategic arms expenditures as the United States sought to build the weapons of the future. SANE responded with a full-page ad in the *New York Times* in June 1974, titled "From the people who brought you Inflation: Humane nuclear war." Using the same war room scene employed by Edward Sorel so successfully in the 1969 ABM ad, this ad alerted readers to the dangers of "limited" nuclear war plans and to the connections between military spending and inflation.

The ad pointed out that "to celebrate President Nixon's generation of peace, the administration is asking taxpayers to finance a record-breaking military budget for fiscal year 1975." At the same time the Pentagon was adding something new—targeting Soviet missiles and bases as well as cities—the highly dangerous "counterforce" strategy that made the adversary fear surprise attack. Ironically, the Pentagon stated this would make nuclear war "more humane," for the loss of life would be less than what would otherwise be the case. "They're mad. They're absolutely mad," the SANE ad screamed out. "They refuse to see that a spiraling arms race leads straight to all-out inflation and bankruptcy, and that a bankrupt America is a weak America." "This has got to be stopped by Congress," the ad concluded, and urged its readers to write their senators to vote for major cuts in military spending and a halt to counterforce weapons.[14]

When Gerald Ford assumed the presidency upon Nixon's resignation in August 1974, he pushed the military budget over $100 billion a year and made plans to develop the Trident submarine fleet, the strategic Cruise missle, and a B–1 bomber. At the same time, Ford and Secretary of Defense James Schlesinger warned that the United States did not rule out the use of nuclear weapons either in a first strike situation or against nations not possessing them. The administration was particularly intrigued by the possibilities of "limited" nuclear war. In January 1975, Schlesinger assured a Senate subcommittee that, while "the psychological impact of a nuclear attack would result in some initial loss in government . . . positive adaptive behavior would prevail."[15]

In response, SANE co-sponsored with Women's Strike For Peace the first pro-disarmament demonstration in front of the Ford White House and stepped up its campaign to oppose "limited nuclear strategies" with new literature and consultation with other peace groups. Representatives Bella Abzug (D-NY) and Tom Harkin (D-IA.), a member of SANE's board, participated in the demonstration along with SANE co-chairman Seymour Melman and executive director Sanford Gottlieb, Women's Strike for Peace coordinator Ethel Taylor, Henry

Niles of Business Executives Move for Peace, and La Donna Harris, social activist and wife of 1976 presidential candidate Fred Harris of Oklahoma. Leaders of the two sponsoring groups sought a meeting with National Security Council officials, but the White House declined. Recognizing that disarmament had not been part of the public dialogue in the United States for over a decade, SANE tried to bring it back as a prelude to pressuring the leaders toward nuclear as well as conventional disarmament.[16]

To this end, in November 1976, SANE sponsored a Conference on "The Arms Race and the Economic Crisis" in New York City. The economic impact of military spending was discussed by Melman and Milwaukee Mayor Henry Maier; Senator Dick Clark of Iowa gave the keynote address on working toward a demilitarized foreign policy; and five action-oriented workshops were held on disarmament, arms trade and aid, the proliferation of nuclear weapons, "limited" nuclear war, and economic conversion. The conference finale included a broad look ahead at "What Changes Would Disarmament Bring?" with Dr. George Rathjens, a former official of the White House and the Pentagon and the Arms Control and Disarmament Agency and one of the nation's foremost experts on the arms race.[17]

During the 1976 presidential election campaign, the SANE board followed the position articulated by Melman and decided to work exclusively on issues—a demilitarized foreign policy, economic conversion of military resources to civilian needs, a settlement on the conflict in the Middle East, international cooperation to international problems, and an unconditional amnesty for Vietnam era draft resisters—without supporting a particular presidential candidate or group of candidates. Their decision reflected the sharp differences between 1968 and 1972 on the one hand and 1976 on the other. Because of the great importance of the Indo-China War in the earlier campaigns, SANE was able to move with unanimity in support of Eugene McCarthy (January 1968) and George McGovern (January 1972), as both of these candidates shared much of SANE's viewpoint. In 1976, however, foreign policy was less an issue to the voters, and the candidates under consideration shared little in SANE's view of the important issues.[18]

Work began immediately to stress these issues in the campaign. SANE's Campaign Issues Packet assembled in one place the most cogent and concise articles designed to be read and given away to opinion makers in the news media, political life, and local communities. In addition, SANE provided background material to presidential candidates and Democratic Convention delegates. Appearing before the Democratic Platform Committee in May, executive director Gottlieb criticized the "one-dimensional notion that Soviet military power is the main threat to U.S. national security." Following such hawks as Admiral Elmo Zumwalt and Eugene Rostow before the Platform Committee, Gottlieb outlined this and other problems as threats to "the security of Americans—and, coincidentally, the security of all other peoples." "A military establishment is not the only source of national security," Gottlieb told the committee. "Our strength is measured also by the health of the economy, by our industrial capacity, by our unequalled agricultural system, by the planet's most advanced technologies, and by the strengths of the people united in purpose and at peace with itself."[19]

SANE, along with other peace groups and labor unions, lobbied the Democratic Platform Subcommittee on a conversion of the arms industry plank that was adopted in the platform in July. After receiving the Democratic nomination, candidate Jimmy Carter sent a letter to SANE stating that he would do his "utmost to implement the economic-conversion plank in the Democratic platform." Following a heated debate on September 18, the SANE board voted 20 to 2 to "cooperate with the Carter-Walter Mondale campaign on issues in an effort to help solidify the campaign's commitment to constructive foreign and military policies," but the Democratic ticket failed to win their necessary two-thirds vote for full support (tantamount to endorsement). The board stated in its resolution that the Carter-Mondale campaign was "not yet close enough to SANE's position to merit full support," but it agreed that Gerald Ford was "clearly unacceptable" and that a Ford-Robert Dole Administration "would reinforce the influence of the Pentagon over our lives and stifle the chances of real arms reduction."[20]

According to executive director Gottlieb, failure to endorse the Carter-Mondale ticket was a serious mistake for SANE. He saw a significant difference between the Democratic and Republican candidates on arms control and disarmament and believed that with Carter as president there would at least be some hope for a new foreign policy, whereas with Ford there was none. When sufficient resistance to this idea among the SANE board manifested itself, Gottlieb chose to campaign for Carter by himself.[21]

At the same time, SANE was suffering a severe financial crisis. Ever since American troops returned from Vietnam, SANE, like other peace organizations, experienced rapidly declining membership until it now stood at a little over 6,000. Income had also fallen to about $150,000, while costs continued to rise and large loans required repayment. For the first time in SANE's history, payrolls were missed for half of the staff on several occasions. Although SANE leaders realized how much needed to be done in reversing the arms race, more and more of their time was taken seeking funds to carry out the most basic of programs.[22]

In this state of financial austerity, SANE began exploring the possibility of merger with other peace organizations which found themselves in similar circumstances. Since 1973, talks were held with the World Federalists, Clergy and Laity Concerned, and the Council for a Liveable World; but all met the same negative result as each organization chose to keep its own identity. By late 1976 a new organization emerged which Gottlieb believed had tremendous possibilities, and he became a member of its board.

New Directions, a citizens' lobby working on the global issues in the fields of arms control, environment, poverty, and human rights, was officially launched in October 1976 with Russell Peterson, past chairman of the Council on Environmental Quality, as full-time president. Gottlieb hoped to bring SANE into New Directions as a major part of the organization's arms control and disarmament voice. At its December meeting, however, the board voted to keep SANE's organizational identity, whereupon Gottlieb submitted his resignation as executive director. On the first day of April Gottlieb left SANE to become arms control and disarmament director for New Directions; and Victor Lloyd, who had been with the organization for the previous two years as director of development, became the administrative director of SANE.[23]

Gottlieb's departure left a vacuum of leadership in SANE. He was one of the original 5,000 respondents to the first SANE ad that created the grass-roots dimension of SANE in 1957, was the organization's first political action director, and had served as its executive director since 1967. As a result, an already severe financial crisis became even worse. By July 1977, an all-time low watermark was reached in the organization as its operating deficit was $28,830; it had only $702 in the bank and $32,373 in loans outstanding and accounts payable. Lloyd and his small staff were subsidizing the organization by working for no pay, and SANE was literally on the verge of closing its doors.[24]

The SANE board decided to continue, however, until a new executive director could be found that might revitalize the organization. On October 29, 1977, the board unanimously voted in David Cortright as the executive director. Cortright, who was just thirty, had his political roots in the antiwar movement of the Vietnam era. Upon graduation from Notre Dame in 1968, he was drafted into the Army. The training shattered his previous assumptions about U.S. military policy, and he plunged into antiwar organizing. He joined with fellow soldiers at Fort Hamilton, New York, to found GIs United Against the War in Vietnam, where they launched a major courtsuit against the Army for suppressing their First Amendment rights. As a result of his antiwar stance, Cortright was transferred to Ft. Bliss, Texas, where he continued his activities with the GIs for Peace, helping to coordinate several antiwar rallies.[25]

After his discharge from the Army, Cortright studied with Marcus Raskin at the Institute for Policy Studies in Washington, D.C. There he devoted almost three years to research and writing about the GI movement, which was published as a book, *Soldiers in Revolt*, by Doubleday in 1975. In 1974, he was selected as a fellow of the Robert F. Kennedy Memorial to study the problems of youth in the military, and before coming to SANE he was working at the Center for National Security Studies, where he delved deeper into military policy.

Cortright stated he was surprised to find out that SANE was still functioning in 1977 but was interested in working for a peace organization; and when the board offered him the job, he gladly accepted. Although he knew the organization was suffering financial hardship, he was shocked to find out how severe it really was. Indeed, the committee had only until December 15 to pay a $10,000 debt to the Internal Revenue Service that had been rolled over several times already. To Cortright's surprise, an anonymous donor sent in a check for the whole amount just three days before the deadline. With that behind them, SANE managed to survive into the early part of 1978, whereupon Cortright wrote the SANE membership, told them he was assembling a new staff, and asked them for their help. Thousands responded to this appeal, and SANE slowly started coming back. Within the next two years, SANE experienced a major resurgence of activity. Membership climbed to 10,000, income more than doubled that of 1977, other debts were being reduced, and the cash flow situation improved dramatically.[26]

As membership grew and the financial situation improved, so did the prospects for enactment of SANE's program. Priorities that would carry SANE into its third decade included a sustained emphasis on two goals— nuclear disarmament and economic conversion. Immediate plans for disarmament included publication of a popular flyer on the Nuclear Club, publication of fact sheets on fallout and arms reduction, and circulation at the local level of a disarmament appeal addressed to President Carter by prominent Americans under the auspices of the Ad Hoc Working Group for Disarmament. At the same time SANE produced a slide show and filmstrip entitled "The Race Nobody Wins." Narrated by actor Tony Randall, the highly professional presentation was a most effective way to communicate the issues of the arms race to the American public. In its first year it was used by 600 schools, churches, and community groups across the country and along with hundreds of thousands of pieces of SANE literature helped to spread the organization's message on nuclear disarmament.[27]

In 1977, SANE also worked closely with the National Campaign to Stop the B–1 Bomber, housing their Washington headquarters in their national office. The committee would not let Jimmy Carter forget his campaign promise. Even after President Carter cut the B–1, arms zealots in Congress attempted to revive the program. SANE and other groups requested greater pressure from the White House and urged representatives to defeat the bomber. The final vote on October 20 was 204 to 194, with the peace organizations' efforts apparently making the difference. Co-chairman Melman sent a telegram to President Carter stating that SANE "applauds your decision to suspend the production and deployment of the B–1 bomber. This decision is hopefully a signal for a continued effort toward reversing the arms race."[28]

SANE's efforts in the House also helped swing thirty to forty votes in favor of an amendment by Congressman Ted Weiss (D-NY.) barring funds for the Neutron bomb, a final vote of 109 against and 297 for. Continuing public and congressional opposition forced the administration to delay deployment. Congressman Weiss thanked SANE for its support and noted in a letter to the organization: "Your active participation was a major factor in our historic effort to delete funding for the Neutron bomb."[29]

Increasingly, however, SANE's disarmament strategy began to focus on two issues—the ratification of the SALT II Treaty and the defeat of the MX missile system. In spite of the agreement's limitations, SANE viewed the ratification of SALT II as an essential step toward reversing the arms race and lobbied energetically for its ratification. In a statement adopted by the national board on June 2, 1979, SANE recommended and supported ratification of the SALT Treaty because it embodied an agreement between the United States and the USSR and set some limits on the future development of certain strategic weapons. "Continued negotiation of arms limitation and reduction agreements was essential to human survival," declared SANE, and "SALT II is part of that process."[30]

While the SANE board had certain reservations about the content and ratification process of SALT II, the alternative to ratification, the organization believed, was "an unrestricted nuclear arms race between the U.S. and the U.S.S.R. which would pose a major threat to the world." SANE's reservations flowed from two separate considerations. For one, SALT II itself was quite limited. It in fact legalized further strategic weapons development and production. The treaty contained no restrictions on nonnuclear forces or nuclear forces, other than those with very long-range delivery systems. Secondly, within the United States, a bargain was being offered by the Carter Administration in order to obtain political support for the ratification of the treaty. That bargain included an acceleration of other armament plans such as the MX missile, the 100,000-man international strike force, and other escalating arms programs. SANE instead strongly favored concrete steps towards demobilization, including adoption of the U.S.-USSR 1962 proposals to reverse the arms race, cut-off production of further nuclear explosives, and unilateral initiatives to end the arms race which it said was "decimating the economic systems of both the U.S. and the U.S.S.R. and the whole world."[31]

To assist the ratification campaign, SANE prepared several publications including a SALT Issues Reading Packet, a SALT Crucial Issues flyer containing concise rebuttals to the common criticism of the treaty, and a flyer called "The Soviet Threat: Myths and Realities" which examined the U.S.-Soviet military balance. SANE also took responsibility for education and lobbying Senators on the treaty. Following on the heels of the Iranian hostage crisis and the Soviet invasion of Afghanistan, however, Congress was in no mood to ratify the SALT Treaty, and it languished in the Senate for want of support until Carter withdrew it from active consideration. Accordingly, SANE turned its emphasis to its other major disarmament program—the Stop the MX Missile Campaign.

In 1979, SANE started quietly laying the groundwork for a national Stop-MX Campaign. Coordinator Michael Mawby started building contacts in the deployment states in the West as well as alerting a wide range of national groups about the upcoming MX fight and trying to enlist their support. In September, the MX moved another step forward when Carter decided on the "racetrack" basing mode idea which involved running the missiles around on circular roadways. With this announcement, the MX issue snapped into sharper focus, and the SANE opposition began in earnest. "At last we know exactly what we're fighting," stated Mawby. "The MX battle lines can now be clearly drawn. This is a fight for environmental responsibility, for budgetary sanity, and—most important of all—for the future of arms control and disarmament." Accordingly, SANE published a colorful, illustrated brochure: "The Mobile Missile: Disaster on Wheels," which discussed the full range of problems posed by the MX system, from arms control difficulties to environmental damage.[32]

In October, Mawby took a nineteen-day organizing trip through the mountains and valleys of the projected deployment states, Utah and Nevada. Toni Stuart of California's Clergy and Laity Concerned and Marilyn McNabb of Nebraskans for Peace accompanied him most of the way. Together or separately, they met with the attorney general of Nevada, editorial boards of the *Las Vegas Sun* and *Salt Lake City Tribune*, numerous newspaper, television, and radio reporters, state and local officials, and environmental and peace activists. Mawby related his belief that the government officials supporting the MX "have not reasoned out the full implications of the massive new defense system. When considered in the context of the U.S.-Soviet defense climate," he concluded, "the new system would mean eventually a big escalation in the need for additional weapons."[33]

In late 1979, Marilyn McNabb became a new staff member to help coordinate the anti-MX effort. On January 24, 1980, Mawby testified on the MX before the Public Lands Subcommittee of the House Interior Committee. He told the committee members that "most local residents view the MX system with fear, trepidation, and abhorrence for a variety of reasons. Following the Nebraska pattern, a Utah and Nevada anti-MX groundswell is growing as more and more information is released to the public," added Mawby. "The SALT factor has thrown a wrench into the MX plans, which by requiring an expanded version of the MX can only lead to ever more opposition on the part of the general public."[34]

The first major legislative battle in SANE's campaign to halt this mammoth new nuclear missile took place on May 15, 1980, in the House of Representatives. Amendments by Ron Dellums (D-CA.), to delete all MX funds, and by Paul Simon (D-IL.), to delete funds for the basing mode, went down to defeat, the latter amendment gaining 152 supporters. According to SANE, congressional debate suggested that there was considerable strength for the anti-MX forces and the campaign now had a solid, proven base of support on which to build in the months and years ahead. Over the next year, McNabb observed, "We've got to go about the business of finding more people who, for their own varied reasons, want to stop the MX. We've got to focus on the economic aspects: cost, inflation, and jobs."[35]

In August, anti-MX forces, including SANE, carried the battle to halt deployment of the mobile missile to the floor of the Democratic Convention. Although President Carter considered the MX a "must win issue," an anti-MX resolution was introduced by Carter delegate Joe Smith of Oregon. Through his efforts, the resolution nearly became part of the original platform, losing by only seven votes. Smith then called SANE and others to assist him in bringing the MX debate to the full convention. SANE staffers distributed literature on the MX and gave back-up support to the anti-MX delegates throughout the convention proceedings. Unfortunately for Smith and SANE the intense lobbying campaign unleashed by the administration paid off when the delegates voted 1,874 to 1,277 to keep MX language in the platform. The publicity generated by the floor fight, however, made the anti-MX resolution a worthwhile effort. Major newspapers covered the floor fight, and network television interviewed Utah delegates about their opposition to the MX. In addition, through SANE's and other efforts, many delegates heard for the first time about the astronomical costs and dangerous risks that MX deployment would entail.[36]

While SANE was heading the early Stop the MX Campaign, executive director Cortright was quickly moving the organization into the forefront of national political efforts on conversion. An economic conversion bill was drafted back in 1977 with Melman and board member Lloyd Dumas, both professors of Industrial Engineering at Columbia University, playing a major role in its design. The Defense Economic Adjustment Act, S 2279, was introduced in Congress in 1978, and SANE sought co-operation from labor groups and others in supporting the bill. The committee also helped to produce a mass distribution pamphlet on conversion, to be circulated in cooperation with the United Auto Workers and the International Association of Machinists, and took over the leadership of the Conversion Committee of the Coalition For A New Foreign and Military Policy in Washington.[37]

SANE was one of the first peace organizations to realize that labor support was essential in order to move toward disarmament. Working to dispel the "Hawk" stigma peace activists attached to labor, along with the accompanying insensitivity to the worker's plight, SANE broke the ice by cooperating closely with the major defense contractor unions in the new economic conversion initiative. The McGovern-Mathias conversion bill that SANE helped to design promoted as a basic principle the need for job security and income guarantees by providing funds for adjustments and retraining assistance for displaced workers. As chairman of the Conversion Committee, SANE was also instrumental in expanding the list of permanent members to include ranking officials from the International Association of Machinists and Aerospace Workers, United Auto Workers, United Electrical Workers, American Federation of Government Employees, and the Oil, Chemical and Atomic Workers.[38]

The committee also arranged for a working group composed of union leaders to refine the McGovern-Mathias legislation and in doing so served as a major catalyst in developing a political consensus for conversion. As a part of this expanded effort on conversion, SANE began publishing a bimonthly newsletter called *The Conversion Planner*, which reported on both the legislative push for conversion and local organizing in communities around the country. SANE, other peace groups, and labor unions also worked together to produce a new brochure on economic conversion, "More Jobs: Converting to a Peaceful Productive Economy." This was the first concise resource on this complex topic, pointing out that more jobs and job security, more resources for basic human needs, disarmament, and a more liveable world are all parts of the promise of a national conversion program.[39]

SANE's platform received a major boost when in March 1979 it was announced to the press that William Winpisinger, President of the million member Machinists Union (IAM), was assuming the co-chairmanship of the committee along with Melman, symbolizing an emerging labor-peace alliance on such common causes as reduced military spending and economic conversion. Citing a new study ("The Impact of Military Spending on the Machinists Union," prepared by economist and SANE board member Marion Anderson), which showed that military spending cost his workers jobs, 12 percent of which are involved in defense work, Winpisinger identified conversion as "a basic self-interest of the Machinists." He declared, "We reached the point long ago where we were no longer enamored of the virtues of defense employment."[40]

In November 1979, the labor-peace alliance pressing for conversion scored its first legislative victory when two conversion related amendments to the Public Works and Economic Development Act of 1979 passed the House of Representatives. The lobbying effort on behalf of the amendments was the first major move in a complex legislative battle by slow but steady increments. While the amendments, offered by Rep. Stewart McKinney (R-CT.) and Rep. Christopher Dodd (D-CT.) did not directly call for conversion, they would pave the way for the overall switch from military to civilian production outlined in the larger McGovern-Mathias conversion bill. While these provisions passed House committee and floor votes with little difficulty, by the time they reached conference committee they began to draw heavy fire from the Carter Administration. But even the House passage of the amendments alone was, as Machinists president and SANE co-chairman Winpisinger put it, "an historic milestone." This debate put conversion on the map as a legislative issue and showed that the labor-peace alliance initiated by SANE and the IAM was a political force to be reckoned with.[41]

Conversion appeared to be well on its way to concrete victories both nationally and locally. Then came the American hostage crisis in Iran and the Soviet invasion of Afghanistan, double-digit inflation, and a recession. In early 1980, Carter committed the nation to a huge, five-year military expansion. Consequently, the conversion legislation was stalled in conference committee, and many local organizers who had been succeeding in pressing the issue locally found the context radically altered. The new spurt in military funding in many cases rejuvenated the military industry, thus undercutting the arguments for alternate use planning.

As the 1980 presidential election campaign commenced, the national board of SANE issued a statement arguing that the Carter Administration had "reneged on its election campaign commitments to de-escalate the arms race." According to SANE,

The military build-up being sponsored by the Carter Administration is a major contributing factor to the widespread inflation now ravaging the U.S. economy.

The President's policies are also fueling an international arms race which threatens American national security and the survival of all humanity.

And this commitment to major new weapons systems, according to SANE, "increased the danger of nuclear holocaust." Because of the administration's unacceptable record on issues of peace and nuclear weapons, SANE declared itself "opposed to the renomination of President Jimmy Carter." The organization agreed, however, that it would continue to focus on questions of peace and human survival and urged political aspirants to address their concerns.[42]

In search of an acceptable alternative, SANE discussed endorsing Senator Edward Kennedy but instead invited all the candidates, declared and potential, to state their position on the following five points: immediate negotiations with the Soviet Union for reversal of the arms race based on the 1962 McCloy-Zorin proposal; appointment of 100 persons as a special staff in the Arms Control and Disarmament Agency to develop concrete steps toward general disarmament; adoption of the Defense Economic Adjustment Act to begin planning for conversion from military to civilian economy; cancellation of the MX missile program; and maintenance of the all volunteer force without draft registration.[43]

After closely monitoring the campaign, in October 1980 SANE offered its view of the upcoming presidential election. According to the committee, "The issues that should be critically examined—nuclear proliferation, economic dislocation, military spending, national priorities—have been put on the back burner, while a furious race to see who is the most 'hawkish' takes place between the Republicans and the Democrats." Representative John Anderson of Illinois, the independent candidate, seemed somewhat better than Carter and Ronald Reagan on this issue, but he still had serious weaknesses from SANE's point of view. Thus SANE continued its policy of nonendorsement of candidates and instead urged its members to use the election as an opportunity to publicize a sane approach to the arms race and national priorities.[44]

Following Reagan's overwhelming victory in November, SANE members received a letter from co-chairman Melman imploring them that this was no time for retreat. He stated that the understanding of what the election meant gave SANE its marching orders for the next period. "We must show the connection between inflation plus unemployment and the operation of the permanent war economy. We must explain why an escalation of military budgets will only worsen these conditions.'' According to Melman, it was SANE's obligation to explain that there was an alternative way to improve America's military security: not by the meaningless enlargement of overkill, but rather by attempting seriously the reversal of the arms race. ''It is our responsibility,'' Melman concluded, ''to rally a population around the idea that the dreaded arms race and danger of nuclear war can be averted, and that by these sane acts we can start the process of reconstruction of the American economy.''[45]

Newly elected President Reagan moved quickly to revitalize the Cold War between the United States and the Soviet Union and to boost American military expenditures to an all-time high. In the process, however, his actions helped to ignite SANE and the long-dormant nuclear disarmament movement. The president unveiled his budget plans on February 18, 1981, asking for a record $200 billion for the Pentagon, at the same time instituting unprecedented cutbacks in social programs. The president also announced plans to develop a whole new generation of deadly and provocative nuclear weapons systems—the MX missile, Trident submarines and missiles, Pershing and ground launched Cruise missiles. There was even an attempt to resurrect the ABM system and the B–1 bomber which, if successful, would have nullified two of SANE's most significant victories. To Reagan's critics, his massive arms buildup made nuclear war more likely than ever before.

Accordingly, SANE once again mobilized to meet the challenge and became the nerve center of a host of disarmament activities. On the educational level, the committee prepared a new twenty-four page booklet on the budget, outlining specific recommendations for military cuts and presenting an alternative view of national security. Within a year, nearly 6,000 copies were sold, largely to trade union officials and members of domestic peace groups. ''Deadly Standoff: The U.S.-Soviet Military Balance'' pointed out with graphs and statistics the myth of Soviet superiority and American weakness and made the case for the nuclear weapons freeze. SANE also expanded the distribution of its successful slide show, ''The Race Nobody Wins,'' which now had a total sales of more than 2,000 to college and high school educators, and continued its weekly ''Consider the Alternatives'' radio broadcasts, with a network of 150 stations and growing steadily.[46]

In March 1980, SANE helped found an independent National Campaign to Stop the MX, as a means of bringing taxpayers, environmentalists, church leaders, and others into a broad coalition against the missile. SANE supported the campaign through funding and by permitting senior staff member Michael Mawby to serve as the campaign's legislative director. Through the Campaign, the organization produced tens of thousands of fact sheets and flyers about the MX, maintained close liaison with local opponents in the great basin of Texas and eastern New Mexico, and coordinated several major legislative challenges in Congress. In addition, SANE presented technical briefings to Capitol Hill staffs, rebutting claims of a so-called "window of vulnerability," and convened several widely covered press conferences.[47]

In October, SANE's three-year fight against the MX scored a major victory when President Reagan cancelled the mobile basing plan, but the administration decided to proceed with the missile itself. At least 100 of the 10-warhead missiles would be produced and deployed initially in existing Titan and Minuteman silos. Following this decision, SANE executive director Cortright travelled to the new potential deployment state of Arizona, speaking against the missile in Tucson and Phoenix and appearing on nearly a dozen radio and television programs and in several newspaper reports.[48]

Following Reagan's August 1981 decision to produce the Neutron bomb, SANE immediately began mobilizing opposition to the new weapon. Within two days, twenty-four organizations, including major religious denominations, the International Association of Machinists, National Association of Social Workers, Friends of the Earth, and several peace and environmental groups had signed SANE's letter of protest to President Reagan and Defense Secretary Casper Weinberger. At a press conference at the National Press Club in Washington, SANE released its letter to Reagan, as well as statements wired to the organization from the two largest European disarmament movements—Britain's Campaign for Nuclear Disarmament and Holland's Interchurch Peace Council. SANE also produced a special fact sheet on the Neutron bomb, distributing over 25,000 to SANE members and supporters within one month of the president's decision, and conducted an extensive lobbying campaign against the bomb that included personally visiting congressional offices and delivering several thousand postcards sent to Congress by SANE members.[49]

SANE also took the lead in supporting the peace movements of Europe and in building opposition to the deployment of Pershing II and Cruise missiles. In December 1981, the committee sponsored a major conference in Washington with four prominent European peace leaders: Jo Richardson, Labor Party Member of Parliament in Britain; Major General (Ret.) Gert Bastian, former commander of the Bundeswehr's 12th Armored Division; Petra Kelly, leader of Germany's Green Party; and Karl-Heinz Hansen, Social Democratic Party Member of Parliament from Germany. The delegates fielded questions from a panel of congressional and State Department aides and presented arguments for cancelling the NATO missile buildup.[50]

With the help of professional public relations consultants, SANE organized an exhaustive itinerary of media interviews for the delegation in New York, Chicago, Los Angeles, and Washington—including meetings with *New York Times* and *Washington Post* reporters and appearances on NBC television's "Today Show," National Public Radio's "All Things Considered," the Studs Terkel program, the Michael Jackson Show, and others. The organization also co-sponsored Capitol Hill briefings in May and September for visiting European military experts Nino Pasti, a retired general and former NATO Commander and then a member of the Italian Senate, and Brigadier (Ret.) Michael Harbottle, retired British military officer and then general secretary of the World Disarmament Campaign.[51]

In cooperation with the International Association of Machinists and other unions, SANE also continued to emphasize the harmful economic effects of excessive arms spending. On March 26, 1981, the committee convened a briefing in the House of Representatives on the "Military Budget and Today's Economy," featuring economists Robert Lekachman, Leslie Nulty, and others. And in June, SANE presented a similar session in the Senate, co-sponsored by Senators Charles Mathias (R-MD.) and Paul Tsongas (D-MA.), focusing on the military budget and inflation and featuring economist John Kenneth Galbraith.[52]

In the fall of 1981 SANE helped to initiate one of the most significant challenges to Reagan's budget priorities in creating a broadly based Fair Budget Action Campaign to mobilize national and grass roots opposition to Reaganomics. Founded by SANE in cooperation with the Food Research and Action Center and Ralph Nader's Congress Watch, the Fair Budget Campaign was endorsed by more than sixty national organizations—including such prominent groups as the United Steelworkers, the National Education Association, National Organization for Women, and the National Urban Coalition. The campaign ads pledged "to work for the maintenance of vital human services, equitable taxation, and sensible military spending.'' The main strategy for achieving these goals was to mobilize ''cooperative grassroots action'' and ''intense public education of the devastating effects of the Reagan budget.'' In April 1982, the campaign sponsored hearings and ''accountability sessions'' with members of Congress in hundreds of communities throughout the country. SANE provided major staff support to the project and insured that these challenges to Reaganomics included a strong plea for reduced arms expenditures.[53]

Events in the spring of 1982, specifically concerning the nuclear freeze campaign, also propelled the nuclear disarmament movement and consequently SANE into the national spotlight. Fueled largely by the rhetoric and policies of the Reagan Administration on nuclear armaments and U.S.-Soviet relations and influenced by the dramatic anti-nuclear demonstration in Western Europe, the nuclear freeze campaign had within a few years mushroomed into a political force. ''This movement is too powerful,'' wrote foreign policy expert George Kennan in the *New York Review of Books*, ''too elementary, too deeply embedded in the natural human instinct for self-preservation, to be brushed aside by the government. It will continue to grow,'' predicted Kennan, ''until something is done to meet it.''[54]

A mutual, verifiable freeze on all testing, production, and deployment of nuclear weapons was first proposed by Randall Forsberg, founder and director of the Institute for Defense and Disarmament Studies in Brookline, Massachusetts, in December 1979 and introduced by her in January 1980 at a town meeting of about thirty peace groups sponsored by the Fellowship of Reconciliation. Although it was rejected by the Democratic National Convention in August 1980, the proposal was revitalized when it swept through Vermont town meetings with skillful organizing help from the American Friends Service Committee. Success in Vermont—and earlier in eight Massachusetts election districts—caught the media's attention and stimulated freeze proponents elsewhere in the country. By the spring of 1982, nuclear freeze resolutions had been passed by 309 New England town meetings, 320 city councils from coast to coast, 56 county councils, one or both houses in eleven state legislatures, and 109 national and international organizations, including the UN General Assembly. In Washington, freeze proposals sponsored by Senators Edward Kennedy (D-MA.), Mark Hatfield (R-OR.), and

Representative Ed Markey (D-MA.) among others, won the support of 24 senators and 166 House members and prompted even greater numbers of legislators to endorse a variety of other arms-control plans.[55]

Early success by the New Jersey SANE committee in its statewide nuclear freeze campaign under the able guidance of longtime director Dorothy Eldridge, spurred the national organization to become involved. In May 1982, President Reagan, forced by the weight of public opinion to acknowledge the need for dialogue with the Soviets, finally offered a proposal for strategic arms reduction talks (START). Although proud that its members and supporters in the nuclear disarmament movement could take partial credit for this shift in the administration's line, SANE sent a statement to the press declaring that the President's plan was seriously flawed for it was a diversion from the call for a nuclear freeze and because it proposed selective reductions which SANE felt had little chance for success. Reagan's proposal, contended SANE, "continues the traditional 'bargaining chip' approach of building new weapons now with negotiating the illusory limits in the future." Instead, SANE proposed the following alternative principles as the basis for a real arms reduction plan: an immediate freeze on the testing, production, and deployment of all new nuclear weapons; negotiations for proportionate, across the board reductions in existing arsenals of the two sides; and economic conversion planning to protect workers and communities dependent on military industry and to speed the transition to socially useful production.[56]

To educate the American people on what it saw wrong with the president's proposal and to garner support for the SANE program for real arms reductions, the Committee placed two full-page ads in the Sunday editions of the May 23 New York Times. Under the headline "How to stop feeling hopeless about preventing nuclear war," SANE told its readers in the second ad, "The time has come for The Great Turnaway From Nuclear War." Although response to the two ads, according to David Cortright, fell short of expectations, it did underscore once again SANE's total commitment to the freeze and the nuclear disarmament campaign.[57]

On June 12, 1982, in a historic outpouring of support for peace and disarmament, some one million people jammed the streets of Manhattan and the Great Lawn of Central Park in the largest antiwar march in American history. The rally, held in conjunction with the United Nations Special Session on Disarmament, featured dozens of speakers and entertainers and participants from throughout the country and the world. SANE had made a major commitment to this event, assigning a full-time staff person, Chad Dobson, to the rally committee and assisting the march with finances and their resources.[58]

"The power of the issue kept the broadest range of groups involved in organizing the rally," said Dobson shortly afterwards. "Our success comes from the efforts of so many people, and I think really reflects the political strength of the nuclear disarmament movement." A SANE contingent, including several members of the board, chapters, and staff, marched up Fifth Avenue after waiting almost four hours to take its place in the march. Other large groups of SANE members poured in from feeder points around the city.[59]

The June 12 rally, calling for the freezing and reduction of nuclear weapons and transferring the military budget to fund human needs, represented the biggest challenge yet to President Reagan's military buildup and nuclear war preparations. Smaller rallies were held in other parts of the country, including some 100,000 people at the Rose Bowl in Pasadena, California, with SANE activists playing a major role in these endeavors.

Filled with media adulation and flushed with at least outward manifestation of their success, the nuclear disarmament movement and national organizations like SANE grew and prospered. Just four days after the massive New York rally, 125 people jammed the SANE offices in Washington, D.C., to help dedicate and celebrate SANE's new Ben Spock Center for Peace. A drive to obtain a permanent building for SANE was concluded when some 1,500 members contributed an astounding $75,000, more than twice what the SANE staff had anticipated. Spock, who had earlier been contacted by David Cortright and asked to again play an active role in SANE, came down from New York for the dedication ceremony and helped in the celebration along with SANE board members Ted Weiss, U.S. representative from New York; Hilda Mason, D.C. City Council member; and Dick Greenwood, assistant to the president of the International Association of Machinists.[60]

At this combined dedication and twenty-fifth anniversary celebration, Spock, after displaying his usual hearty good humor and taking some blasts at the Reagan Administration, told the people gathered that he was very proud to have the building named after him and of the work SANE had been doing. After sketching briefly the history of his involvement in the organization, Spock declared, "Just as SANE persisted since 1957 in not being defeated, the rest of us have to do the same. It's our only chance to fend off nuclear annihilation.'' Executive director Cortright concluded the festivities by saluting the membership for their magnificent support and participation that had made the Ben Spock Center for Peace possible. ''This is a great day for all of us,'' Cortright stated in appreciation, ''and we will go forward to continue and expand our work for reducing and eliminating the threat of nuclear war.''[61]

SANE at twenty-five was a healthy, viable, moderately influential peace committee that had almost quadrupled its membership in just two years and was well on its way to becoming again, as it was two decades and a half before, the largest nuclear disarmament organization in the country. The harder question remained, however, as to whether it and the anti-nuclear movement had become in the process a potent political force and one that would have an impact on public policy.

7

Conclusion: SANE and the Revival of the Nuclear Disarmament Movement, 1982–1985

Because everything we do and everything we are is in jeopardy, and because the peril is immediate and unremitting, every person is the right person to act and every moment is the right moment to begin, starting with the present moment.
—Jonathan Schell, 1982[1]

During the summer of 1982, citizen disarmament activity continued to grow dramatically. Despite the vehement opposition of the Reagan Administration, a CBS *New York Times* poll in May found that 72 percent of the American public favored a bilateral nuclear freeze. As SANE celebrated its twenty-fifth anniversary, the committee launched a major campaign "to transform the current groundswell of public concern about nuclear war into a well organized sustained citizens' movement for peace." "We're going to undertake a drive for nuclear sanity that is unprecedented in its scope and scale," executive director David Cortright wrote the SANE membership in the fall of 1982. Through intense political action and massive media outreach, peace liberals in SANE thus initiated their 1,000-day program to build a powerful network to turn America away from nuclear war.[2]

To begin this ambitious program, SANE immediately created a political action committee. Candidates supported by SANE PAC won in sixteen of thrity-two elections, as SANE members contributed $50,000 and enormous amounts of time and energy to races in their areas. Among the winners were four candidates—Bob Carr (D-MI.), Pete Kostmayer (D-PA.), Bob Mrazek (D-NY.), and Doug Basco (D-CA.)—who represented important new leadership on SANE issues. "Considering that we only got moving three months before the election, we made a very impressive showing," declared Mike Mawby, SANE PAC director. "Our strength lies not with megabucks, but with committed and concerned individuals. We can look forward to making an even bigger impact in 1984."[3]

The November mid-term elections climaxed a year of spectacular success for the nuclear freeze campaign and for the efforts of SANE and other disarmament groups. Nuclear freeze referendums were approved by a lopsided 3 to 2 margin around the nation, and at the same time, the number of pro-freeze representatives was substantially increased, providing the necessary margin for the House to pass a freeze resolution by a vote of 278 to 149 the following May. SANE members were justifiably proud of their accomplishments, but Cortright reminded them that "most of their successes so far have been largely symbolic." November's election victories did not stop a single nuclear weapon. Neither did the giant June 12 rally in New York. Many of the same politicians who said they supported a freeze continued to vote funds for first-strike nuclear weapons. In the midst of the most extensive outpouring of peace sentiment in American history, Congress approved the largest peacetime military budget in American history.[4]

"We must move now to make the freeze a concrete reality. We have a majority of the American people on our side," declared Cortright, "and we must use that support to achieve an actual change in policy." This meant focusing on two vital levers of power—control over funding and the ability to win elections. "If we want to stop the arms race," concluded Cortright, "we must show that we can challenge the funding of nuclear weapons and that we have clout at the voting booths to back that up."[5]

During 1983, SANE's membership, staff, and influence skyrocketed beyond what its leadership dreamed possible. The committee's membership more than doubled during the previous two years to 75,000 and its Washington staff doubled in size from ten to twenty, making it necessary to purchase the building next door to provide additional office space for the thriving organization. SANE had enrolled 1,700 activists in a Rapid Response Network, a nationwide phone tree and grass-roots legislative alert system with branches in 375 of the country's congressional districts, and now had two full-time lobbyists representing SANE members on Capitol Hill and working to reduce the military budget, halt the MX missile, and freeze and reduce nuclear weapons.[6] An advisory council was also formed which included several prominent people in the nuclear disarmament movement such as Randall Forsberg, Coretta Scott King, Linus Pauling, Benjamin Spock, and Jerome Wiesner.

At the same time, SANE initiated the first permanent door-to-door canvass campaign for peace in the nation. By early 1984 this campaign employed fifty full-time organizers who contacted one-quarter-of-a-million households and in the process recruited nearly 10,000 new activists and contributors to SANE. An innovative new minority outreach project was also started to broaden the constituency for peace to include Black and Hispanic communities. SANE participated in voter registration drives in low-income communities, translated the organization's materials including its monthly newsletter into Spanish, and appeared widely on Spanish language radio and television programs. The committee also hosted a reception for Coretta Scott King at its national headquarters to further strengthen the link between the civil rights movement and the movement for peace and participated in the Twentieth Anniversary Mobilization on August 27, 1983, in commemoration of the historic civil rights March on Washington.[7]

As membership and activities mushroomed, new SANE chapters developed and others reemerged making the total forty-five, stretching from Anchorage, Alaska, to Augusta, Georgia. SANE's field-organizing department grew from one part-time to four full-time staff positions, people who were constantly on the road, forming new chapters, speaking on campuses, appearing on local media programs, and providing assistance to grass-roots freeze groups. After a twenty-two-year absence, a Hollywood for SANE chapter was established when Max Youngstein was contacted by the SANE national office and enlisted Jimi Kaufer to head the organizing committee. A full-page ad for the committee appeared in *Variety*, the popular entertainment industry publication in December 1983; and among the more than 250 sponsors of the ad were Debra Winger, Jack Lemmon, Burt Lancaster, James Earl Jones, Sally Field, Jean Stapleton, Shirley MacLaine, Dana Andrews, Patty Duke Austin, Anne Bancroft, Ed Asner, and Ralph Bellamy. Hollywood for SANE pledged to make its talents available to all other groups who shared their concern for bilateral nuclear disarmament and in October

1984 sponsored several performances of a staged reading, *Handy Dandy, A Comedy But . . .* , in theatres in Los Angeles, New York, and London with proceeds benefiting the Nuclear Freeze Campaign.[8]

An Arms Control Computer Network was established in SANE's national offices linking seven national peace organizations into a common telecommunications and grass-roots lobbying system. Participating groups included SANE, Physicians for Social Responsibility, the Nuclear Weapons Freeze Campaign, Coalition for a New Foreign and Military Policy, Council For a Liveable World, Friends of the Earth, and Greenpeace. The publications department was also growing rapidly, now selling one-half million brochures and flyers annually, spreading its message to every state in the country. SANE was also reaching millions of radio listeners a week through its 140-station ''Consider the Alternatives'' public affairs broadcasts and in its new program of paid radio advertisements.[9]

SANE's initial effort in this behalf was in North Carolina where the committee sponsored seventeen billboard ads and nearly 300 sixty-second radio spots on behalf of a bilateral nuclear weapons freeze. The radio spots were narrated by the popular head basketball coach of the University of North Carolina, Dean Smith. Coach Smith's participation attracted widespread publicity to the SANE campaign as articles appeared in every major newspaper in the state, and the SANE campaign was the lead story on television news in Charlotte and elsewhere. The SANE media campaign reached hundreds of thousands of people in North Carolina and surrounding states and set the pattern for bringing the peace movement into the age of modern mass communications.[10]

Although the ongoing political battle to stop the dangerous and wasteful MX missile remained SANE's top legislative priority, the organization increased its opposition to the destabilizing Cruise and Pershing II missiles, focused major attention on the harmful effects of excess arms spending and the need for economic conversion, and commenced educating and organizing the American people in opposition to intervention in Central America. The committee's policy opposed all U.S. military involvement in Central America, including covert aid to overthrow the Nicaraguan government, military aid to El Salvador, and the militarization of Honduras and Costa Rica. Peace liberals in SANE believed that poverty and repression were at the root of problems in the region, not the ''export of revolution'' by Communists. The organization supported the Contadora group (Colombia, Mexico, Panama, and

Venezuela) in their efforts to begin serious negotiations to resolve the region's turmoil, beginning with a halt to all outside support for groups fighting in the area.[11]

The year 1984 offered the peace movement and SANE an unprecedented opportunity to shift away from nuclear war and move instead toward peace. There was a widespread feeling among liberal peace activists that the November elections could well be a turning point in citizen efforts to halt the nuclear arms race, as individuals and organizations all over the country mobilized to elect a Congress that they hoped would respond to the overwhelming majority of Americans who wanted a nuclear freeze. National SANE declared to its membership that through SANE PAC it would continue to focus on electing a more progressive Congress and work to unseat the Reagan Administration. "We must assure that the voice of peace is heard loudly in 1984," David Cortright wrote to the members in late 1983, "and that the popular mandate for nuclear arms reduction is finally translated into political reality."[12]

To give peace activists the needed expertise to ensure election of peace candidates, SANE sponsored an election skills training conference, "Peace is Primary," in March 1984 where hundreds of SANE members from thirty-two states came to Washington, D.C., to learn about making peace the primary issue in the 1984 elections. "This kind of conference had never been held before," stated Cortright. "It will be an invaluable help to activists who are going to exercise the growing power of the peace movement by electing a Congress that will say no to dangerous, wasteful weapons spending." Major speakers included Rep. Les AuCoin (D-OR.), leader of the MX fight in Congress; Eleanor Smeal, former president of the National Organization of Women; Mary Crisp, former co-chairman of the Republican National Committee; William Winpisinger, president of the IAM and co-chairman of SANE; and Rep. Mike Lowry (D-WA.), a committed voice for peace on Capitol Hill.[13]

The conference was preceded by a meeting of the national board of SANE. The board decided to launch a major campaign to mobilize SANE members for election year activity for peace. Members were urged to participate in voter registration efforts, to lobby, to work with local candidates, and to help sign up new SANE members. To make this a reality, SANE's political staff first selected fifty key House and Senate races—closely contested races where it was felt the votes of the peace movement could make a real difference. SANE PAC decided to especially concentrate on elections which involved members of the powerful Appropriations and Armed Services Committees, for "by changing just a few dozen strategically placed House and Senate seats," SANE felt it could dramatically change the political climate on Capitol Hill and assure much greater support for arms reduction.[14]

In the presidential race, SANE worked to unseat Ronald Reagan and to make sure the Democratic party was firmly committed to halting the arms race. In January 1984, Cortright was among a group of peace movement leaders who met with former Vice President and Democratic presidential candidate Walter Mondale and gained his commitment to the freeze and a nuclear test ban. Similar sessions were arranged with the two other Democratic candidates, Colorado Senator Gary Hart and the Reverend Jesse Jackson, and met with the same success. On behalf of fourteen national peace organizations and several prominent individuals, Cortright released a letter on July 12, after meeting with Jesse Jackson in Chicago, addressed to delegates of the Democratic National Convention in San Francisco urging support for two minority planks to the party platform which advocated "no first use" of nuclear weapons and substantial real reductions in military spending. "We feel it is morally and politically imperative that the delegates approve these two additions to the party platform," wrote Cortright, "and thereby put the Democratic Party squarely behind a comprehensive peace program."[15]

By mid-summer, SANE PAC was involved in nearly 100 House and Senate races aiding candidates by donating staff time to campaigns, sending their professional door-to-door canvass to key races, making direct financial contributions to some campaigns, and mobilizing the energy and talents of SANE's membership. In just over a year, the SANE canvass had grown from two people in a six-feet-by-ten-feet office to over 200 paid, professional staff knocking on doors five nights a week in ten cities, with the goal of reaching one million households by the November elections. In the process, two to three million people found out about SANE and its work and tens of thousands were being activated in the Rapid Response Network and mobilized to join in other SANE activities.[16]

At the same time, SANE published a six-page color brochure "Help Wanted" that documented the critically important national policy areas in which Ronald Reagan had been a dangerous failure. Stating that this brochure "may be the most important publication SANE has ever produced,'' the committee's new literature was designed to show the president's personal responsibility for the growing threat of nuclear war in the hope that people would look at the policies rather than the man. By the November election SANE printed and distributed more than one million copies of this brochure to the delegates at the Democratic Convention through the canvassing program, and through the mail with requests topping off at 20,000 for one single day.

As part of this continuing educational effort, SANE also published research reports, conducted press conferences, and broadcasted a series of radio documentaries over SANE's ''Consider the Alternatives'' radio network now heard weekly on 150 stations by an estimated two million listeners. In early 1984, SANE hired a full-time press secretary to enhance its media communications activities. Press releases and background fact sheets were now mailed regularly from SANE to nearly 1,000 reporters, editors, and broadcast journalists throughout the country. In return, SANE received increasingly prominent press coverage during 1984. On April 17, the *New York Times* published a feature article on SANE and its anti-nuclear lobbyist Laurie Duker, and on May 16, the lead story on the CBS Television Evening News featured SANE's MX radio spots in North Carolina and Washington, D.C.[17]

In August, *Newsweek* reported that ''for the first time, various groups in the American peace movement, including SANE, the Nuclear Weapons Freeze Campaign, and the Council for a Liveable World, are pooling their resources to bring their common message to voters.'' An umbrella group called the Committee for a Strong Peaceful America retained Peter Fenn and Associates, a Washington-based consulting firm, to create the ad campaign and was on its way to raising one million dollars to bankroll the project. Without endorsing any candidates or party, the thirty and sixty second radio and TV spots focused on the need for arms control and the dangers of nuclear proliferation and ''Star Wars'' weaponry. The campaign kicked off in seven target states in mid-August and went nationwide after Labor Day and featured celebrity spokespersons.[18]

As the *New York Times* article pointed out, a ''new image'' was being created by SANE and other anti-nuclear organizations ''allowing it to be more competitive with well-financed military industry lobbyists and has helped mold what was an unorganized and ideologically divided movement into a more effective lobbying force.'' SANE was also hailed in the *Congressional Quarterly* as an important and effective part of the liberal arms control coalition that was putting ''the squeeze'' on the

Reagan Administration's arms policies and for its ambitious goals for achieving election day results. The article declared that administration critics were planning election-year strategy based on the belief that President Reagan is politically vulnerable to public fear that his combative stance toward Moscow increases the risk of nuclear holocaust. Their goal was "to make Reagan look like a bomb-thrower and keep the level of public distrust as high as we can," stated Michael Mawby, political action director of SANE. "The bomb-throwing image is on people's minds and it's our job to keep it there. . . . Ultimately, people will not trust Reagan on this issue."[19]

Mawby was one of SANE's representatives at the Democratic Convention in July and wrote a report to the committee's membership stating that "the new Democratic platform represents the most progressive program for halting and reversing the nuclear arms race ever taken by one of the major parties." Mawby pointed out that the platform fully endorsed a nuclear freeze and called for specific steps to reach that goal, promised to terminate two of the most wasteful nuclear programs— the MX missile and the B–1 bomber—and prohibited nerve gas production. A full arms control agenda was set forth by the party, including promises to conclude a Comprehensive Test Ban Treaty and to pursue a ban on space weapons and an international ban on production of weapons-grade nuclear materials like plutonium and uranium. The platform also reaffirmed U.S. commitment of the ABM Treaty and pledged to resubmit such unratified treaties as SALT II and the Threshold Test Ban to the Senate.[20]

Mawby applauded the Democrats for opposing a peacetime draft or draft registration, for supporting pulling back battlefield nuclear weapons from Europe's frontlines, and for promising to "provide national leadership" for economic adjustment to workers, communities, and industries affected by weapons cutbacks which could result in the first step toward an economic conversion policy. The platform also promised to end the covert war against Nicaragua, supported the Contadora peace process in Central America, and restricted the use of military force in that region and elsewhere. The Democratic platform was far from perfect, declared Mawby, as it failed to pass the Jesse Jackson minority planks to substantially reduce military spending and establish a no first-use policy, but it "does address the concerns of the peace movement" and "stands in stark contrast to the Reagan record of stonewalling on arms control and sharply increasing nuclear tensions. . . . It is the best the disarmament movement ever had,'' concluded Mawby, ''and is one that SANE members can support.''[21]

Meanwhile, in a major upset for the Reagan Administration, the MX program came to a screeching halt on September 30 when, after marathon negotiations between congressional leaders and the administration, the White House finally conceded to put the MX on ice until the following spring. The agreement, which House Speaker Tip O'Neill (D-MA.) characterized as ''a death knell for the MX,'' required affirmative votes in both the House and Senate in April 1985 before any new MX production money could be released.[22] Reagan's original request of forty MX missiles in February 1984 was flatly repudiated because of the groundswell of public opposition to the program, and grass-roots activists deserved major credit for the victory. ''The progress made in knocking out the centerpiece of the President's nuclear buildup has given us the political clout and sophistication to broaden our agenda next year,'' wrote SANE field organizer Jerry Hartz. ''The ability of peace supporters to influence Congress can no longer be taken lightly.''[23]

Flushed with success on placing at least a temporary stranglehold on the MX, SANE liberals and their allies in the nuclear disarmament movement prepared themselves for an uphill battle to unseat President Reagan in the upcoming general election. On November 6, the president won a landslide victory over Walter Mondale by a margin of 59 percent to 41 percent of the popular vote, capturing a record 525 electoral votes and sweeping everything except Washington, D.C., and Mondale's home state of Minnesota. There were mixed results in Congress, however, with the Democrats gaining two Senate seats and the GOP picking up fourteen seats in the House, not enough for the ideological majority Reagan had asked for in the campaign's final days.

Furthermore, most political analysts agreed, and exit polling confirmed, that Reagan's landslide was largely a personal victory with little precise policy mandate or clear ideological underpinning. In the Senate contest, Representatives Paul Simon of Illinois and Tom Harkin of Iowa, Democrats who boasted solid records on arms control, were able to defeat incumbent Republicans who strongly supported Reagan's nuclear arms policies. And in the House, most of the representatives who made up the informal arms control bloc—such as Les AuCoin, Bob Edgar (D-PA.), Bruce Morrison (D-CT.) and George Brown Jr.—survived Reagan's massive victory and won reelection, many in spite of strong and well-financed opponents who had clutched Reagan's coattails. Every one of the forty-five incumbents with 100 percent SANE voting records were returned to office, and fourteen of the seventeen incubments who received SANE PAC staff and substantial financial support won ree-lection. Overall, of the 167 House and Senate candidates endorsed by SANE PAC, 106 won.

Despite the fact that the continuation of Reagan's policies was now a sobering reality for the peace and justice movement, activists found solace in the fact that they would not be without allies in Congress. SANE and other disarmament organizations cited their ability to raise more funds and motivate a substantial number of volunteers as a sign of the ever growing political sophistication of the movement. "The peace movement emerged as a mature and effective force in American politics this election," declared SANE PAC's director Michael Mawby. "Members of Congress who take leadership positions on peace issues now know that there is a growing movement behind them."[24]

SANE PAC raised $250,000 for this election, five times the amount raised for the 1982 congressional elections. The Council for a Livable World and its affiliate Peace PAC raised slightly over $1 million for pro-arms control candidates—just about double the amount it raised in 1982; and Freeze Voter 84 raised over $2.6 million, signed up 1,000 full-time volunteers, and fielded a paid staff of close to 200. Further-more, this organizational clout gave the movement a political base to build on in anticipation of the off-year elections in 1986 when peace activists declared that they would have a good shot at ousting up to twenty-two senators opposed to the nuclear freeze.[25]

Following his victory, Senator-elect Simon noted the movement's contribution to his campaign and a spokesperson for the Harkin cam-paign also cited a "very active peace constituency" as one reason for the new Iowa senator's victory. The campaign manager for Represent-ative Les AuCoin, a leading MX opponent who won a tough reelection fight, maintained that "staff support from the peace movement had a major impact on the outcome of the race" and was later quoted by SANE as stating, "we'd be packing our bags if it weren't for the peace movement support we got."[26]

There remains, however, the hard reality that the arms control issue—as a paramount concern—never took off on its own and that the move-ment was just not able to push the arms race to the center stage in the national political debate. Perhaps it was unrealistic to expect such an outcome, for the movement, though certainly making dramatic gains over the last four years, was not nearly strong enough yet to yield much political clout in halting a forty-year-old nuclear arms race. For SANE's executive director Cortright, the movement's ability to channel national policies in a more rational direction lay in the strength of its numbers. To this end, SANE had already initiated a massive membership recruitment drive, which by December 1984 resulted in over 100,000 paid-up members—a tripling of SANE's membership in just eighteen months. At the same time, the activist network of citizens who had committed their time and energies to stopping the arms race in SANE's Rapid Response Network had increased sixfold in that same eighteen months to 36,000. This increase was so encouraging that, over the next five years SANE envisioned the creation of a permanent, large-scale, American peace movement of more than one million members that would be able to effectively influence U.S. arms control and defense policies.[27]

While participating in the Nuclear Weapons Freeze Campaign's Fifth National Conference in St. Louis on December 7–9, SANE announced its 1985 agenda which included the continuation of its Arms Control Computer Network, expanded and more comprehensive leadership training sessions and educational campaigns, and a legislative strategy focused on a major campaign to halt nuclear testing as a first step toward implementing the nuclear freeze. The agenda also included plans to finally defeat the MX, to block the administration's "Star Wars" initiatives, and to end U.S. military intervention in Central America. At the same time, the committee declared that it would take a leading role in organizing a broad coalition of peace, labor, church, and civil rights organizations in direct action protest events for peace, jobs, and justice to take place in Washington, D.C., in April 1985 and that it would initiate a project to urge the U.S. government to establish an Endowment for Peace by the end of the decade. The proposed endowment would have four chief goals: nuclear disarmament, improved U.S.-Soviet relations, peaceful resolutions of international conflicts, and conversion from a military to a civilian economy.[28]

On January 3, 1985, major citizen peace organizations including SANE released a statement welcoming the resumption of talks between the United States and the Soviet Union and urging that the following objectives be achieved through the negotiations: an agreement not to undercut existing arms control treaties; a ban on extending the arms race into space; a halt to testing nuclear weapons; a freeze on testing, production, and deployment of nuclear weapons systems; and deep reductions in the existing arsenals of nuclear weapons. The statement also included interim steps that could be taken immediately as a way of working towards these objectives including a reaffirmation of current arms agreements, such as the ABM Treaty of 1972; the continuation of the moratorium on ASAT (anti-satellite) weapons testing; and a suspension of nuclear testing. When the talks opened on March 12, leaders of major international peace organizations—SANE (USA), The Campaign for Nuclear Disarmament (United Kingdom), The Green Party (West Germany), and the Inter-Church Peace Council (Holland)—met with representatives of the U.S. and Soviet delegations in Geneva to set forth their comprehensive strategy for arms reduction.[29]

In 1963, SANE was in the forefront of successful fight to ban atmospheric nuclear testing when the United States and Soviet Union signed the Limited Test Ban Treaty. It therefore seemed appropriate that two decades later SANE, along with several other arms control and disarmament groups, would return to its original concern and help spearhead a new effort to halt all nuclear tests as a meaningful, attainable, and verifiable step towards ending the nuclear arms race. Although none of the weapons currently being build or deployed would be stopped, SANE declared that a Comprehensive Test Ban Treaty would severely limit new technical improvements, would bar development of some of the new "Star Wars" technology, and would gradually reduce confidence in existing nuclear stockpiles to the point that over several years, neither side would be sure their weapons still worked. According to the committee, over 900 nuclear weapons tests have taken place worldwide since 1963 and represent the driving force behind the arms race. "By taking the long overdue step of stopping them now," SANE contended, "part of the nuclear freeze would be in place, U.S.—Soviet tensions would be reduced, and a real foundation would have been set on which to achieve a comprehensive freeze and reductions in nuclear weapons."[30]

The fortieth anniversary of Hiroshima Day, August 6, 1985, was appropriately set aside by SANE and other peace groups throughout the country for a solemn commemoration of the first use of nuclear weapons, as well as a time to focus on the dangers of U.S. and Soviet current nuclear policy. SANE members throughout the country participated in numerous events that highlighted the need for a comprehensive end to the arms race by pushing for a halt to all nuclear weapons testing. When the Geneva summit meeting between President Reagan and Soviet General Secretary Mikhail Gorbachev opened in November, 1985, SANE board member Jesse Jackson, on behalf of SANE, the Nuclear Weapons Freeze Campaign, and other peace organizations, presented the two world leaders a nationwide petition with over one million signatures urging an end to nuclear testing and the reversal of the nuclear arms race.[31]

Since World War II, the American peace movement has developed, according to historian Lawrence Wittner, a political as well as a moral relevance and in the process has generated new assumptions, a higher level of effectiveness, and a greater maturity.[32] The history of the National Committee for a Sane Nuclear policy has confirmed this analysis. SANE was a new kind of peace organization which sprang into existence simultaneously in the United States and abroad around 1957–1958. As "survivalists" concerned with the immediate problem of avoiding nuclear war and ensuring the continuation of the human race, individuals involved in organizations like SANE gave new hope and meaning to citizen action for peace and provided a needed respite from the McCarthyite insistence on political uniformity. The intense nuclear arms competition and the almost continuous atmosphere of crisis, which characterized the period when these groups began, created a sense of urgency and immediacy which was not being met fully by older pacifist and world order organizations.

The fact that SANE was dealing in a direct, pragmatic, and political way with immediate issues ensured a membership of concerned, aware, and active people. Not even Senator Dodd's accusations in 1960 of Communist infiltration in the nuclear test ban movement could greatly diminish the fervor that energized peace liberalism in this period. The same sensitivity to political currents has also meant, however, periodic exhaustion of interest, energies, and funds after a particular crisis had been met. Thus, after SANE's and the world's greatest arms control triumph to date, the signing and ratification of the 1963 partial Nuclear Test Ban Treaty, the tide of peace activism began to wane.

In the period of detente that followed, SANE saw its task as being constructive advocacy rather than unrelieved protest. SANE liberals believed that the initiatives for peace belonged in the hands of those groups which were willing to do the difficult, day-to-day job of public education and the slow task of building political power within the establishment, in order to generate the necessary mandate to implement policies which had been accepted. Therefore, when Lyndon Johnson assumed the mantle of peace candidate in the 1964 election, many peace activists in SANE and other peace groups rallied to his campaign.

Then came Vietnam, which shattered the liberal consensus, polarized the country, and radicalized many peace liberals in the process. Peace liberals in SANE were put on the defensive and vilified as the enemy by a government that deeply resented their criticisms as well as by a more militant wing of the antiwar movement that was offended by their unwillingness to work with radicals and by their timidity in attacking America's interventionist policies. Unwilling to make a frontal assault against the central premise of Cold War liberalism in regards to nuclear war, or against the unjust and unnecessary war in Vietnam, SANE reluctantly was forced to relinquish a leadership role in the antiwar movement. Peace liberals regrouped, however, under the banner of responsible protest and found alternatives to radicalism under Democratic presidential candidates Eugene McCarthy in 1968 and later George McGovern in 1972. Although antiwar groups exhibited remarkable political strength in both campaigns, they did not manage to capture the presidency. Only after a barrage of antiwar activity in the streets, on the campuses, and later in the Congress, was President Nixon forced to bring American troops home and arrange a "peace" settlement. In the process, however, antiwar activities and sentiment declined substantially, and SANE nearly collapsed.

Although the anti-nuclear emphasis of the peace movement had been derailed by Soviet-American detente and by the fierce struggle over the Vietnam War, what Norman Cousins called the "nightmare of nuclear war" remained as possible as ever. Due in large part to the efforts and concern of peace liberals like Cousins, Benjamin Spock, Sanford Gottlieb, and David Cortright, the issue was not allowed to lie completely dormant. Thus, when Ronald Reagan assumed the presidency in 1981 and immediately commenced the largest military buildup in our history, the nuclear disarmament movement and groups like SANE flourished once again.

Ever more importantly, the movement that germinated in the early 1980s, through the leadership of groups like SANE, had learned some important lessons from the recent past and thus were more likely to be successful in the future. The new movement was careful not to give unnecessary offense in its demonstrations and public rallies and accordingly was much more broadly based than the antiwar movement of the 1960s had been. It attracted participation and support from a wide range of new people and organizations not previously involved in the peace movement. SANE and the nuclear disarmament movement of the 1980s not only focused on individual weapons systems like the MX but on the dynamics of the nuclear arms race as a whole. Contemporary liberal peace activists stressed the connections between nuclear deterrence and an interventionist foreign policy and between the nuclear weapons budget, the federal deficit, and unemployment; this in the belief that the more the public understood about the causes and the consequences of the nuclear arms race the faster they would be able to stop it. The present movement is also less naively optimistic than the antiwar movement of the 1960s, realizing the necessity of long-term solutions and fully cognizant of the resiliency of conservative elites deeply committed to "winning" the arms race and the struggle for global supremacy. As Randall Forsberg stated in her keynote address to the December 1984 National Conference of the Nuclear Freeze Campaign, "Our goal of a more stable world in which peace has a footing more secure than the need to avoid a nuclear holocaust will be better served if we directly confront the superpowers' Cold War imperialistic policies."[33]

Although SANE and the nuclear disarmament movement have energized substantial numbers of committed people as in the late 1950s and early 1960s, measuring its progress is a difficult matter. As Randall Kehler, national coordinator of the Nuclear Weapons Freeze Campaign, pointed out, if we use as our gauge the actual number of nuclear weapons that have been cancelled by either nuclear superpower, it would appear there has been no progress at all. In fact, by this measurement the movement slipped backwards, as recently we have seen a massive buildup of nuclear weapons on both sides. But perhaps this is an unrealistic and inappropriate way to measure the movement's progress. If it is assumed that the U.S. government will become committed to pursuing a mutual freeze and other steps towards nuclear disarmament only when enough pressure has been brought to bear and if it is understood that such pressure can only be mounted after there has been a demonstrated shift in public consciousness, then there is no doubt that the movement's progress has been substantial.[34]

In 1984, the nuclear freeze became an important election issue as seven of eight Democratic presidential contenders endorsed it publicly, and it certainly played a key role in several congressional campaigns. A recent public opinion poll by the right wing Committee on the Present Danger revealed that almost everyone had indeed heard of the freeze and that nearly 80 percent approved of it. Even more importantly, a national study conducted by the Public Agenda Foundation to probe attitudes towards nuclear arms reported "that Americans have come to believe that nuclear war is unwinnable and unsurvivable" and that for the average American "the danger (of nuclear war) is real and immediate—far more so than among elites and experts." Daniel Yankelovich and John Doble of the Public Agenda Foundation concluded from this study that "the American electorate is now psychologically prepared to take a giant step toward real arms reductions" and that "the public finds the long-term risks of continuing the way we are going simply unacceptable."[35]

Translating public opinion into concrete and substantial steps towards nuclear disarmament is another matter, however, and despite their unprecedented scope and progress, SANE and like-minded groups have yet to exhibit sustained influence on U.S. foreign and military policy. As Charles DeBenedetti has pointed out, "The peace movement stands as a minority reform in America because it constitutes a subculture opposed to the country's dominant power culture and power realities." And yet, SANE and the liberal nuclear disarmament movement have had and still have importance. SANE exists principally because it functions as a foreign policy opposition group (that is, partly what the old political parties used to do in the days before "bipartisanship") in a country where democratic debate does not like to range often into foreign policy matters. The organization's role has been to articulate foreign policy alternatives of the kind that U.S. ruling authorities decline to propose. Traditionally that was the job of the opposition party. But, for any number of reasons, neither the Republican nor the Democratic parties assume the oppositional role that is needed in Cold War society; and therefore, SANE has been improvised by foreign policy liberals to fill in the space.[36]

SANE's work is also significant, for over the years it has helped to establish a climate of opinion in which governmental decisions are made. On the national level liberal peace activists in SANE and other organizations disseminate information Congress needs to make key policy decisions. And on the community level their literature and representatives alert citizens to critical military and economically related issues and organize them into action in the political process. They also have earned the respect of influential policy makers as they are being perceived by foreign policy elites in the State Department and Congress as becoming increasingly sophisticated in their assessment of the dangers of the nuclear arms race. Indeed, as Lawrence Wittner recently wrote, although peace sentiment has remained a minority impulse throughout American history, "the popularity and resilience of the peace movement may indicate that peace is gradually becoming a more realistic option than war."[37]

But movements whose ultimate success is vital to the survival of the human race need to try to be truthful about their limitations in practice as well as their potential for the future. Throughout its history, SANE has functioned on the cutting edge of current issues of public concern, and its story lends insight into the evolution and importance of liberal peace movements in American history. For over a quarter of a century the committee has evolved into the nation's largest peace membership organization that has left its elitist and exclusionist policies far behind. Far from eschewing mass action, it now actively encourages citizen action and grass-roots activism. At the same time, these peace liberals have retained their basic belief in democracy and in the common sense and goodwill of the American people, working through the system, placing communication and dialogue with the public and the power structure at the center of their approach. Reflecting these liberal assumptions about how American politics works, SANE's strategy and tactics, though limited by their own parameters and having only minimal effect in influencing government policy, have helped to legitimize the anti-nuclear protest and thereby to enlarge the area of accepted political action. Its greatest challenge remains, however, in translating its energy and resources into power that can win at the polls and sustaining a movement that flourishes beyond the times when it appears to be needed the most—during the atmospheric testing debate, the Vietnam War, and Reagan's military buildup. It is a political as well as a moral imperative that liberal peace activists become even more unrelenting in working to transform these immediate issues into long-range policy alternatives, including a comprehensive approach to stopping the nuclear arms race.

With conservatism, increased militarism, and a combative Cold War posture the dominant strains in American politics today, it is also essential that nuclear disarmament organizations like SANE maintain their momentum, deepen their analysis, and articulate their criticisms more forcefully. The concern with nuclear weapons and with peace must become more integrated within a larger movement which can construct a true basis for real national "security." The elimination of nuclear arsenals would mean the reversal of a pattern of human behavior—the search for security in better weapons—that is as old as recorded history. It is therefore necessary that the movement continue to sharpen its debate concerning broad and difficult questions of how society could be transformed to a point where renouncing nuclear weapons has the possibility to be taken up as a realistic and desirable objective by a majority of the American people. Only then will the government be forced to consider SANE's foreign policy prescriptions as an integral part of U.S. nuclear policy.

To build upon its considerable success in changing public opinion and attitudes, it is also fundamental that nuclear arms control organizations like SANE come to the realization that no irreversible progress is likely without major institutional reforms to loosen the grip of the military-industrial complex on U.S. security policy. As Christopher Paine emphasized in the fortieth anniversary issue of the *Bulletin of Atomic Scientists*;

New laws are needed: to increase congressional control over the military budget; to drastically curb official secrecy; to limit contractor campaign contributions; to lock the revolving door between Pentagon and its contractors; and to withdraw from the defense industry the task of evaluating new weapons systems.

Although this certainly presents a formidable task for the American peace movement, such legislation is essential to any long-run strategy to end the nuclear arms race, contends Paine, and to reduce the threat of nuclear war.[38]

Finally, nuclear disarmament activists in SANE and other organizations must come to grips with the irony of a rapidly accelerating nuclear arms race occurring in the midst of the nuclear disarmament revival of the 1980s. It has become increasingly clear that the cultivation of public anxieties and fears about nuclear weapons is an inadequate strategy for reversing the arms race. Whatever repugnance can be evoked toward these weapons, if a greater concern can be raised about enemy capabilities and intentions, that will determine arms policy. At the same time, ''arms control'' can be incorporated into the rhythms of a burgeoning arms race. In the past new weapons systems were brought into development as ''bargaining chips'' in the arms control process. Now, in a far more audacious move, the Reagan Administration lays claim to being the true nuclear disarmers. The Strategic Defense Initiative is offered as the realistic pathway to a world in which nuclear weapons have been rendered impotent. This poses a very different challenge for SANE and other nuclear disarmament groups. In the past they simply offered an alternative vision to the Pentagon's version of peace and security. Now that the Pentagon seeks to move into the "disarming" of nuclear weapons via Star Wars, SANE will have to persuade anew that the only real hope for genuine peace and security lies in "beating swords into plowshares."[39]

Twenty-eight years after the committee's first advertisement, the world is still "facing a danger unlike any danger that has ever existed."[40] Sane and realistic, liberal nuclear pacifists have persevered in their effort to realize their ideals of real security, peace, and justice in a world careening toward nuclear disaster. In spite of its failure thus far to steer this nation on a course of nuclear sanity and peace, SANE remains fervently committed to fulfilling its historic goal of creating a conscious public awareness of nuclear disarmament as the only alternative open to humankind if it is likely to overcome its own obsolescence and have a long-term future. At a time when many historians and political analysts are hastily proclaiming the exhaustion of liberalism, peace activists in SANE, the Nuclear Freeze Campaign, and similar organizations continue to work together and to struggle against the Cold War neoconservative tide. By their efforts, they continue to affirm the possibilities of liberal peace activism in contemporary America. Four decades after the first nuclear bomb was dropped on Hiroshima, we are just beginning to come to terms with the reality that sanity and survival in the nuclear age are essential human concerns that transcend all our differences. Perhaps now is the time to consider reviving the "Ban the Bomb" slogan of the late 1950s and early 1960s, moving beyond the goal of the nuclear freeze to that of the total abolition of all nuclear weapons. As Jonathan Schell has written, no less than the fate of the earth is hanging in the balance.[41]

Notes

PREFACE

1. Dwight D. Eisenhower, Statement to Prime Minister Harold Macmillan, British Broadcasting System television interview, August 3, 1959.

2. "Giving Peace a Chance," *Newsweek* 100 (June 21, 1982): 40; *New York Times*, November 15, 1957, p. 54.

3. Donald Keys, "What Is Sane to You?" *SANE World* 5 (June 1966): 4. See also Homer Jack, "What SANE Is and Is Not," *SANE World* 1 (December 15, 1962): 2.

4. Norman Cousins to Trevor Thomas, June 13, 1958, National Committee for a Sane Nuclear Policy Manuscripts, Swarthmore College Peace Collection, Swarthmore, Pennsylvania, Document Group 58, Series B (Hereafter cited as SANE MSS); Charles DeBenedetti, *The Peace Reform in American History* (Bloomington: Indiana University Press, 1980), p. 163.

5. DeBenedetti, *The Peace Reform*, p. 199; Minutes of the Organizing Committee of SANE, October 1, 1957, SANE MSS, Series A.

CHAPTER 1

1. Lewis Mumford, "Gentlemen: You are Mad!" *Saturday Review* 24 (March 2, 1946): 5, 6.

2. Norman Cousins, *Modern Man Is Obsolete* (New York: Viking Press, 1945), p. 10.

3. Lawrence Wittner, *Rebels Against War: The American Peace Movement,*

1933–1983 (Philadelphia: Temple University Press, 1984), p. 139; Cousins, *Modern Man Is Obsolete*, pp. 20, 23.

4. *New York Times*, October 17, 1945, p. 4.

5. Norman Cousins, "Report From Oslo," *Saturday Review* 50 (August 26, 1967): 22, 42. The standard work in this field is Grenville Clark and Louis B. Sohn, *World Peace Through World Law* (Cambridge: Harvard University Press, 1968).

6. Dexter Perkins, *The American Approach to Foreign Policy* (Cambridge: Harvard University Press, 1952), p. 113; Jon Yoder, "United World Federalists: Liberals For Law and Order," in Charles Chatfield, ed., *Peace Movements in America* (New York: Schocken Books, 1973), p. 79.

7. Yoder, "United World Federalists," p. 100.

8. *New York Times*, February 23, 1947, p. 25 and February 24, 1947, p. 3.

9. *New York Times*, November 15, 1948, p. 17 and April 4, 1948, sec. IV, p. 8.

10. *U.S. Congressional Record*, 80th Cong., 1st sess., 1947, 93, part 7: 8506; *New York Times*, June 10, 1949, p. 3.

11. "The Atomic Scientists of Chicago," and "The National Organizations of Scientists," *Bulletin of Atomic Scientists* 1 (December 10, 1945): 1, 2.

12. *New York Times*, December 11, 1945, p. 15.

13. Wittner, *Rebels Against War*, p. 150; Roy Finch, "The New Peace Movement," part 2, *Dissent* 15 (Spring 1963): 138.

14. Wittner, *Rebels Against War*, p. 174.

15. Ibid, p. 175.

16. Eugene Rabinowitch, "Five Years After," *Bulletin of Atomic Scientists* 7 (January 1951): 3; "Council of Federation of American Scientists Meets," *Bulletin of Atomic Scientists* 1 (May 1, 1946): 16; Albert Einstein, "The Real Problem is in the Hearts of Men," *New York Times Magazine* (June 23, 1946): 7.

17. Otto Nathan and Heinz Norden, eds., *Einstein on Peace* (New York: Simon and Schuster, 1960), p. 380.

18. Ibid., pp. 410–411, 471–472, 481.

19. A.J. Muste to Albert Einstein, May 28, 1946; Einstein to Muste, November 4, 1946; Leo Szilard to Muste, December 18, 1946, quoted in Wittner, *Rebels Against War*, pp. 176–177.

20. Albert Einstein to A.J. Muste, November 4, 1946, and Leo Szilard to A.J. Muste, December 18, 1946, quoted in Nathan and Norden, *Einstein on Peace*, pp. 175, 176.

21. Norman Cousins, *Who Speaks For Man?* (New York: The MacMillan Co., 1953), p. 25; Rabinowitch, "Five Years After," p. 3.

22. Norman Cousins and Thomas Finletter, "A Beginning For Sanity," *Bulletin of Atomic Scientists* 2 (July 1, 1946): 11–14; Wittner, *Rebels Against War*, p. 169.

23. Robert Gilpin, *American Scientists and Nuclear Weapons' Policy* (Princeton: Princeton University Press, 1962), pp. 35, 64–73.

24. Ralph E. Lapp, *Kill and Overkill: The Strategy of Annihilation* (New York: Basic Books, Inc., 1962), pp. 19, 20.

25. Nathan and Norden, *Einstein on Peace*, pp. 504–505, 557–558; Rabinowitch, "Five Years After," p. 4.

26. Wittner, *Rebels Against War*, pp. 201, 210.

27. *New York Times*, March 30, 1967, p. 30.

28. See Harry Kalven, Jr., "The Case of J. Robert Oppenheimer Before the Atomic Energy Commission," *Bulletin of Atomic Scientists* 10 (September 1954) in Morton Grodzins and Eugene Rabinowitch, eds., *The Atomic Age: Scientists in National and World Affairs* (New York: Basic Books, Inc., 1963), pp. 442–465; Albert Einstein's Letter to the Editor, *Reporter* 11 (November 18, 1954): 8.

29. Yoder, "United World Federalists," p. 106; Wittner, *Rebels Against War*, pp. 222, 223.

30. "The Myth That Threatened One American Town," *The Federalist* 3 (April 1953): 8–10.

31. Norman Cousins, "The Climate of Freedom," *Saturday Review* 35 (December 13, 1952): 22.

32. Ibid.; Norman Cousins, "No," *Saturday Review* 33 (October 7, 1950): 28, 29.

33. Norman Cousins, "Worse Than The H-Bomb," *Saturday Review* 35 (December 13, 1952): 20.

34. Norman Thomas to A.J. Muste, January 15, 1951, and A.J. Muste to Norman Thomas, February 19, 1951, quoted in Wittner, *Rebels Against War*, p. 224.

35. DeBenedetti, *The Peace Reform In American History*, p. 151; I.F. Stone, "First Call For A Test Ban," *I.F. Stone's Weekly* (November 1, 1954): 1.

36. Robert A. Divine, *Blowing On The Wind: The Nuclear Test Ban Debate, 1954–1960* (New York: Oxford University Press, 1978), pp. 32, 33, 34.

37. *New York Times*, July 10, 1955, p. 1.

38. Divine, *Blowing On The Wind*, pp. 59, 66.

39. Ibid., pp. 72, 84–112. Stevenson officially thanked Norman Cousins for his help in reference to nuclear testing in a letter December 15, 1956. Walter Johnson, ed., *The Papers of Adlai Stevenson* (Little, Brown, & Co., 1976), 6: 346.

40. Norman Cousins, Interview, July 25, 1983; Norman Cousins, *Present Tense: An American Editor's Odyssey* (New York: McGraw-Hill, 1967), p. 266.

41. Norman Cousins, *Dr. Schweitzer of Lambaréné* (New York: Harper and Row, 1960), pp. 18, 130, 165, 173.

42. *New York Times*, April 24, 1957, p. 1.; and *Saturday Review* 40 (May 18, 1957): 13.

43. *New York Times*, April 26, 1957, p. 4.

44. *Time* 69 (May 6, 1957): 24; *New York Times*, April 26, 28, 1957; *Bulletin of Atomic Scientists* 13 (June 1957): 201, 206–207, quoted in Divine, *Blowing On The Wind*, pp. 122–123.

45. Linus Pauling, Interview, February 9, 1983; Linus Pauling, *No More War* (New York: Dodd, Mead, and Co., 1958), pp. 160–178.

46. *New York Times*, June 4, 1957, p. 17.

47. Divine, *Blowing On The Wind*, pp. 129–137.

48. Eugene J. Rosi, "Mass and Attentive Opinion on Nuclear Weapons Tests and Fallout, 1954–1963," *Public Opinion Quarterly* 29 (Summer 1965): 283–290; and *Newsweek* 49 (May 6, 1957): 51–58.

49. Cousins, *Present Tense*, p. 60; Cousins, Interview.

50. Norman Cousins, "The Great Debate Opens," *Saturday Review* 40 (June 5, 1957): 24; Divine, *Blowing On The Wind*, pp. 140–141.

51. Divine, *Blowing On The Wind*, p. 141.

52. Norman Cousins, "The Debate Is Over," *Saturday Review* 42 (April 4, 1959): 25.

CHAPTER 2

1. Sir Charles (C.P.) Snow, Speaking to the American Association for the Advancement of Science, New York, December 26, 1960.

2. Robert Gilmore, Interview, October 13, 1971; Lawrence Scott, "Memo-One—Shared Thinking," April 30, 1957, SANE MSS, Series A.

3. Lawrence Scott, Interview, September 24, 1971; Scott, "Memo-One—Shared Thinking."

4. Scott, "Memo-One—Shared Thinking."

5. Lawrence Scott, "Meeting of Initiating Committee," May 29, 1957, SANE MSS, Series A.

6. Minutes of the Committee to Stop Nuclear Tests, June 21, 1957, SANE MSS, Series A.

7. Ibid.

8. Divine, *Blowing On The Wind*, p. 166; Cousins, Interview.

9. Minutes of the Provisional Committee to Stop Nuclear Tests, September 24, 1957, SANE MSS, Series A.

10. Catherine Cory to Norman Cousins and Clarence Pickett, September 20, 1957, SANE MSS, Series B.

11. Ibid.; Minutes of the Provisional Committee to Stop Nuclear Tests, September 24, 1957, SANE MSS, Series A.

12. Erich Fromm to Norman Cousins, October 27, 1957, SANE MSS, Series B.

13. Minutes of the Organizing Committee, October 8, 1957, SANE MSS,

Series A; Minutes of the Executive Committee, December 2, 1957, SANE MSS, Series A.

14. Minutes of Organizing Committee, October 1, 1957, SANE MSS, Series A.

15. *New York Times*, November 15, 1957, p. 54.

16. Divine, *Blowing On The Wind*, pp. 167, 168; Advertisement No. 1, SANE MSS, Series A.

17. Arlo Hurth, "Response to the First Statement Issued by the National Committee for a Sane Nuclear Policy: November 15-December 31, 1957," January 1958, SANE MSS, Series A.

18. Ibid.

19. Trevor Thomas to the Editors of *Time* Magazine, April 30, 1958, SANE MSS, Series A.

20. Hurth, "Response to the First Statement Issued by SANE"; Sanford Gottlieb, "National Committee for a Sane Nuclear Policy," *New University Thought* 2, (Spring 1962): 156.

21. Nathan Glazer, "The Peace Movement in America," *Commentary* 31 (April 1961): 290.

22. Hurth, "Response to the First Statement Issued by SANE." SANE's membership was unrepresentative of the country as a whole in other ways also. In the beginning, at least, its membership was categorized as upper-middle class, professional and semi-professional, white collar, Protestant and Jewish, and white. Sanford Gottlieb, Interview, January 8, 1972.

23. Memorandum of conference with Hubert Humphrey, January 11, 1958; Memorandum of telephone conversation between Trevor Thomas and Thomas Hughes, January 30, 1958, SANE MSS, Series B.; *New York Times*, February 19, 1958, p. 26.

24. *New York Herald American*, March 24, 1958, p. 9; Bill Attwood to Norman Cousins, April 4, 1958; Lewis Mumford to Trevor Thomas, March 10, 1958, SANE MSS, Series B.

25. Norman Cousins, "Neither Suicide, Nor Surrender," *Saturday Review* 41 (April 12, 1958): 26; Norman Cousins, "Double Disaster," *Saturday Review* 41 (April 19, 1958): 26, 58; *New York Times*, April 11, 1958, p. 15.

26. Cousins, "Neither Suicide, Nor Surrender," p. 26; *New York Times*, April 18, 1958, p. 32.

27. "How Sane the SANE?" *Time* 71 (April 21, 1958): 13, 14; George H. Gallup, *The Gallup Poll: Public Opinion, 1935–1971* (New York: Random House, 1972), pp. 1541, 1552–53; Eugene J. Rossi, "Mass and Attentive Opinion on Nuclear Weapons Tests and Fallout, 1954–1963," *Public Opinion Quarterly* 29 (Summer 1965): pp. 280–297; Divine, *Blowing On The Wind*, p. 205.

28. Minutes of the Executive Committee, June 8, 1958; Clarence Pickett and Norman Cousins to Dwight D. Eisenhower, August 22, 1958, General

File, White House Central Files, Dwight D. Eisenhower Library, Abilene, Kansas; Minutes of the First National Conference, September 29, 1958, SANE MSS, Series A.

29. Wittner, *Rebels Against War*, p. 253.

30. Minutes of the First National Conference.

31. For CND's history and relationship to SANE, see Frank E. Myers, "The Failure of Protest Against Postwar British Defense Policy," in Solomon Wank, ed., *Doves and Diplomats: Foreign Offices and Peace Movements in Europe and America in the Twentieth Century* (Westport, Conn: Greenwood Press, 1978), p. 243.

32. *New York Times*, October 31, 1958, p. 21.

33. Divine, *Blowing On The Wind*, p. 239; Dwight Eisenhower, *Waging Peace*, quoted in Charles Alexander, *Holding the Line in the Eisenhower Era, 1952–1961* (Bloomington: Indiana University Press, 1976), p. 209.

34. *New York Times*, February 13, 1959, p. 15.

35. "Time to Act For Sanity," *SANE-USA* 2 (March 1959): 1.

36. *New York Times*, March 29, 1959, p. 16.

37. Sanford Gottlieb to Donald Keys, March 24, 1959, SANE MSS, Series B; Dan Wakefield, "Beached on 42nd St," *Nation* 188 (April 25, 1959): 357–359; *SANE-USA* 2 (May, 1959): 2.

38. *New York Times*, April 28, 1959, p. 34; Norman Cousins, "The Debate Is Over," *Saturday Review* 42 (April 4, 1959): 26; Norman Cousins, "Science and Moral Illiteracy," *Saturday Review* 42 (May 2, 1959): 28.

39. Divine, *Blowing On The Wind*, pp. 275, 276; "Report on Fallout Hearings," *SANE-USA* 2 (September 1959): 4, 6.

40. *New York Times*, August 13, 1959, p. 17.

41. "Nuclear Test Moratorium Continued," *SANE-USA* 2 (September 1959): 1.

42. Minutes of the Second National Conference, October 25, 26, SANE MSS, Series A. *New York Times*, February 8, 1960, p. 10; George Gallup, *Gallup Poll*, p. 1643; Divine, *Blowing On The Wind*, p. 291.

43. Lists of Sponsors, SANE MSS, Series A.

44. Minutes of the Second National Conference.

45. *New York Times*, October 20, 1959, p. 45; Steve Allen to author, May 28, 1982; Max Youngstein, Interview, April 6, 1984.

46. Michael Arons, "On The Campus," *SANE-USA* 2 (March 1959): 2.

47. H. Stuart Hughes, Interview, January 7, 1972; I.F. Stone, "Peace is Becoming Respectable," *I.F. Stone's Weekly* (October 5, 1959): 1.

48. *U.S. Congressional Record*, Senate, June 5, 1985, p. 9055; Donald Keys, "Parameters of an American Peace Movement," 1963, p. 6, SANE MSS, Series A; Divine, *Blowing On The Wind*, p. 212; Minutes of the Second National Conference.

CHAPTER 3

1. Senator Thomas J. Dodd, U.S. Congress, Senate Internal Security Sub-committee of the Committee of the Judiciary, *Communist Infiltration in the Nuclear Test Ban Movement*, 86th Cong., 2nd sess., 1960, part 1: 39.

2. For a review of the rally, see "The Other Summit Conference," *Nation* 190 (June 4, 1960): 482; Glazer, "The Peace Movement in America," p. 290.

3. Dodd, U.S. Congress, p. 39.

4. Scott, "Memo-One—Shared Thinking."

5. Norman Cousins to Trevor Thomas, June 13, 1958, SANE MSS, Series B.

6. Trevor Thomas to Norman Cousins, June 19, 1958, SANE MSS, Series B.

7. FBI, Office Memorandum, July 30, 1958, SAC to Director, FBI File, National SANE Office, Washington, D.C.

8. Norman Thomas to Norman Cousins, January 11, 1960, Norman Thomas Collection, New York Public Library, New York City (Hereafter cited as Thomas MSS); Norman Cousins to Edmund C. Berkeley, June 30, 1960, SANE MSS, Series B; Minutes of the National Board Meeting, January 20, 1960, SANE MSS, Series A.

9. Norman Cousins to Donald Keys and Norman Thomas, January 25, 1960, SANE MSS, Series B.

10. A.J. Muste, "The Crisis in SANE, *Liberation* 5 (July-August 1960): 10; *New York Times*, October 13, 1960, p. 11.

11. Norman Cousins, Interview, January 6, 1972; Steve Abrams, Interview, June 14, 1982; Dori Loewi, Letter to the author, June 23, 1982.

12. Cousins, Interview; *U.S. Congressional Record*, Senate, May 25, 1960, p. 10237; *New York Times*, May 26, 1960, p. 11.

13. Cousins, Interview.

14. Barbara Deming, "The Ordeal of SANE," *Nation* 192 (March 11, 1961): 201; *New York Times*, May 26, 1960, p. 11; Norman Cousins to Edmund C. Berkeley, June 30, 1960.

15. Minutes of the National Board Meeting, May 26, 1960, SANE MSS, Series A.

16. "Standards for SANE Leadership," May 26, 1960, SANE MSS, Series A; "Implementation of the May 26 Policy Statement," July 29, 1960, SANE MSS, Series A.

17. Donald Keys, Executive Director to the Committee, May 27, 1960, SANE MSS, Series A; Norman Cousins and Clarence Pickett to all local Committee Chairmen, July 29, 1960, SANE MSS, Series A.

18. "Implementation of the May 26 Policy Statement."

19. Walter Lear to Dear Friend, November 14, 1960, SANE MSS, Series

A; Sanford Gottlieb to Norman Cousins, October 18, 1960, SANE MSS, Series A; Walter Lear, Interview, June 20, 1983.

20. Lear, Interview.

21. See U.S. Congress, Senate Internal Security Subcommittee on the Judiciary, Testimony of Linus Pauling, 86th Cong., 2nd sess., June 21, 1960, Part 1, pp. 1–360; and *Report on the Hearing of Dr. Linus Pauling*, 87th Cong., 1st sess., 1961, pp. 1–60, National Committee to all local committees about the case of Linus Pauling, n.d., SANE MSS, Series A. At the hearing on August 9 and again on October 11, Pauling refused to turn over the information the subcommittee had requested. The committee changed their position accordingly and he was not cited for contempt.

22. Letter to the Editor from Norman Cousins, *Liberation* 5 (December 1960): 3; Norman Cousins to Edmund Berkeley, June 30, 1960; Walter Lear to Dear Friend, September 29, 1960, SANE MSS, Series A.

23. Policy Statement from National SANE, September 29, 1960, SANE MSS, Series A.

24. Policy Statement from National SANE, October 24, 1960, SANE MSS, Series A; Edward Meyerling to Steve Allen, November 1, 1960, SANE MSS, Series B.

25. See *U.S. Congressional Record*, Senate, March 8, 1961, pp. 3465–3466.

26. *New York Times*, March 9, 1961, p. 17; U.S. Congress, Senate, Internal Security Subcommittee on the Judiciary, *Communist Infiltration of the Nuclear Test Ban Movement*, 87th Cong., 1st sess., 1961, part 2, pp. 1–150.

27. Statement adopted by the National Board on April 17, 1961, SANE MSS, Series A.

28. See Subcommittee Report, 1960, 1961, parts I and II; Director J. Edgar Hoover to Jack Valenti, special assistant to the president, November 13, 1964, FBI File, National SANE Office, Washington, D.C.

29. Gottlieb, Interview; Donald Keys, Interview, January 5, 1972.

30. Norman Cousins to Edmund Berkeley, Implementation of May 26 Policy Statement, July 29, 1960, SANE MSS, Series B.

31. Statement of Donald Keys, executive director, May 27, 1960, SANE MSS, Series A; Gottlieb, Interview.

32. Gottlieb, Interview; Keys, Interview; Stuart Meacham, Interview with Charles Chatfield, May 7, 1969, loaned to the author; Cousins, Interview.

33. Deming, "The Ordeal of SANE," p. 201; Robert Gilmore to National SANE Board of Directors, June 27, 1960, SANE MSS, Series B; Stewart Meacham to Norman Cousins, October 18, 1960, SANE MSS, Series B.

34. Cousins, Interview; Norman Cousins to Linus Pauling, August 4, 1961, SANE MSS, Series B; Linus Pauling, Interview, February 9, 1983.

35. Robert Gilmore, Stewart Meacham, A.J. Muste, "Right of Dissent Upheld," Letter to the Editor, *New York Times*, July 27, 1960, p. 28.

36. A.J. Muste, "The Crisis in SANE," *Liberation* 5 (July-August 1960): 10–14; and A.J. Muste, "The Crisis in SANE: Act II," *Liberation* 5 (November 1960): 5–8; A.J. Muste to David Riesman, December 21, 1960, A.J. Muste papers, Swarthmore College Peace Collection, DG50, Box 37, "SANE." (Hereafter cited as Muste MSS.)

37. Washington Executive Board to National Committee, n.d., SANE MSS, Series B.

38. Queens Committee to the National Board, n.d., SANE MSS, Series B; E. Russel Stabler to National Board, December 20, 1960, Muste MSS, Box 37.

39. John W. Darr to Board of Directors, September 9, 1960, SANE MSS, Series B; Edmund C. Berkeley to Friends, October 20, 1960, SANE MSS, Series B; Chicago Committee to National Board, September 19, 1960, SANE MSS, Series B. Berkeley wanted Dr. Linus Pauling to lead this movement, but it never did get started.

40. Brooklyn Student Committee to National SANE, n.d., SANE MSS, Series B. There are no records of numbers of students who left SANE at this time; the only indication is that it was a considerable amount. Gottlieb, Interview.

41. Norman Thomas, Letter to the Editor, *Nation*, March 15, 1961, SANE MSS, Series B; Homer Jack to Barbara Deming, February 28, 1961, SANE MSS, Series B; Gottlieb, Interview.

42. Steve Allen to Mortimer Frankel, October 25, 1960, SANE MSS, Series B. Indeed, Allen would not work side by side with a Communist in an organization and consistently defended his anti-Communist position. For instance, see Steve Allen to Ed Meyerling, September 26, 1960, Steve Allen files, Van Nuys, California, and his autobiography, Steve Allen, *Mark It and Strike It* (New York: Holt, Rinehart and Winston, 1960), pp. 406–426.

43. Cousins, Interview; quoted in Deming, "Ordeal of SANE," pp. 202, 203.

44. A.J. Muste to John Swomley, Jr., January 30, 1961, Muste MSS, Box 37; Homer Jack, Interview, January 29, 1972.

45. Muste to Swomley, January 30, 1961.

46. Cousins, Interview; A.J. Muste to John Swomley, January 30, 1961; A.J. Muste to Homer Jack, March 7, 1961, SANE MSS, Series B.

47. Cousins, Interview; Norman Cousins, Letter to the Author, February 8, 1973; Norman Thomas to Benjamin Spock, June 17, 1966, Benjamin Spock Collection, George Arents Memorial Library, Syracuse University, Syracuse, New York. (Hereafter cited as Spock MSS.)

48. Glazer, "The Peace Movement in America," p. 294.

49. Norman Thomas to Norman Cousins, June 2, 1960, SANE MSS, Series B; quoted in Deming, "The Ordeal of SANE," pp. 202, 204, 205.

50. Quoted in Divine, *Blowing On The Wind*, pp. 315–316.

CHAPTER 4

1. Albert Schweitzer, November 11, 1960, quoted in *SANE-USA* 4 (January 1961): 2.

2. Homer Jack, "New Frontier," *SANE-USA* 4 (February 1961): 2.

3. Clarence Pickett and Norman Cousins, "Greetings to JFK, NK," *SANE-USA* 4 (January 1961): 2.

4. "Americans Walk for Peace: Demonstrations in Many Cities," *SANE-USA* 4 (March 1961): 1.

5. "25,000 March L.A. to Boston," *SANE-USA* 4 (April-May 1961): 1.

6. *New York Post*, April 2, 1961, p. 15.

7. "Brief Summary of Discussion," Special National Board Meeting of SANE, June 16, 17, 1961, SANE MSS, Series A.

8. Ibid.

9. "SANE's Solution on Berlin Published Coast to Coast," *SANE-USA* 4 (July-August 1961): 1.

10. Charles J. Sommerhouser to SANE, July 20, 1961, SANE MSS, Series B; J.B.S. to SANE, July 22, 1961, SANE MSS, Series B; Marshall D. Moscott to SANE, n.d., SANE MSS, Series B.

11. Norman Cousins and Clarence Pickett to John F. Kennedy, August 31, 1961, Name File, White House Central Files, John F. Kennedy Library, Boston, Massachusetts. (Hereafter cited as JFKL.)

12. "Nuclear Tests Resumed!" *SANE-USA* 4 (September-October, 1961): 1.

13. "Kennedy Challenges U.S.S.R. To 'Peace Race,' " *SANE-USA* 4 (October-November 1961): 1; "Brief Summary of Discussion."

14. "Kennedy Challenges U.S.S.R. To Peace Race," *SANE-USA*, p. 1.

15. "The Peace Race," A Statement of Policy for 1961–1962 adopted on October 30, 1961, by the National Board of Directors of the National Committee for a Sane Nuclear Policy, SANE MSS, Series A.

16. "SANE Approves Turn Toward Peace," *SANE-USA* 4 (October-November 1961): 4.

17. Homer Jack to John F. Kennedy, October 31, 1961, and November 14, 1961, Name File, JFKL; "World Leaders in Appeal," *SANE-USA* 4 (January 14, 1962): 1.

18. Norman Cousins to Homer Jack, March 7, 1962, SANE MSS, Series B.

19. "Initiatives to Break the Geneva Impasse," *SANE World* 1 (April 15, 1962): 6.

20. *New York Times*, April 10, 1962, p. 36; *New York Times*, April 18, 1962, p. 36.

21. Benjamin Spock, Interview, March 6, 1972; Lynn Bloom, *Doctor Spock:*

Biography of a Conservative Radical (N.Y.: Bobbs, Merrill Co., 1972), pp. 245–46.

22. Ibid.

23. *New York Times*, April 16, 1962, p. 30.

24. "SANE—and Others," *Time* 80 (April 27, 1962): 22.; "Dr. Spock's Worry," *Newsweek* 59 (April 30, 1962): 21.

25. Guy-Michael Davis to Benjamin Spock, May 31, 1962; Stephanie May to Benjamin Spock, April 17, 1962; Nell Lee Litvak to Benjamin Spock, May 1, 1962, Spock MSS.

26. Norman Thomas to John F. Kennedy, April 20, 1962, and John F. Kennedy to Norman Thomas, April 28, 1962, Name File, JFKL. "Atomic Clouds Darken Pacific Skies," *SANE World* 1 (May 1, 1962): 1.

27. "The Peacemakers," *SANE World* 1 (May 1, 1962): 4, and (June 1, 1962): 5.

28. "Concern Grows on Fallout Hazard," *SANE World* 1 (May 15, 1962): 1; *New York Times*, July 5, 1962, p. 54; Ernest B. Kellog to Clarence Pickett, July 16, 1962, SANE MSS, Series B.

29. "Seven Years For A Sane Nuclear Policy," *SANE World* 3 (April 15, 1964): 3.

30. Walter LaFeber, *America, Russia, and the Cold War*, 3rd ed., (New York: John Wiley and Sons, 1976), p. 228.

31. "Crisis Strengthens War Group," *SANE World* 1 (November 1, 1962): 1.

32. Homer Jack to John F. Kennedy, October 24, 1962, Name File, JFKL; "The U.S.-Cuban Crisis," A National Policy Statement Issued October 24, 1962, SANE MSS, Series A; *New York Times*, October 25, 1962, p. 34, and October 28, 1962, p. 59.

33. "Talks Trigger Nuclear Test-Ban Hopes," *SANE World* 2 (February 1, 1963): 1; "A World of Flux and New Opportunities," *SANE World* 2 (February 15, 1963): 1.

34. "The Roosevelt Peace Award," *SANE World* 1 (December 1, 1962): 2.

35. *New York Times*, April 7, 1963, 4, p. 10. "Pacem In Terris" was published on April 11 and was reprinted in its entirety in *SANE World* 2 (May 1, 1963); "An Easter-Passover Appeal," *SANE World* 2 (April 1, 1963): 4.

36. Norman Cousins, *The Improbable Triumvirate: Pope John, John F. Kennedy, Nikita Khrushchev* (New York: W.W. Norton, 1972), pp. 48–50.

37. Ibid., pp. 78–110.

38. Cousins, Interview, July 25, 1983. Ted Sorenson in his book *Kennedy* (New York: Bantam Books, 1966), p. 882, wrote how the president valued in particular the April 30 letter from Cousins in preparing for his American University speech; Theodore Sorensen, Oral History Transcript, April 15, 1964, p. 72, JFKL; Norman Cousins to Pierre Salinger, June 10, 1963, and Norman Cousins to John F. Kennedy, June 11, 1963, President's Office Files, General Correspondence, JFKL.

39. Cousins, Interview.

40. *New York Times*, August 2, 1963, p. 28.

41. "Statement on Test-Ban Treaty," August 7, 1963, Name File, JFKL; Cousins, *Improbable Triumvirate*, p. 127. For a list of other organizations contributing more than 75,000 letters to the president on behalf of the treaty, see "Test-Ban: So Near and Yet So Far," *SANE World* 2 (July 1, 1963): 1, 6.

42. Cousins, *Improbable Triumvirate*, pp. 144–147.

43. Arthur Schlesinger, Jr., *A Thousand Days: John F. Kennedy in the White House* (New York: Fawcett, Crest, 1967), p. 834.

44. John F. Kennedy to Norman Cousins, October 7, 1963, Name File, JFKL.

45. Homer Jack, "Test-Ban Treaty: Beginning of Detente?" *SANE World* 2 (September 1, 1963): 1, 6; Norman Cousins, "Just The Beginning," *Saturday Review* 46 (September 21, 1963): 28, 29; Donald Keys, "A Shaft of Light," *SANE World* 2 (September 1, 1963): 2.

46. See Wittner, *Rebels Against War*, p. 277; and Paul Boyer, "From Activism to Apathy: The American People and Nuclear Weapons, 1963–1980," *Journal of American History*, 70 (March 1984): 821–844; Norman Cousins to Homer Jack, March 7, 1963, SANE MSS; Series B; Homer Jack "SANE Tasks Ahead," *SANE World* 2 (October 15, 1963): 2.

47. Donald Keys, "Difficulties of Measuring Success," *SANE World* 3 (April 15, 1964): 4.

48. "Policy Statement for 1964," Adopted by the National Board of Directors, November 25, 1963, SANE MSS, Series A.

49. Richard Hudson, ed., *War/Peace Report* 1 (September 1963) reprinted in *SANE World* 2 (November 1, 1963): 2. Also see Donald Keys, "SANE, UWF, and the Future, 1964," n.d., SANE MSS, Series A.

50. "Comparison Between Major Policy Pronouncements: UWF and SANE," 1964, SANE MSS, Series A; Erich Fromm to Homer Jack, November 15, 1963, SANE MSS, Series B.

51. National Board Meeting of SANE, May 20, 1965, SANE MSS, Series A; "Terminate Consolidation Negotiations," *The Federalist* 15 (June 1965): 2.

52. Sanford Gottlieb, "A Broader Framework for SANE," 1961, SANE MSS, Series A.

53. Norman Thomas, "Should SANE Endorse Political Candidates? Yes," July 10, 1962, SANE MSS, Series A; William J. Butler, "Should SANE Endorse Political Candidates? No," July 10, 1962, SANE MSS, Series A; Sanford Gottlieb Political Action Director to All Local Committees, Political Action Chairmen, and Members of the National Board, July 10, 1962, SANE MSS, Series A.

54. "Peace and Politics," *SANE World* 2 (March 1, 1963): 3; Sanford Gottlieb, "Peace is Good Politics in 1964 Elections," *SANE World* 3 (October 1, 1964): 1, 4.

55. Homer Jack, "Democratic Platform Marks Policy Retreat," *SANE World* 3 (October 1, 1964): 1.

56. "The President's Mandate for Peace," *SANE World* 3 (December 1964): 1.

57. "SANE Conference Sets New Policies," *SANE World* 4 (January 1965): 1; George Herring, *America's Longest War: The United States and Vietnam, 1950-1975* (New York: John Wiley and Sons, 1979), p. 125.

58. Herring, *America's Longest War*, pp. 129, 130.

CHAPTER 5

1. Richard Reeves, "Peace, Man, Says Baby Doctor Spock," *New York Times Magazine* (July 16, 1967): 49.

2. John E. Mueller, *War, Presidents, and Public Opinion* (New York: John Wiley and Sons, 1973), p. 164. Also see William Berkowitz, "The Impact of Anti-Vietnam Demonstrations Upon National Public Opinion and Military Indicators," *Social Science Research* 2 (March 1973): 1–14; Howard Schuman, "Two Sources of Antiwar Sentiment in America," *American Journal of Sociology* 78 (November 1972): 515–520; E.M. Schreiber, "Anti-War Demonstrations and U.S. Public Opinion," *British Journal of Sociology* 27 (June 1976): 225–235; Milton Rosenberg, Sidney Verba, and Phillip Converse, *Vietnam and the Silent Majority: A Dove's Guide* (New York: Harper and Row, 1970); George Ball, "The Lessons of Vietnam," *New York Times Magazine* (April 1, 1973): 43.

3. Godfrey Hodgson, *America In Our Time* (New York: Doubleday and Co., 1976), p. 371; and Jules Witcover, "Where Washington Reporting Failed," *Columbia Journalism Review* 9 (Winter 1970–1971): 11.

4. Allen Matusow, *The Unraveling of America: A History of Liberalism in the 1960s* (New York: Harper and Row, 1984).

5. "Policy Paper on Southeast Asia," June 27, 1962, SANE MSS, Series A; "Policy Statement on South Vietnam," September 27, 1963, SANE MSS, Series A; "The U.S. and Vietnam: Which Way Now?" *SANE World* 14 (April 1, 1964): 1; "Educators Appeal for Neutralized Vietnam," *SANE World*, 14 (July 1964): 1; "Southeast Asia and Vietnam," November 15, 1964, SANE MSS, Series A.

6. Hodgson, *America In Our Time*, p. 285.

7. Lyndon Johnson to Benjamin Spock, December 1, 1964; Benjamin Spock to McGeorge Bundy, February 7, 1965; Benjamin Spock to President Johnson, March 23, 1965; and President Johnson to Benjamin Spock, March 30, 1965, Name File, White House Central Files, Lyndon Baines Johnson Library, Austin, Texas (hereafter cited as LBJL); Spock, Interview; Thomas Powers, *The War At Home: Vietnam and the American People 1964–1968* (New York: Grossman, 1973), p. 54.

8. *New York Times*, February 19, 1965, p. 21; "SANE's Vietnam Rally Fills Garden," *SANE World* 5 (January 1966): 1.

9. Carl Oglesby to Sanford Gottlieb, October 24, 1965, and Sanford Gottlieb to Carl Oglesby, October 27, 1965, SANE MSS, Series B; Fred Halstead, *Out Now!: A Participant's Account of the American Movement Against the War* (New York: Monarch Press, 1978), p. 100.

10. Ibid., p. 95.

11. Todd Gitlin, *The Whole World Is Watching: Mass Media in the Making and Unmaking of the New Left* (Berkeley: University of California Press, 1980), p. 117; Memo, Chester Cooper to the President, November 29, 1965, Name File, National Security Files, LBJL; Chester Cooper, *The Lost Crusade: America in Vietnam* (New York: Dodd, Mead & Co., 1970), pp. 289, 290.

12. Kirkpatrick Sale, *SDS* (New York: Random House, 1974), p. 242. See also the criticism voiced in the letter from Elizabeth Most Bobrick to Spock, Thomas, and Keys, December 21, 1965, Spock MSS.

13. Carl Oglesby to Sanford Gottlieb, December 17, 1965; Sanford Gottlieb to Carl Oglesby, January 4, 1966, SANE MSS, Series A; Oglesby's speech is analyzed in Sale, *SDS*, pp. 242–245.

14. Sanford Gottlieb, "35,000 March for Negotiations," *SANE World* 5 (January 1966): 1; Gitlin, *The Whole World*, pp. 117–123.

15. Shana Alexander, "Evolution of a Peace Creep," *Life* 59 (December 10, 1965): 35; "March for Peace," *The Christian Century* (December 8, 1965): 1501; Robert Sherrill, "Patriotism of Protest," *Nation* 201 (December 13, 1965): 465; Memo, Hubert Humphrey to the President, December 2, 1965, Name File, National Security File, LBJL.

16. The tensions between the early New Left and SANE are developed further in Paul Boyer, "From Activism to Apathy: The American People and Nuclear Weapons, 1963–1980," pp. 838–844.

17. Staughton Lynd, "The Substance of Victory," *Liberation* 11 (January 1966): 3; Robert Wolfe, "American Imperialism and the Peace Movement," *Studies On the Left* 6 (May-June 1966): 41. Also see Andrew Kopkind, "Radicals on the March," *The New Republic* 153 (December 11, 1965): 15–19.

18. Sanford Gottlieb to Bill Moyers, January 19, 1966, Benjamin Spock to the President, January 27, 1966, Sanford Gottlieb to the President, February 1, 1966, Name Files, White House Central Files, LBJL.

19. *New York Times*, May 16, 1966, p. 1. For the radicals critique of SANE's demonstration, see John Gerassi, "SANE, Civil Rights, and Politics," *Liberation* 11 (June 1966): 44.

20. Sanford Gottlieb, "Lessons of the 1966 Primary Races," *SANE World* 5 (November 1966): 1, 3, 4.

21. "Draft of Prologue to Call for Spring Mobilization," January 1967, SANE MSS, Series A; Seymour Melman, Interview, January 5, 1972; Walter Goodman, "Liberals vs. Radicals: War in the Peace Camp," *New York Times Magazine* (December 3, 1967): 49, 177.

22. Benjamin Spock to Donald Keys, Sanford Gottlieb, and Mary Temple, November 25, 1966, Spock MSS; Norman Thomas to Donald Keys, January 3, 1967, Thomas to A.J. Muste, February 8, 1967, Thomas to Benjamin Spock, March 10, 1967, Thomas MSS; April 15 "Demonstrations of Spring Mobilization Committee," February 12, 1967, SANE MSS, Series A.

23. See letters from various local chapters to Benjamin Spock and National Board of SANE, Spock MSS; Abe Bloom, Interview, April 30, 1972; Spock, Interview, March 6, 1972; *The Washington Post*, April 7, 1967, p. 1.

24. *San Francisco Chronicle*, April 13, 1967, p. 11; *New York Times*, April 13, 1967, p. 3.

25. "Statement of National SANE Regarding the Spring Mobilization," April 14, 1967, SANE MSS, Series A.

26. H. Stuart Hughes to Benjamin Spock, April 20, 1967, Norman Thomas to Benjamin Spock, April 12, 1967, Spock MSS; Benjamin Spock to H. Stuart Hughes, May 2, 1967, Spock interview.

27. "Resolutions Passed by the National Board of SANE," April 27, 1967, SANE MSS, Series A; Benjamin Spock to H. Stuart Hughes, May 2, 1967.

28. Ibid.; Robert Schwartz, Interview, February 23, 1984.

29. Homer Jack, "To Members of the Corporation of SANE; One Sane Direction," May 15, 1967, SANE MSS, Series A.

30. SANE Policy and Strategy for Peace, Statement of Members of the Corporation, May 1967, p. 9, SANE MSS, Series A.

31. "Negotiations Now," *SANE World* 6 (April 1967): 1.

32. "U Thant Advances SANE Campaign," *SANE World* 6 (May 1967): 1.

33. Minutes of the National Board, September 14, 1967, *SANE MSS*, Series A; "A Message from Dr. Spock," September 1967, SANE MSS, Series A; Spock, Interview; Schwartz, Interview.

34. "American Resistance," *Liberation* 12 (November 1967): entire issue; Noam Chomsky, "Resistance," *New York Review of Books* 9 (December 7, 1967): 4–12; Goodman, "Liberals vs. Radicals," p. 194.

35. *New York Times*, October 20, 1967, p. 1.

36. Sanford Gottlieb, Interview, January 19, 1972; *New York Times*, October 21, 1967, p. 8.

37. Donald Keys, executive director, to Members of the Board of SANE, November 13, 1967, SANE MSS, Series A; Cousins, Interview; Benjamin Spock, Interview, March 6, 1972, and May 20, 1982; and H. Stuart Hughes, Interview, January 7, 1972, See also Hughes to SANE Board, Sponsors and Chapters, "The State of SANE," November 28, 1967, SANE MSS, Series A.

38. Sanford Gottlieb, Interview, January 19, 1972. Also see Gottlieb, "SANE's Road: Another Assessment," *War/Peace Report* 6 (February 1968): 18.

39. "Political Policy for 1968," June 27, 1967, SANE MSS, Series A; "Statement of Support for Eugene McCarthy," January 27, 1968, SANE MSS, Series A.

40. Richard T. Stout, *People* (New York: Harper and Row, 1970), pp. 43, 44.

41. Ibid., p. 63.

42. "Political Policy for 1968," *New York Times*, July 18, 1967, p. 17.

43. "SANE Political Strategy: 1968," Adopted by The National Board, October 19, 1967, SANE MSS, Series A.

44. "Statement of Support for Eugene McCarthy"; Matusow, *The Unraveling of America*, p. 390.

45. On the antiwar movement's impact on Johnson's March 31 decision, see Melvin Small, "The Impact of the Antiwar Movement on Lyndon Johnson, 1965–1968," *Peace and Change*, 10 (Spring 1984): 20; "Statement by SANE Chairman H. Stuart Hughes," April 1, 1968, SANE MSS, Series A.

46. "SANE Truth Squads to Track HHH, Nixon as Democratic Insurgents Look Beyond 1968," *SANE World* 7 (September 1968): 1; "The Long Range Political Role of SANE," Adopted by the National Board on September 21, 1968, SANE MSS, Series A.

47. Matusow, *The Unraveling of America*, p. 379; Mike Sletson to Sanford Gottlieb, September 20, 1968, SANE MSS, Series A; and Roy Bennet to National SANE Policy Committee, November 7, 1968, SANE MSS, Series A.

48. "Resolution on Immediate Partial Withdrawal from Vietnam," December 8, 1968, SANE MSS, Series A.

49. "New Vietnam Resolution," June 7, 1969, SANE MSS, Series A.

50. "SANE Policy on Withdrawal from Vietnam," September 20, 1969, SANE MSS, Series A.

51. *New York Times*, September 21, 1969, p. 3. Dr. Spock's conviction was later reversed.

52. "SANE Supporting Two Autumn Actions," *SANE World* 8 (September 1969): 3.

53. Tad Szulc, *Illusion of Peace: Foreign Policy in the Nixon Years* (New York: Viking, 1978), p. 158.

54. "SANE Urges U.S. End Saigon Support as Path to Peace in Vietnam, Laos," *SANE World* 9 (April 1970): 4.

55. Sanford Gottlieb, "Will Cambodia Be Nixon's Tet?" *SANE World* 9 (May 1970): 1; "Sunday Times Ad Nets Big Response," *SANE World* 9 (June 1970): 2.

56. "Anti-War Movement to go Local?" *War/Peace Report* 8 (May 1970): 20.

57. Sam Brown, "The Politics of Peace," *The Washington Monthly* 2 (August 1970): 20; Sanford Gottlieb, "Probing the Silent Majority," *SANE World* 9 (July 1970): 1, 5.

58. A Dove's Guide to Communications," *SANE World* 9 (September 1970): 1.

59. "Joint Resources Tapped for New Drive," *SANE World* 9 (October

1970): 1. SANE backed thirteen senatorial and congressional candidates, but only four emerged victorious: Senators Vance Hartke (D-IN.) and Harrison Williams (D-NJ.), Congresswoman Bella Abzug (D-NY.), and Congressman Robert Drinan (D-MA).

60. SANE Endorses April 24 Demonstration, April 6, 1971, SANE MSS, Series G.

61. By the summer of 1971 disillusionment with the war reached an all-time high. A near majority felt that the pace of troop withdrawals was too slow, and a substantial majority approved the removal of all troops by the end of the year even if the result was a Communist takeover of South Vietnam. See Louis Harris, *Anguish of Change* (New York: W.W. Norton, 1973), p. 73.

62. Michael Harrington, "The Peace Movement Is Using the Wrong Strategy," *New York Times Magazine* (May 30, 1971): 10, 21, 23.

63. "Resolution of Peace Politics of 1972," November 17, 1971, SANE MSS, Series G.

64. "SANE's Evaluation of 1972 Presidential Candidates," January 29, 1972, SANE MSS, Series G.

65. "Vietnam Record," *SANE World* 12 (February 1973): 5; *SANE Action*, December 21, 1972, SANE MSS, Series G; Henry Kissinger, *White House Years* (Boston: Little, Brown and Co., 1979), p. 261.

66. DeBenedetti, *The Peace Reform in American History*, p. 193; see "War Powers Bill, Arms Cut Offer Chance to Restrain President," *SANE World* 12 (March 1973): 1, 3.

67. *New York Times*, December 21, 1976, p. 4; "Lest We Forget . . . An Appeal for Reconciliation," *SANE World* 16 (February 1977): 4.

68. Michael Walzer, "The Peace Movement: What Was Won By Protest?" *The New Republic* 168 (February 10, 1973): 25; Charles DeBenedetti, "On the Significance of Citizen Peace Activism: America, 1961–1975," *Peace and Change* 9 (Summer 1983): 14. For other retrospective analysis on the impact of the antiwar movement, see Sam Brown, "The Defeat of the Anti-war Movement," in Anthony Lake, ed., *The Vietnam Legacy* (New York: New York University, 1976), pp. 120–127; James O'Brien, "The Anti-war Movement and the War," *Radical America* 8 (May-June 1974): 53–86; Irving Howe and Michael Walzer, "Were We Wrong About Vietnam?" *The New Republic* 181 (August 18, 1979): 15–18; and Melvin Small, "The Impact of the Antiwar Movement on Lyndon Johnson, 1965–1968: A Preliminary Report," pp. 1–22.

69. Schuman, "Two Sources of Antiwar Sentiment," p. 515.

70. Susan Sontag, "The Meaning of Vietnam," *New York Review of Books* 22 (June 12, 1975): 27.

71. "Offbeat Policemen," *New Yorker* 47 (August 8, 1970): 23. Peter Berger makes a similar point in "Indo-China and the American Conscience," *Commentary* 69 (February 1980): 35.

72. "Gottlieb Stresses Coalition on Needs," *SANE World* 9 (February 1970): 7.

73. David McReynolds, *We Have Been Invaded by the 21st Century* (New York: Grove Press, 1971), p. 170.

74. Robert Schulzinger, "The Political Impact of Vietnam," *Peace and Change* 9 (Summer 1983): 2.

75. *Washington Star*, February 19, 1973, p. A–8.

76. Ibid.; "A Sane World Begins At Home: Demilitarizing American Society," Adopted January 16, 1971, SANE MSS, Series G; *New York Times*, June 20, 1971, p. 14E.

CHAPTER 6

1. Lenore Marshall, *Latest Will: New and Selected Poems of Lenore Marshall* (New York: W.W. Norton and Co., 1969), p. 42.

2. Boyer, "From Activism to Apathy: The American People and Nuclear Weapons, 1963–1980," p. 821.

3. Norman Cousins, "The Nightmare That Won't Go Away," *Saturday Review* 59 (April 17, 1976): 14.

4. Jerome Frank to Donald Keys, June 13, 1965, SANE MSS, Series B.

5. Donald Keys to Jerome Frank, June 24, 1965, SANE MSS, Series B.

6. Donald Keys, "What is SANE to You?" *SANE World* 5 (June 1966): 4; Minutes of SANE National Board Meeting, July 21, 1966, SANE MSS, Series A.

7. *New York Times*, July 22, 1965, p. 39; SANE National Board Meeting, January 27, 1968, SANE MSS, Series A; *New York Times*, March 24, 1969, p. 12.

8. "The Story of an Ad," *SANE World* 8 (July 1969): 3.

9. "Arms Cuts: Leashing the Complex," *SANE World* 8 (June 1969): 1, 2, 3.

10. Minutes of the National Board Meeting, June 7, 1969, SANE MSS, Series A.

11. "One and a Half Cheers for SALT," *SANE World* 11 (May 1972): 1, 2.

12. "Missile Pact Gets Tepid Response," *SANE World* 11 (August 1972): 3.

13. Ibid.

14. *New York Times*, June 2, 1974, p. 23.

15. "Limited Nuclear War Plans," *SANE World* 14 (July-August 1975): 1, 2.

16. Ibid.; "People Must Pressure Their Leaders Toward Nuclear Disarmament," *SANE World* 14 (October 1975): 1, 2.

17. *SANE World* 14 (December 1975): entire issue.

18. Minutes of the National Board Meeting, May 15, 1976, SANE MSS, Series G.

19. "Lobbying Improved Democrat's Platform," *SANE World* 15 (August 1976): 1, 3.

20. Minutes of the National Board Meeting, September 18, 1976, SANE MSS, Series G.

21. Sanford Gottlieb, Interview, July 27, 1979.

22. "The State of SANE," October 7, 1976, SANE MSS, Series G.

23. Gottlieb, Interview. See also SANE's farewell to Gottlieb in *SANE World* 16 (April 1977): 1, 2, 3. Gottlieb was a mainstay of New Directions until it disbanded in 1981. He then became executive director of United Campuses to Prevent Nuclear War.

24. Minutes of SANE Executive Committee Meeting, July 19, 1977, SANE MSS, Series G.

25. David Cortright, Interview, June 7, 1982.

26. Ibid.; Minutes of National Board Meetings, September 8, 1979, and December 1, 1979, SANE MSS, Series G.

27. "Twenty Years in the Struggle for Peace: A Report to the Members," 1977, SANE MSS, Series G.

28. Seymour Melman to President Jimmy Carter, June 30, 1977, SANE MSS, Series G.

29. "The Neutron Bomb Moves Through Congress," *SANE World* 16 (September-October 1977): 1; "Twenty Years in the Struggle for Peace."

30. "SALT II Statement Adopted by the National Board," June 2, 1979, SANE MSS, Series G.

31. "SALT II Showdown in the Senate," *SANE World* 18 (July-August 1979): 1–4.

32. "Basing Choice Moves MX Forward," *SANE World* 18 (October 1979): 1, 2.

33. "A Tour Through the MX Deployment States," *SANE World* 18 (December 1979): 2.

34. "A Period of Transition," *SANE World* 19 (March 1980): 4.

35. Minutes of the National Board Meeting, June 7, 1980, SANE MSS, Series G.

36. Minutes of the National Board Meeting, September 6, 1980, SANE MSS, Series G.

37. "Labor-Peace Alliance: New Hope for Conversion," *SANE World* 17 (April 1978): 1, 2.

38. Ibid.

39. Seymour Melman and David Cortright to SANE Members, December 28, 1978, SANE MSS, Series G.

40. "Winpisinger Becomes New SANE Co-Chairman," *SANE World* (April 1979): 1, 2.

41. Minutes of the National Board Meeting, December 1, 1979, SANE MSS, Series G.

42. Statement of SANE National Board, September 8, 1979, SANE MSS, Series G.

43. Ibid.

44. "A Sane View of the 1980 Elections, *SANE World* 19 (October 1980): 1, 2, 4.

45. "No Time For Retreat," *SANE World* 19 (December 1980): 1, 2.

46. SANE 1981 Activities Report, SANE MSS, Series G.

47. Minutes of the National Board Meeting, March 21, 1981, SANE MSS, Series G.

48. "The Reagan Master Plan: Missiles, Missiles, and More Missiles," *SANE World* 20 (November 1981): 1, 2.

49. "Neutron Bomb Gets Green Light: SANE Launches Opposition Campaign," *SANE World* 20 (September 1981): 1, 4.

50. "Europeans Bring Disarmament Message to America," *SANE World* 21 (January 1982): 1, 2, 3.

51. Ibid.

52. "Galbraith Addresses SANE Briefing," *SANE World* 21 (July-August 1981): 1, 4.

53. "Fair Budget Campaign Launches Offensive," *SANE World* 21 (April 1982): 1, 3.

54. George Kennan, "On Nuclear War," *New York Review of Books* 28 (January 21, 1982): 8.

55. Statement on the Nuclear Weapons Freeze Campaign, 1983, Nuclear Weapons Freeze Campaign, St. Louis, Missouri.

56. "Reagan's START Proposal—Will It Stop the Arms Race?" *SANE World* 21 (June 1982): 1, 4.

57. *New York Times*, May 23, 1982, p. 24E.

58. For coverage of the march, see *New York Times*, June 13, 1982, pp. 1, 42, 43; and Fox Butterfield, "Anatomy of the Nuclear Protest," *New York Times Magazine* (July 11, 1982): 14–17, 32–39.

59. "Rally for Disarmament: June Actions A Major Success," *SANE World* 21 (July-August 1982): 1.

60. Benjamin Spock, Interview, May 20, 1982; Cortright, Interview; "SANE Celebrates Dedication of Ben Spock Center for Peace," *SANE World* 21 (July-August 1982): 3.

61. "SANE At 25," Consider the Alternatives, tape #520, SANE Education Fund, Philadelphia, Pennsylvania.

CHAPTER 7

1. Jonathan Schell, *The Fate of the Earth* (New York: Avon Books, 1982), p. 226.

2. *New York Times*, June 13, 1982, p. 43; David Cortright to SANE Members, Fall 1982, SANE MSS, Series G.

3. "The Elections," *SANE World* 21 (December 1982-January 1983): 4.

4. David Cortright, "Next Steps for the Freeze," *SANE World* 21 (December 1982-January 1983): 3.

5. Ibid.

6. 1983 SANE Activities Report, SANE MSS, Series G.

7. Ibid.

8. *Variety*, December 16, 1983, p. 25; Max Youngstein, Interview, April 6, 1984; Jimi Kaufer, Interview, April 6, 1984.

9. 1983 SANE Activities Report.

10. "SANE Takes to the Airways," *SANE World* 22 (April 1983): 4; see *Raleigh News and Observer*, February 8, 1983, and February 9, 1983.

11. "Reagan's War to 'Save Democracy,' " *SANE World*, 22 (July-August 1983): 1, 2; "The U.S. War in Central America," *SANE World* 23 (June 1984): 2.

12. David Cortright to SANE Members, Winter 1983, SANE MSS, Series G.

13. "Campaign Report, SANE PAC," Spring 1984, SANE MSS, Series G.

14. David Cortright to SANE Members, Spring 1984, SANE MSS, Series G.

15. "Statement of SANE Executive Director, David Cortright on Peace Movement Support for Minority Planks," July 12, 1984, "Dear Democratic Party Delegate," July 12, 1984, SANE MSS, Series G.

16. David Cortright, Interview, July 20, 1984.

17. *New York Times*, April 17, 1984, p. 18; National SANE Education Fund, Progress Report, June 1984, SANE MSS, Series G.

18. "The Peace Movement Is Buying Time," *Newsweek* 102 (August 6, 1984): 13.

19. *New York Times*, April 17, 1984; "Reagan Faces Squeeze on Nukes," *Congressional Quarterly* (January 21, 1984): 101; "Nuclear Freeze Groups Focus on Candidates," *Congressional Quarterly* (May 5, 1984): 1021.

20. Michael Mawby, "Post Convention Report: The Democrats and the Peace Movement," *SANE World* 23 (September 1984): 1, 4.

21. Ibid.

22. In late March 1985 the fiscal year funding request for 21 MX Missiles was narrowly approved by Congress (219 to 213 and 217 to 210 in the House and 55 to 45 in the Senate). It was significant that the Coalition to Stop the MX (spearheaded by SANE and Common Cause) held nearly half the House and was able to influence more Republicans to vote against the MX than ever before, indicating the long-term future of the MX was indeed in doubt.

23. Jerry Hartz, "Major Victory in the Battle to Stop MX," *SANE World* 23 (October 1984): 34.

24. Michael Mawby, "1984 Election Wrap-Up: Presidential Loss, Congressional Victories," *SANE World* 23 (November-December 1984): 3, 12, 13.

25. David Corn, "Election Lessons to Build On," *Nuclear Times* 3 (December 1984): 12, 13.

26. Ibid.

27. David Cortright, Interview, December 9, 1984; SANE 1984 Member Report, SANE MSS, Series G; Information supplied by Beth Leopold of the SANE organization staff in early November 1985 indicated that although SANE's 130,000 members could be found throughout the country, five states comprised more than 50 percent of the entire membership: Maryland, 16,000; Massachusetts, 14,000; New York, 13,500; Michigan, 12,500; and California, 12,000. Other areas with strong SANE support included Virginia, and Pennsylvania, Illinois, Oregon, New Jersey, and Washington, D.C.

28. David Cortright, "The New SANE Agenda," *SANE World* 23 (November-December 1984): 1, 8; Endowment for Peace, SANE MSS, Series G.

29. "Arms Talks to Resume," *SANE World* 24 (February 1985): 1; "SANE Goes to Geneva," *SANE World* 24 (April 1985): 1.

30. Ed Glennon, "Unfinished Business—SANE Tackles Nuclear Testing," *SANE World* 24 (February 1985): 1, 2.

31. "Stop All Nuclear Explosions," *SANE Action* (July-August 1985): 8; *New York Times*, November 20, 1985, p. 1.

32. Wittner, *Rebels Against War*, pp. 301, 302.

33. Randall Forsberg, Keynote address to the Nuclear Weapons Campaign's Fifth National Conference, December 7, 1984.

34. Randall Kehler, "The Freeze: Three Years After," *Fellowship* 50 (July/August 1984): 8, 9; Randall Kehler, "Address to the Nuclear Weapons Campaign's Fifth National Conference," December 7, 1984.

35. Daniel Yankelovich and John Doble, "The Public Mood: Nuclear Weapons and the U.S.S.R.," *Foreign Affairs* 63 (Fall 1984): 34, 36, 46.

36. DeBenedetti, *The Peace Reform in American History*, p. 199; also see Bob Overy, *How Effective Are Peace Movements?* (Montreal: Harvest House, 1982).

37. Conversation with State Department officials John W. McDonald and Joseph Montville on September 21, 1984, confirm this point; Wittner, *Rebels Against War*, p. 306.

38. Christopher Paine, "Lobbying for Arms Control," *Bulletin of Atomic Scientists* 41 (August 1985): 130.

39. See "Space: The Final Frontier," April 1985, a SANE brochure written by Jerry Hartz highlighting the fallacies of the Star Wars program, SANE MSS, Series G.

40. *New York Times*, November 15, 1957.

41. On the exhaustion of liberalism and the neoconservative revival, see, for example, the Epilogue in Alonzo Hamby, *Liberalism and Its Challengers: F.D.R. to Reagan* (New York: Oxford University Press, 1985), pp. 339–354; Schell, *The Fate of the Earth*.

Bibliography

MANUSCRIPT COLLECTIONS

Allen, Steve. Personal Papers, Van Nuys, California.

Cousins, Norman. Brooklyn College Library, Brooklyn, New York.

Dwight D. Eisenhower Library, Abilene, Kansas.

John F. Kennedy Library, Boston, Massachusetts.

Lyndon Baines Johnson Library, Austin, Texas.

Muste, A.J. Swarthmore College Peace Collection, Swarthmore, Pennsylvania.

National Committee for a Sane Nuclear Policy. Swarthmore College Peace Collection, Swarthmore, Pennsylvania.

SANE: Committee for a Sane Nuclear Policy. National SANE office, Washington, D.C.

Spock, Benjamin. Arents Memorial Library, Syracuse University, Syracuse, New York.

Thomas, Norman. New York City Public Library, New York.

PUBLIC DOCUMENTS

U.S. *Congressional Record*.

U.S. Senate. Internal Security Subcommittee of the Committee on the Judiciary. *Communist Infiltration in the Nuclear Test Ban Movement*. 86th Cong., 2d sess., 1960, part 1.

U.S. Senate. Internal Security Subcommittee of the Committee on the Judiciary.

Communist Infiltration in the Nuclear Test Ban Movement. 87th Cong., 1st sess., 1961, part 2.

U.S. Senate. Report on the Hearings of Dr. Linus Pauling. 87th Cong., 1st sess., 1960.

U.S. Senate. Testimony of Dr. Linus Pauling. 86th Cong., 2d sess., June 21, 1960, part 1.

U.S. Senate. Testimony of Dr. Linus Pauling. 86th Cong., 2d sess., 1961, part 2.

BOOKS

Allen, Steve. *Mark It and Strike It.* New York: Holt, Rinehart and Winston, 1960.

Berman, Ronald. *America in the Sixties: An Intellectual History.* New York: Harper and Row, 1968.

Bloom, Lynn. *Dr. Spock: Biography of a Conservative Radical.* New York: Bobbs, Merrill, Co., 1972.

Boulton, David, ed. *Voices From the Crowd: Against the H-Bomb* Philadelphia: Dufour Editions, 1964.

Brock, Peter. *Twentieth-Century Pacifism.* New York: Van Nostrand Reinhold Co., 1970.

Chatfield, Charles, ed. *Peace Movements in America.* New York: Schocken Books, 1973.

Cousins, Norman. *Dr. Schweitzer of Lambaréné.* New York: Harper and Row, 1960.

———. *The Improbable Triumvirate: Pope John, John F. Kennedy, Nikita Khrushchev.* New York: W.W. Norton, 1972.

———. *Modern Man Is Obsolete.* New York: Viking Press, 1945.

———. *Who Speaks for Man?* New York: The MacMillan Co., 1953.

DeBenedetti, Charles. *The Peace Reform in American History.* Bloomington: Indiana University Press, 1980.

Divine, Robert. *Blowing On The Wind: The Nuclear Test Ban Debate, 1954–1960.* New York: Oxford University Press, 1978.

———. *Second Chance: The Triumph of Internationalism in World War II.* New York: Athenum, 1967.

Finn, James, ed. *Protest: Pacifism and Politics.* New York: Random House, 1967.

Gallup, George. *The Gallup Poll: Public Opinion, 1935–1971.* New York: Random House, 1972.

Gilpin, Robert. *American Scientists and Nuclear Weapons' Policy.* Princeton: Princeton University Press, 1962.

Gitlin, Todd. *The Whole World Is Watching: Mass Media in the Making and*

Unmaking of the New Left. Berkeley: University of California Press, 1980.

Grodzins, Morton, and Eugene Rabinowitch, eds. *The Atomic Age: Scientists in National and World Affairs*. New York: Basic Books, 1963.

Halstead, Fred. *Out Now!: A Participant's Account of the American Movement Against the War*. New York: Monarch Press, 1978.

Hamby, Alonzo. *Liberalism and Its Challengers: F.D.R. to Reagan*. New York: Oxford University Press, 1985.

Harris, Louis. *Anguish of Change*. New York: W.W. Norton, 1973.

Hentoff, Nat. *Peace Agitators: The Story of A.J. Muste*. New York: The MacMillan Co., 1963.

————. ed, *The Essays of A.J. Muste*. New York: Bobbs-Merrill, 1967.

Herzog, Arthur. *The War-Peace Establishment*. New York: Harper and Row, 1965.

Hodgson, Godfrey. *America In Our Time*. New York: Doubleday and Co., 1976.

Hollis, Elizabeth, ed. *Peace Is Possible*. New York: Grossman, 1967.

Jacobs, Paul, and Saul Landau, eds. *The New Radicals*. New York: Random House, 1965.

Jacobson, Harold, and Eric Stein. *Diplomats, Scientists and Politicians: The United States and the Nuclear Test Ban Negotiations*. Ann Arbor: University of Michigan Press, 1966.

Kaufman, Arnold. *The Radical Liberal: New Man in American Politics*. New York: Atherton Press, 1968.

Keniston, Kenneth. *Young Radicals: Notes on Committed Youth*. New York: Harcourt, Brace, Jovanovich, 1968.

LaFeber, Walter. *America, Russia, and the Cold War*. New York: John Wiley and Sons, 1976.

Lapp, Ralph E. *Kill and Overkill: The Strategy of Annihilation*. New York: Basic Books, Inc., 1962.

McReynolds, David. *We Have Been Invaded By the 21st Century*. New York: Grove Press, 1971.

Mailer, Norman. *The Armies of the Night: History as a Novel*. New York: New American Library, 1968.

Matusow, Allen. *The Unraveling of America: A History of Liberalism in the 1960s*. New York: Harper and Row, 1984.

Melman, Seymour. *The Peace Race*. New York: George Braziller, 1962.

Mueller, John E. *War, Presidents, and Public Opinion*. New York: John Wiley and Sons, 1973.

Mumford, Lewis. *In The Name of Sanity*. New York: Harcourt, Brace, and Co., 1954.

Nathan, Otto, and Heinz Norden, eds. *Einstein on Peace*. New York: Simon and Schuster, 1960.

Newfield, Jack. *A Prophetic Minority*. New York: New American Library, 1966.

O'Neill, William. *Coming Apart: An Informal History of the 1960s*. Chicago: Quadrangle Books, 1971.

Overy, Bob. *How Effective Are Peace Movements?* Montreal: Harvest House, 1982.

Pauling, Linus. *No More War!* New York: Dodd, Mead, and Co., 1958.

Powers, Thomas. *The War At Home: Vietnam and the American People, 1964–1968*. New York: Grossman, 1973.

Robert, Chalmers. *The Nuclear Years: The Arms Race and Arms Control, 1945–1970*. New York: Praeger, 1970.

Rosenberg, Milton, Sidney Verba, and Phillip Converse. *Vietnam and the Silent Majority: A Dove's Guide*. New York: Harper and Row, 1970.

Russell, Bertrand. *Has Man A Future?* New York: Simon and Schuster, 1961.

Sale, Kirkpatrick. *SDS*. New York: Random House, 1974.

Salisbury, Harrison, ed. *Vietnam Reconsidered: Lessons From A War*. New York: Harper and Row, 1984.

Schell, Jonathan. *The Fate of the Earth*. New York: Avon Books, 1982.

Schlesinger, Arthur, Jr. *A Thousand Days: John F. Kennedy in the White House*. New York: Fawcett, Crest, 1967.

Skolnick, Jerome. *The Politics of Protest*. New York: Simon and Schuster, 1969.

Sorenson, Theodore. *Kennedy*. New York: Bantam Books, 1966.

Spock, Benjamin. *Decent and Indecent: Our Personal and Political Behavior*. New York: Fawcett, Crest, 1971.

Stout, Richard. *People*. New York: Harper and Row, 1970.

Teodori, Massimo. *The New Left: A Documentary History*. New York: Bobbs-Merrill, Co., 1969.

United World Federalists. *Unity and Diversity*. New York: World Government House, 1947.

Viorst, Milton. *Fire in the Streets: America in the 1960s*. New York: Simon and Schuster, 1969.

Wank, Solomon, ed. *Doves and Diplomats: Foreign Offices and Peace Movements in Europe and America in the Twentieth Century*. Westport, Connecticut: Greenwood Press, 1978.

Weinberg, Arthur, and Lila Weinberg, eds. *Instead of Violence*. New York: Grossman Pub. Inc., 1963.

Wittner, Lawrence. *Rebels Against War: The American Peace Movement, 1933–1983*. Philadelphia: Temple University Press, 1984.

Zaroulis, Nancy, and Gerald Sullivan. *Who Spoke Up: American Protest Against the War in Vietnam, 1963–1975*. New York: Doubleday, 1984.

ARTICLES

Alexander, Shana. "Evolution of a Peace Creep." *Life* 59 (December 10, 1965): 35.

"Anti-War Movement to go Local?" *War/Peace Report* 8 (May 1970): 20.

"The Atomic Scientists of Chicago." *Bulletin of Atomic Scientists* 1 (December 10, 1945): 1.

Bantell, John F. "Grenville Clark and the Founding of the United Nations: The Failure of World Federalism." *Peace and Change* 10 (Fall-Winter 1984): 97–116.

Berger, Peter. "Indo-China and the American Conscience." *Commentary* 69 (February 1980): 34–35.

Berkowitz, William. "The Impact of Anti-Vietnam Demonstrations Upon National Public Opinion and Military Indicators." *Social Science Research* 2 (March 1973): 1–14.

Boyer, Paul. "From Activism to Apathy: The American People and Nuclear Weapons, 1963–1980." *Journal Of American History* 70 (March 1984): 821–844.

Brown, Harrison. "The World Government Movement in the US." *Bulletin of Atomic Scientists* 3 (June 1947): 156, 157.

Brown, Sam. "The Defeat of the Antiwar Movement," in Anthony Lake, ed. *The Vietnam Legacy.* New York: New York University Press, 1976, pp. 120–127.

———. "The Politics of Peace." *Washington Monthly* 2 (August 1970): 24–46.

Butterfield, Fox. "Anatomy of the Nuclear Protest." *New York Times Magazine* (July 11, 1982): 14–17, 32–39.

Chatfield, Charles. "Peace Research in History: The Ecology of Choice." *Peace and Change* 2 (Summer 1974): 1–8.

Corn, David. "Election Lessons to Build On." *Nuclear Times* (December 1984): 12–15.

"Council of Federation of American Scientists Meets." *Bulletin of Atomic Scientists* 1 (May 1, 1946): 16.

Cousins, Norman. "The H-Bomb and World Federalism." *The Federalist* 2 (January 1953): 14–15.

———. Various articles. *Saturday Review* (1957–1976).

Cousins, Norman, and Thomas Finletter. "A Beginning for Sanity." *Bulletin of Atomic Scientists* 2 (July 1946): 11–14.

DeBenedetti, Charles. "On the Significance of Citizen Peace Activism: America, 1961–1975." *Peace and Change* 9 (Summer 1983): 6–20.

Deming, Barbara. "The Ordeal of SANE." *Nation* 192 (March 11, 1961): 201–204.

Ecker, Paul. "SANE: A Portrait of Autocracy in Action." *Contemporary Issues* 2 (May-June 1961): 27–28.

Einstein, Albert. "The Real Problem is in the Hearts of Men." *New York Times Magazine* (June 23, 1946): 7, 42–44.

Finch, Roy. "The New American Peace Movement, Part I." *Dissent* 15 (Winter 1963): 86–95.

———. "The New American Peace Movement, Part II." *Dissent* 15 (Spring 1963): 138–148.

Gerassi, John. "SANE, Civil Rights, and Politics." *Liberation* 11 (June 1966): 44.

"Giving Peace a Chance." *Newsweek* 100 (June 21, 1982): 40, 41.

Glazer, Nathan. "The Peace Movement in America." *Commentary* 31 (April 1961): 288–296.

Goodman, Walter. "Liberals vs. Radicals: War in the Peace Camp." *New York Times Magazine* (December 3, 1967): 48, 49, 177–195.

Gottfried, Alex, and Sue Gottfried. "The New Movement: Peace Without Pacifism." *Liberation* 9 (February 1964): 17–21.

Gottlieb, Sanford. "National Committee for a Sane Nuclear Policy." *New University Thought* 2 (Spring 1962): 155–157.

———. "SANE's Road: Another Assessment." *War/Peace Report* 6 (February 1968): 18.

Harrington, Michael. "The Peace Movement Is Using the Wrong Strategy." *New York Times Magazine* (May 30, 1971): 10, 21–23.

"How Sane the SANE?" *Time* 62 (April 21, 1958): 13–14.

"How the Scare Over US Atom Tests Exploded." *US News and World Report* 43 (July 5, 1957): 23–26.

Howe, Irving, and Michael Walzer. "Were We Wrong About Vietnam?" *New Republic* 181 (August 18, 1979): 15–18.

"Is There a Pacifist Revival?" *Liberation* 3 (May 1958): 3, 18.

Jack, Homer. "Where Do We Go From Here?" *War/Peace Report* 1 (September 1963): 21, 28.

Katz, Milton S. "Norman Cousins: Peace Advocate and World Citizen." In Charles DeBenedetti, ed., *Peace Heroes in Twentieth-Century America.* Bloomington: Indiana University Press, 1986.

———. "Peace Liberals and Vietnam: SANE and the Politics of 'Responsible' Protest." *Peace and Change* 9 (Summer 1983): 21–39.

———, and Neil H. Katz. "Pragmatists and Visionaries in the Post-World War II American Peace Movement: SANE and CNVA." In Solomon Wank, ed., *Doves and Diplomats: Foreign Offices and Peace Movements in Europe and America in the Twentieth Century.* Westport, Conn.: Greenwood Press, 1978, pp. 265–288.

Kehler, Randall. "The Freeze: Three Years After." *Fellowship* 50 (July/August 1984): 8–10.

Kennan, George. "On Nuclear War." *New York Review of Books* 28 (January 21, 1982): 8–10.

Keys, Donald. "SANE's Wayward Drift to the Left." *War/Peace Report* 6 (January 1968): 14, 16.

Kopkind, Andrew. "Radicals on the March." *New Republic* 158 (December 11, 1965): 15–19.

Lens, Sidney. "Ban the Bomb." *Progressive* 46 (August 1982): 24, 25.

"Letter to the Editor." *Liberation* 5 (December 1960): 3.

"The Lobbying Establishment." *Washingtonian Magazine* 8 (November 1972): 67–73.

Lynd, Staughton. "The Substance of Victory." *Liberation* 11 (January 1966): 3.

Mitzman, Arthur. "Not SANE Enough." *Liberation* 4 (October 1959): 16–18.

Murphy, J.V. "What We Gave Away in the Moscow Arms Agreement." *Fortune* 86 (September 1972): 201–206.

Muste, A.J. "The Crisis in SANE." *Liberation* 5 (July-August 1960): 10–13.

———. "The Crisis in SANE: Act II." *Liberation* 5 (November 1960): 5–8.

———. "Pacifism Enters A New Phase." *Fellowship* 26 (July 1, 1960): 21–25, 34.

"The Myth That Threatened One American Town." *The Federalist* 3 (April 1953): 8–10.

"The National Organization of Scientists." *Bulletin Of Atomic Scientists* 1 (December 10, 1945): 2.

New York Times. (1945–1985).

"No News: SANE Peace Rally and the New York Times." *Nation* 203 (December 26, 1966): 692.

O'Brien, James. "The Antiwar Movement and the War." *Radical America* 8 (May-June 1974): 53–86.

"Offbeat Policemen." *New Yorker* 47 (August 8, 1970): 22, 23.

"The Other Summit Conference." *Nation* 190 (June 4, 1960): 482.

Paine, Christopher. "Lobbying for Arms Control." *Bulletin of Atomic Scientists* 41 (August 1985): 125–130.

Rabinowitch, Eugene. "Five Years After." *Bulletin of Atomic Scientists* 7 (January 1951): 3, 5, 12.

Reeves, Richard. "Peace Man, Says Baby Doctor Spock." *New York Times Magazine* (July 7, 1967): 8, 9, 39, 46–51.

Rosi, Eugene. "Mass and Attentive Opinion on Nuclear Weapons Tests and Fallout, 1954–1963." *Public Opinion Quarterly* 29 (Summer 1965): 283–290.

SANE USA. (1958–1961).

SANE World. (1962–1985).

Schreiber, E.M. "Antiwar Demonstrations and American Public Opinion on the War in Vietnam." *British Journal of Sociology* 27 (June 1976): 225–235.

Schulzinger, Robert. "The Political Impact of Vietnam." *Peace and Change* 9 (Summer 1983): 1–5.

Schuman, Howard. "Two Sources of Antiwar Sentiment in America." *American Journal of Sociology* 78 (November 1972): 515–520.

Schweitzer, Albert. "Declaration of Conscience." *Public Opinion Quarterly* 29 (Summer 1965): 283–290.

"Senator Dodd, Norman Cousins, and SANE." *Liberation* 5 (December 1960): 4, 5.

Sherrill, Robert. "Patriotism of Protest." *Nation* 201 (December 13, 1965): 463–466.

Small, Melvin. "The Impact of the Antiwar Movement on Lyndon Johnson, 1965–1968." *Peace and Change* 10 (Spring 1984): 1–22.

Stone, I.F. "First Call for a Test Ban." *I.F. Stone's Weekly* (November 1, 1954): 1.

———. "Peace is Becoming Respectable." *I.F. Stone's Weekly* (October 5, 1959): 1.

———. "What Should The Peace Movement Do?" *Liberation* 10 (August 1965): 27, 28.

"Student Peace Groups." *New University Thought* 1 (Spring 1961): 75–80.

Teller, Edward, and Albert Latter. "The Compelling Need for Nuclear Tests." *Life* 44 (February 10, 1958): 64–66, 69, 72.

"Terminate Consolidation Negotiations." *The Federalist* 2 (June 1965): 2.

"United World Federalist's Birthday Marks Half a Decade of Progress." *The Federalist* 1 (February 1952): 6, 7.

Wakefield, Dan. "Beached on 42nd St." *Nation* 188 (April 25, 1959): 357–359.

Walzer, Michael. "The Peace Movement: What Was Won By Protest?" *New Republic* 168 (February 10, 1973): 24–26.

Washington Post. (1960–1965).

Wicker, Tom. "The Politics Before Us." *New York Review of Books* 16 (February 11, 1971): 16.

Witcover, Jules. "Where Washington Reporting Failed." *Columbia Journalism Review* 9 (Winter 1970–1971): 10–15.

Wolf, Robert. "American Imperialism and the Peace Movement." *Studies on the Left* 6 (May-June 1966): 5, 39–41.

Yankelovich, Daniel, and John Doble. "The Public Mood: Nuclear Weapons and the USSR." *Foreign Affairs* 63 (Fall 1984): 34–46.

Yoder, Jon. "United World Federalists: Liberals for Law and Order." *American Studies* 8 (Spring 1972): 109–130.

PERSONAL COMMUNICATIONS

Abrams, Steve. Interview. New York City, June 14, 1982.

Allen, Steve. Letters to the author. May 28, 1982.

Bloom, Abe. Interview. Wheaton, Maryland, April 30, 1972.

Cortright, David. Interview. Washington, D.C., June 7, 1982, and July 20, 1984.

Cousins, Norman. Interview. New York City, January 6, 1972, and Los Angeles, California, July 25, 1983.

Gilmore, Robert. Interview. New York City, October 13, 1971.

Gottlieb, Sanford. Interview. Washington, D.C., January 19, 1972, and July 27, 1979.

Hughes, H. Stuart. Interview. Cambridge, Massachusetts, January 7, 1971.

Jack, Homer. Interview. New York City, January 29, 1972.

Keys, Donald. Interview. New York City, January 5, 1972.

Lear, Walter. Interview. Philadelphia, Pennsylvania, June 20, 1983.

Loewi, Dori. Interview. New York City, June 14, 1982.

Lynd, Staughton. Interview. Boston, December 29, 1971.

Melman, Seymour. Interview. New York City, January 6, 1972.

Pauling, Linus. Interview. Palo Alto, California, February 9, 1983.

Schwartz, Robert. Interview. New York City, February 23, 1984.

Scott, Lawrence. Interview. Philadelphia, September 24, 1971.

Spock, Benjamin. Interview. New York City, March 6, 1972, and Rogers, Arkansas, May 20, 1982.

Stone, I.F. Interview. Washington, D.C., June 7, 1972.

Youngstein, Max. Interview. Los Angeles, California, April 6, 1984.

Index

UWF, 4; on Barach plan, 9; opposes McCarthyism, 12, 13; on arms race, 14; and Adlai Stevenson, 15, 16; on fallout, 16; and Schweitzer appeal, 16; on USSR nuclear test suspension, 19, 20; called Communist dupe, 20; on radiation, 21; and formation of SANE, 22, 23, 25, 30; writes SANE ads, 26, 31, 32; on U.S. nuclear test suspension, 34; on Strontium–90, 38, 39; and Hollywood SANE, 42; at SANE conference, 44; at Madison Square Garden rally, 45; and Communist infiltration issue, 46–48, 51, 60, 61; and Henry Abrams, 48, 49, 56; and Thomas J. Dodd, 49, 50, 54, 56, 63; and Linus Pauling, 52, 57; on civil liberties, 55; and A.J. Muste, 58, 62; Geneva talks, 67, 71; peace award, 81; role in test ban negotiations, 81, 83, 84; role in ratification process, 84, 86; on signing of treaty, 86, 87; merger with UWF, 88, 89; March on Washington, 99; on Spring Mobilization, 101; on internal split in SANE, 103, 104; Negotiations Now, 106; on National Conference for New Politics, 106; resigns from SANE, 108; on nuclear threat, 128; opposes nuclear war, 166

Crane, Henry Hitt, 22, 23
Crisp, Mary, 157
Cruise missile, 134, 147, 156
Cuban Missile crisis, 77, 80, 81

Dahlberg, Edwin T., 98
Darr, John W., 59
Dartmouth Conferences, 83
DeBenedetti, Charles, 120, 121, 168

Dellums, Ron, 141
Dentists for SANE, 81
Divine, Robert, 17, 18, 24, 26, 34
Doble, John, 168
Dobson, Chad, 150, 151
Dodd, Christopher, 144
Dodd, Thomas J., 165; attacks SANE, 45, 46, 48, 53, 55, 57; and Norman Cousins, 49, 50, 56; attacks Linus Pauling, 52; Committee Report, 54; protests against, 58–63
Dominican Republic, 128
Douglas, William O., 5
Draft registration, 145, 160
Drugger, Ronnie, 98
Duffy, Joseph M., Jr., 98
Duker, Laurie, 159
Dumas, Lloyd, 142
Dump Johnson movement, 109

Eastland, James, 46
Economic conversion, 142–144, 156, 160, 163
Eichelberger, Clark, 25
Einstein, Albert: and Federation of American Scientists, 5; on world government, 6; Emergency Committee of Atomic Scientists, 7–10; on Cold War, 7, 8; on *Bulletin of Atomic Scientists*, 10; on McCarthyism, 11, 12; on arms race, 14; appeal with Bertrand Russell, 15; biography of, 72
Eisenhower, Dwight: nuclear testing, 19; anti-test ban, 31; clean bomb, 36; and SANE ad, 36; and SANE appeal, 41; national security, 20, 43; Summit meeting, 43, 45; testing moratorium, 64
Eldridge, Dorothy, 150
Ellsberg, Daniel, 81

ABOUT THE AUTHOR

MILTON S. KATZ is Associate Professor of American Studies in the Liberal Arts Department at Kansas City Art Institute, Missouri. His earlier work on SANE appeared in *Doves and Diplomats: Foreign Offices and Peace Movements in Europe and America in the 19th and 20th Centuries* (Greenwood Press, 1978), *Peace Heroes in Twentieth-Century America*, and *Peace and Change: A Journal of Peace Research.* His articles have appeared in the *Journal of American Culture* and *Phylon: A Review of Race and Culture.*